RELIGION & SOCIETY IN SOUTH ASIA SERIES

Also in the same series:

Female Ascetics
Hierarchy and Purity in Indian Religious Movements
Wendy Sinclair-Brull

Religious Traditions in South Asia
Interaction and Change
Edited by Geoffrey A. Oddie

Paths of Dalit Liberation in Kerala
Interaction with Christianity and Communism, 1854–1966
George Oommen

Religious Conversion Movements in South Asia

Continuities and Change, 1800–1900

Geoffrey A. Oddie

CURZON

First Published in 1997
by Curzon Press
15 The Quadrant, Richmond
Surrey, TW9 1BP

© 1997 Geoffrey A. Oddie

Typeset in Baskerville by LaserScript Ltd, Mitcham
Printed and bound in Great Britain by
TJ International, Padstow, Cornwall

British Library Cataloguing in Publication Data
A catalogue record for this book is available from the British Library

Library Cataloguing in Publication Data
A catalogue record for this book has been requested

ISBN 0–7007–0472–8 (hbk)

Contents

v

Introduction

Geoffrey A. Oddie

Ever since the publication of Hardgrave's book on *The Nadars of Tamilnad*[1] in the 1960s there has been increasing scholarly recognition of the importance of religious conversion movements as a product of change, process and catalyst in South Asian history. The growth of a rich diversity of religious traditions within what we now call 'Hinduism', the spread of Buddhism, Jainism and 'Sikhism', as well as the spread of exotic religions such as Islam and Christianity, have all been to a considerable extent the result of some kind of conversion process. The emergence of these new forms of religious identity, involving different ways of understanding the individual, community and cosmic order have been closely linked with the development of new types of ethical and social behaviour. Most of these movements, with the possible exception of some types of asceticism, involved the development of new forms of social organization, while the new adherents invariably developed their own distinctive forms of culture, historical consciousness and attitudes to a range of general issues including economic activity. Last but not least, the rise and expansion of the new movements, also had a profound effect on political developments, whether one is thinking of the influence of Buddhist ideas in state formation under the Mauryas, the role of Islam in the political process in Medieval India, or the development of 'communal' politics in the present century.

Most of the contributions to the present volume are modified versions of papers delivered at a panel organized in connection with the proceedings of the 13th European Conference on Modern South Asian Studies which was held in Toulouse, 31st. August–3rd. September 1994. Contributors came from Europe,

1

Australia and North America as well as from South Asia. They are mostly concerned with the conversion of 'Hindus' and Muslims to Christianity though the collection also includes a paper on conversion and non-conversion experiences associated with Theosophy.

It is impossible to convey to readers within the confines of any single volume the exciting complexity, range and varied nature of South Asian conversion movements. All one can do is complement existing knowledge, highlight questions and issues, stimulate enquiry and, hopefully in the end, enlarge our scholarly vision and understanding. Although the main focus of this collection is on the Christian (mostly Protestant) conversion phenomenon it is also an attempt to identify, raise and explore many of the central concepts and issues associated with conversion movements in general. Indeed it is anticipated that this book will be of special interest to scholars and others attempting to understand religious change not only in South Asia but also in other parts of the non-Western world.

One of the major problems has always been the question of definition. What is conversion and what are conversion movements? At the simplest and popular level most commentators seem to be referring to some sort of change in religious belief and/or affiliation, a change which is often thought of as communal and which is expressed symbolically through the performance of ritual.[2] In South Asia as in other parts of the world, 'conversion' in the social sense of a change in communal affiliation is, in fact, usually marked by some sort of ritual. For Christians it might be the act of baptism, for Muslims or Buddhists a very simple statement or confession of faith and for modern 'Hindus', involvement in ceremonies associated with 'shuddi'. But whatever the case, there are usually special rituals of admission which underline the social and corporate nature of the process involved.

The frequency with which the term 'conversion' is used to describe these changes of fellowship, has probably been encouraged by the fact that it links the idea of conversion with some kind of observable phenomenon. It is easy for scholars and other observers to talk about 'the shifting of camps' and the way in which people either 'opted out of and joined' or simply 'joined' a new community. Converts, missionaries and others have often highlighted the baptism or moment of admission to membership

2

of the community, while scholars continue to scrutinize member-ship lists, tables of the number of adherents and census data in order to find something tangible which will provide evidence of change and trends in religious development. And yet one may ask whether this is evidence of 'conversion', and what all this data on changes in communal affiliation really means?

In his recent book *Understanding Religious Conversion*, Lewis Rambo places his emphasis not so much on change of fellowship but on an inner and radical religious transformation.[3] He points out that the word 'conversion' which can be translated as 'a turning' is of Jewish and Christian origin, that its precise meaning is disputed even among Christians and he argues that, in the last analysis, conversion is 'what a faith group says it is'.[4] In his own definition he makes allowance for a wide range of different types of experience in different contexts and cultures:

> Conversion is a process of religious change that takes place in a dynamic force field of people, events, ideologies, institutions, expectations, and orientations . . . (a) conver-sion is a process over time, not a single event; (b) conversion is contextual and thereby influences and is influenced by a matrix of relationships, expectations, and situations; and (c) factors in the conversion process are multiple, interactive, and cumulative. There is no one cause of conversion, no one process, and no one simple consequence of that process.[5]

If we accept Rambo's suggestion that conversion has a variety of meanings but take, as a starting point, popular usage and the idea of conversion as the act or process of joining a new religious community, then what more can be said about the practice in India and the people involved?

The main challenge facing the thoughtful enquirer in this case is neither to read too much nor too little into what appears to have been going on.

In his book *The Muslims of British India* Peter Hardy endorses the view that in Indian life 'conversion' means 'more a change of fellowship than of conduct or inner life'; but he then adds a significant rider, that 'the latter [the change in conduct or inner life] may in time occur'.[6] Even in cases where admission to the new community was 'a mere formality' there was always the possibility of growth and development in the inner or spiritual life of the 'convert'. It could perhaps be argued that a great deal of

Catholic and Islamic policy was based on the assumption that once admitted to fellowship or identified as belonging to the community then the individuals concerned were more likely to respond to the advocate's preaching. The important initial step was to gain the people's allegiance, and once this was done then religious change (it was hoped) might follow. Catholic bishops and priests and the leaders of Islamic revival movements were all able to operate on the assumption that they had some sort of pool of 'adherents' who, even if nominal and knowing little about the faith, could be encouraged to respond and rise to greater heights. Even if admission into a new community meant nothing or very little spiritually at the time, it appears in many cases to have symbolized some degree of commitment or openness to further teaching. It not only opened up further avenues of communication between the teachers and missionaries on the one side and adherents on the other, but could also be the beginning of a long process of acculturation into a new tradition. Thus when the Parava fishermen of the Coromandel threw in their lot with the Portuguese in the sixteenth century and in return for Portuguese protection, agreed to accept baptism, they could hardly have known much about the Catholic faith: and yet this was an important stage in their religious journey – the beginning of a process which resulted in their becoming one of the most staunchly Catholic communities in India.

While 'baptism' and other rituals of admission were outward and visible signs of a new status, and, for some, the first step in a genuine spiritual journey, they have also been appropriated and used by individuals and groups as a sign of their sense of dissatisfaction and desire for a change in what might be described as 'tradition identity'. As is well known, census reports have been used in the same way, to express and claim new forms of social or religious identity. Hence instead of dismissing all 'returns on religion' as data which tells us much about the colonizers and *nothing* about the people listed in the reports, as some scholars are apt to do, a careful critical analysis of the material can yield useful results and provide some evidence about the way in which indigenous people described themselves. Unlike the census statistics on the number of 'Hindus' which the reports indicate were calculated by outsiders adding together the number of people in different indigenous categories (eg. vaishnavites, saivites etc) the figures on Christians and probably also Muslims are a direct reflection of the way in which the people described themselves. This is precisely the reason why the census findings and missionary calculations on the number of Christians were sometimes at variance. The Protestant missionary statistics, for example those compiled by the Calcutta Missionary Conference in the nineteenth century, were usually based on the European missionary records and estimates of the number of people under instruction and/or belonging to different congregations etc. The missionary figures, therefore, were based very largely on the missionary's own decision as to whether to include or exclude certain individuals from 'the Christian' category. On the other hand the census takers (at least when dealing with Christians and some of the other non-Hindu people) took seriously what people said about themselves. One example of this is the figures on the Tanjore Christians. After hundreds of 'sudra' Christians were forced to leave the Anglican churches over the caste issue in the second half of the nineteenth century, the number of Protestant Christians recorded in Protestant statistical tables showed a marked decline, as the European missionaries no longer considered them *bona fide* Christians. However, the 'dissidents' as they were sometimes called, continued to think of themselves as Christians and hence the number of Christians recorded in the census (which measured the indigenous response) remained much the same.[7] The census reports therefore, can be useful in telling us at least something about the insiders' sense of allegiance, communal affiliation and feelings about religious identity.

A final issue relating to conversion as something which involves a change of fellowship is the idea that it necessarily involves an opting out as well as a joining in. In some cases it did involve a burning of bridges and a deliberate opting out. One of the classic illustrations of this process is the Basel Mission Christians of the west coast. As Rudolf Fischer has argued in a recent and important paper the mission succeeded in establishing its own economic and social system which was virtually sealed off from all contact with 'Hindu' society.[8] The BM converts who were drawn from different caste backgrounds wore the same distinctive attire. They worked in mission workshops and on other mission projects, lived on the mission property and interacted and intermarried with other members of the BM or Protestant community. But there can be little doubt that this form of extreme isolation or quaranteening was unusual and that most other Christians kept up (to a greater or lesser degree) some form of contact with their pre-conversion associates. As Avril Powell shows in her paper, there were some cases where Protestants of brahmin or asraf Muslim origin, normally expelled from their community, continued or managed to re-establish some degree of contact with their families and former Hindu or Muslim friends. The crucial point is that the adoption of a new identity did not necessarily mean a complete rejection of the old. Most 'Hindus' who joined a new community (whether a Kartabhaja, Christian or Muslim fellowship) continued to relate in some way to their community of origin. For many of them it was not a case of either/or but of striking the right balance between the old and new, or perhaps of adopting an additional identity. Some Christians for example were quite adamant in describing themselves as 'Indian' or 'Hindu' Christians. They were rather like people who keep 'dual citizenship' where the experience, memories and culture of the old world continue to permeate and flavour the new and where the old concerns and values are not always left behind. What Susan Bayly has argued in her recent book is that in the examples she has studied Muslims and Christians continued to share in what she describes as the 'indigenous moral order'.[9] The most obvious examples of this type of continuity were Nadar converts who remained within the caste system and who continued to compete with 'Hindus' in their attempts to improve their status within the caste hierarchy.

Apart from raising questions about the nature of religious identity and community and the processes involved in joining new types of religious fellowship, the following papers also raise the not unrelated questions about transition in belief.

One of the most influential exponents of conversion as transition in belief is Robin Horton who writes about African religion and who has explored the relationship between social change and developments in African cosmology.[10] According to Horton, traditional African religions incorporate a belief in a two-tiered structure, 'the first tier being that of the lesser spirits and the second that of the supreme being'. The lesser spirits he suggests, 'underpin events and processes in the microcosm of the local community and its environment, while the supreme being underpins events and processes in the macrocosm i.e. in the world as a whole'. The world of the lesser spirits was especially appropriate in communities which were comparatively isolated and dominated by subsistence farming. However, as the communities became increasingly exposed to the wider world and as communications improved, so people gradually began to feel the need for more satisfactory systems of 'explanation, prediction and control'. The attention paid to the lesser spirits slowly shifted to a focus on the character and cult of the supreme being- towards a cosmology which appeared to be more meaningful and appropriate in the macrocosm. Notions of a supreme being were however, more highly developed in Christianity and Islam than in African religions, with the result that these exogenous movements seemed to offer a world view (including a system of conduct) which would better equip the African villager to cope with the problems of the wider world.

I have argued elsewhere that Horton's specific model of conversion can hardly be applied in any great detail to the process of conversion from 'Hinduism' to Christianity; and the same argument also applies to the conversion of Hindus to Islam.[11] Apart from the question about the role of caste, economic and other non-ideational factors in prompting Indian conversion, there is also the problem of basic differences between the so-called 'Hindu' and African cosmology. Unlike African cosmology, 'Hinduism' was more a multi-tiered than two-tiered system (a divine hierarchy), and the issue that requires particular attention in relation to conversion is not so much the African problem of explaining the transition from an emphasis on the lower tier to a focus on the supreme deity (most fully and satisfactorily represented in Christianity and Islam), but why belief in one kind of supreme deity, e.g. Vishnu or Shiva, was replaced by a belief in some other kind of 'non-Hindu' supreme being. Unlike Africans (as described by Horton), Hindus seeking more developed ideas of God had no need to search outside their own scriptures and traditions, which encompassed an extremely wide range of religious options.

Nevertheless, the Horton thesis is important for South Asian studies. In the first place, Horton's views may prove to be more fruitful for scholars studying conversion movements among tribals than among the so-called 'Hindus'. Richard Eaton, for example, has already published an article entitled 'Conversion to Christianity among the Nagas 1876–1971' in which he acknowledges his indebtedness to Horton's work.[12] Secondly, and irrespective of how far the Horton model can be applied to conversion movements in the South Asian region, one of the more significant aspects of the debate is that it does challenge scholars to think more about preconversion systems of thought and belief and the way in which indigenous ideas and perceptions relate to conversion. Horton himself reminds us that the mind is not a *tabula rasa* 'automatically registering the imprint of external cultural influences' but rather 'the locus of thought-patterns and values that determine rather closely which of these influences will be accepted and which rejected.'[13]

Oddie's paper which reflects the influence of Horton's theory is largely concerned with the changing context and role of ideas in Kartabhaja conversion in Bengal in the nineteenth century. While he places some emphasis on the parallel ideas and concepts which facilitated understanding, he also points out that it was the perception of differences 'which seemed to make the transfer of faith worth while'. Oommen, who has also been considering the applicability of Horton's 'intellectualist approach', addresses the issue of the role of ideas and related issues in Pulaya conversion in Travancore during much the same period. His findings are, however, somewhat different. He argues that in their preaching and teaching of Pulayas the missionaries [in contrast to those in Bengal] experienced special difficulties in attempts to convey the Christian message. The problems involved in attempting to teach a people who spoke their own peculiar brand of Malayalam were, in this latter instance, compounded by very different pre-conversion ideas of God and of the world around. These ideas not only failed to facilitate the Christian message but acted as a serious obstacle to the Pulayas' understanding of missionary preaching. For this reason, Oommen suggests that earlier historians may well have been correct in arguing that sociological factors were more important in conversion than cosmological considerations.

Though these discussions are directed at what was happening at the 'mass movement' level, they also raise questions about the role of ideas and the comparative importance of belief systems in the conversion of individuals – an issue touched on in Powell's paper and even more central in Moulton's discussion of Hume's relationship with Theosophy where the author outlines in graphic detail one man's struggle with problems of belief.

A third important and inter-connected issue raised in this volume (apart from questions of corporate allegiance and the role of belief) involves the underlying causal factors in conversion and change. What, one may ask, are contributors saying about why people were so often dissatisfied, in transition or on the move?

While there are no obvious or generally agreed forms of explanation most of the papers highlight or, at the very least, imply some kind of personal or corporate crisis which preceded, or was, in some way, interlinked with conversion. The connection between conversion and crisis in tribal societies, a linkage which is central in Horton's model of African conversion, has already been noted by several scholars of Christian conversion in tribal societies in India. Downs[14] and Eaton have both explored a combination of crises in the north-eastern hills region where the pressures of colonial rule and of the outside world threatened traditional cultures and ways of life and led to the rapid spread of Christianity among the various tribes in some parts of the region. Also relevant is Fidelis De Sa's study of religious conversion among tribals in Chota Nagpur in a book which is very pointedly entitled 'Crisis in Chota Nagpur'.[15]

This theme of general or societal crisis is taken up and developed by Bugge in this present volume where she draws attention not to what was happening in so-called tribal societies, but to the situation in what is usually thought of as Hindu caste society. In her paper, in which she compares Catholic and Protestant missions in Tamil Nadu, she suggests that, contrary to generally accepted views, mass movements were less of a response to the inequalities within the caste system and more a reaction of different groups attempting to adapt to the challenges of social and economic change. While, in most of the areas where Protestant movements took place, 'we find social and economic change resulting in marginalization of the poorest sections of society' who looked to Christianity 'for social and religious security', the situation in the French Catholic mission in the dry regions of North and South Arcot, she suggests, was different. There the poorer sections of society took advantage of economic development and 'modernization' to improve their economic and commercial position and 'to establish new religious identities for themselves.' Oddie, who also points to a nexus between rapid political, social and economic change on the one hand and the rise of new religious movements on the other, argues that it was in an atmosphere of economic hardship, social disruption and 'crisis' that the Kartabhaja movement grew and flourished, and paved the way for some of the less satisfied and committed Kartabhajas to seek out and adopt Christian teaching.

In their papers Powell and Moulton also draw attention to the link between crisis and conversion. However, their interest is more in the way in which crisis was linked with changes in the religious life of specific individuals rather than with the nature of the more general contextual social or cultural crisis affecting the life of large numbers of people. Powell whom as we have seen discusses the case of four eminent converts, declares that they left accounts of long drawn-out, gradual conversion processes 'marked in most cases by signs of an intense spiritual or intellectual "crisis".' Thus for Goreh there is abundant evidence that he 'suffered deep, prolonged and multi-faceted "crisis", spiritual, intellectual and social before accepting baptism'. Ram Chandra was one who struggled with increasing doubts and became a leader of sceptical opinion before he accepted Christianity, while 'Imad ud-din was involved in 'a long-drawn out and often despairing process' during which 'he first tried to find satisfaction within the parameters of Islam, at the end of which, after reading the New Testament and aided by various Europeans, he decided for baptism'. But Moulton's account of Hume's restlessness, doubts and agonies of indecision spells out in even greater detail the vicissitudes of a long-term emotional and intellectual crisis.

All of these accounts will remind the reader of the wide range of psychological factors involved in religious change and conversion. We are also reminded of Nock's definition of the process of conversion as 'the re-orientation of the soul of the individual, his deliberate turning from indifference or from an earlier form of piety to another, a turning which implies a consciousness that a great change is involved, that the old was wrong and the new is right.'[16] And yet one may question how far these Indian examples are similar to the European examples Nock had in mind. In India the intellectual and spiritual struggles were taking place in a context where Christianity was not the dominant religion. Individuals such as those discussed in Powell's paper had a wider range of non-Christian options which they could consider for adoption. Linked with this broader pluralistic religious context is the fact that 'Hindu' or Muslim converts to Christianity in India did not necessarily have the same popular or pseudo Christian ideas or assumptions with which to interpret their intellectual and spiritual experience. For example, phraseology to describe one's experience such as having had a 'conviction of sin' or 'a sense of forgiveness', did not come so readily to mind among people unfamiliar with Christian terminology and living in a non-Christian environment. Indeed there is room for a great deal more research on the use of language and the nature of individual experience of crisis and religious change. How far, for example, was the convert's inner struggle and experience of conversion to Islam similar to that of converts to Christianity in the same general social and cultural environment? Was there much difference in the 'Hindu's' inner or psychological experience of 'conversion' to Christianity and Islam? How far did different teachings or expectations make a difference?

Finally, it needs to be stressed that almost all of the contributors emphasize continuities as well as change. Scholars generally are now much more aware that conversion was usually a long-term process even in an evangelical context and in places like Britain, and while some converts might have 'felt' that all things are new there were continuities, patterns and styles of thought which linked the convert with his or her past. There were the kind of parallels and continuities in thought that helped facilitate Kartabhaja conversion to Christianity. There were also the continuities between indigenous Indian religions and Theosophy – a point which is emphasized in Moulton's paper where he explains that Theosophy had become Indianized so that, unlike Europeans, Indian elites were able to become a part of the inner circle 'without modifying religious beliefs'. There were also remarkable continuities in the thought and lifestyle of the converts described in Powell's paper – most of whom continued to use their original name and to dress and live in much the same fashion as they had before. For example, Shaikh Salih, who seemed to attribute some of his own success in Christian evangelism 'to his maintenance of the physical appearance and the aura of a sufi Muslim' continued 'to cling to his familiar appearance and life style'. While Powell produces evidence of continuities in the life of elite converts, Oommen draws attention to the persistence of what was from the missionaries' point of view less acceptable customs among dalit converts in Travancore in the nineteenth century. In fact the question of how far converts should be expected to change their forms of worship, dress and life style became a major issue in different parts of the mission field during this period.

It is Antony Copley's paper on the missionaries and Tanjore Christians in the eighteenth and nineteenth centuries which highlights different interpretations of what conversion to Christianity really meant. As Rambo has pointed out there is a fundamental difference between the views of Western missionaries who seek to find the 'pure' convert and the converts' assimilation of the faith 'in categories relevant to them, not to the dictates of the advocate.'[17] Copley, however, not only focusses on the differences of opinion as between the missionaries on the one side and the Tanjore Christians on the other, but also demonstrates that the missionaries were very much divided over what constituted the true convert and what was required of converts after acceptance into the Christian church. He contrasts the Catholic and Lutheran 'old mission' ethos of accommodation with the new spirit of confrontation as exemplified in the 'new mission' and especially in G. U. Pope who was involved in a bitter and long-running campaign against the Tanjore poet Vedanayagam Sastriar. The source of this conflict was of course the conviction on the part of Vedanayagam and others that discipleship did not necessarily involve cultural transformation and that Indian Christians had every right to continue to interpret Christianity in their own way and to enjoy a lifestyle and customs which in their opinion were not in conflict with the fundamentals of the Christian Gospel.

NOTES

1 Robert L. Hardgrave, *The Nadars of Tamilnad: the Political Culture of a Community in Change*, (Berkeley and Los Angeles, 1969).
2 The use of the word 'conversion' in this sense was not uncommon even among missionaries in India in the nineteenth century. For example, speaking at a conference in Bangalore in 1879 a Methodist missionary, the Rev. W. Burgess lamented the conventional use of the term 'conversion', which, together with 'the loose way' in which missionaries themselves sometimes used the word, tended to foster 'the mere nominal profession of Christianity' and to encourage people 'to lose sight of the tremendous heart-change which the word implies', *The Missionary Conference: South India and Ceylon*, (Bangalore, 1879), p. 294.
3 Lewis R.Rambo, *Understanding Religious Conversion*, (New Haven, 1993).
4 *Ibid.*, p. XIV.
5 *Ibid*, p. 5.
6 P.Hardy, *The Muslims of British India*, (Cambridge, 1972), p. 8.

7 G.A. Oddie, 'Christians in the Census: Tanjore and Trichinopoly Districts, 1871–1901' in N.G. Barrier, (ed.) *The Census in British India. New Perspectives*, (Delhi, 1981), pp. 129–130.

8 Rudolph H. Fischer, 'Christianization and Social Mobility in Nineteenth Century South Kanara and Malabar: a Look at the Basel Mission Experience', in G.A. Oddie (ed.), *Religion in South Asia: Religious Conversion and Revival Movements in South Asia in Medieval and Modern Times* (second rev. and enl. edition) Delhi 1991, pp. 125–154.

9 Susan Bayly, *Saints, Goddesses and Kings. Muslims and Christians in South Indian society, 1700–1900*, (Cambridge, 1989), p. 8.

10 See especially 'African Conversion', *Africa*, Vol. XLV, No. 2, April 1971 and 'On the Rationality of Conversion', Part 1, *Africa*, Vol. 45, No. 3, 1975.

11 D.M. Schreuder and G.A. Oddie, 'What is "Conversion"? History, Christianity and Religious Change in Colonial Africa and South Asia,' *Journal of Religious History*, Vol. 15, No. 4, December 1989.

12 Richard M. Eaton, 'Conversion to Christianity among the Nagas, 1876–1971', *Indian Economic and Social History Review*, Vol. XXI, No. 1, January–March 1984.

13 Robin Horton, 'On the Rationality of Conversion', Part 1, *Africa*, Vol. 45, No. 3, 1975, p. 221.

14 Frederick S. Downs, 'Christian Conversion Movements among Hills Tribes of North East India in the Nineteenth and Twentieth Centuries,' in G.A. Oddie (ed.), *Religion in South Asia, op.cit.*, pp. 155–174.

15 *Crisis in Chota Nagpur With special reference to The Judicial Conflict between Jesuit Missionaries and British Government Officials, November 1889–March 1890*, (Bangalore, 1975).

16 A.D. Nock, *Conversion: The Old and the New in Religion from Alexander the Great to Augustine of Hippo*, (London, 1933), p. 7.

17 Rambo, p. 5.

Chapter 1

Processes of Conversion to Christianity in Nineteenth Century North-Western India

Avril A. Powell

OBJECTIVES

The purpose of this study is to examine some examples of conversion from Islam and Hinduism to Christianity, which occurred in north-western India in the mid-nineteenth century.[1] Conversions will be considered within the period c.1813 to the late 1860s, the former date marking the commencement of Protestant missionary enterprise in this region, and the latter the beginning of the 'mass movements' towards Christianity in this and other regions of India which are beyond the scope of the present study. The focus is on the conversions of individual males belonging to high caste and *ashraf* backgrounds, all of whom left accounts of long drawn-out, gradual conversion 'processes' marked in most cases by signs of an intense spiritual or intellectual 'crisis'. There is insufficient data to take up the issue of female conversion, although some comments will be made about the wives of male converts. It is hoped that study of these conversion experiences will allow the situating of the processes observed in this particular region of India within a broader perspective of recent debate about the dynamic of conversion in other contexts, historical and current, in various parts of the Afro-Asian world.

An examination of 'process' has been facilitated by the existence of some detailed accounts, written either at the time, or very soon afterwards, by the converts themselves, usually in Urdu or Hindi, but then translated into English for publication in missionary journals. Some, but not all, of the original vernacular accounts survive. There are, of course, problems in the interpretation of texts often translated and edited by others, which had been written 'after the event' and often as part of the ongoing evangelistic programme. In some significant cases converts who had previously been prominent within a traditional Indian religious hierarchy from which stance they had published attacks on Christianity before their own conversions, then became vociferous tract writers on behalf of Christianity after baptism, often including in their apology or polemic an explanation of their own rejection of their former religious identity. These, nonetheless very useful 'before and after' statements of faith are particularly characteristic of the several converts who subsequently joined the Christian ecclesiastical hierarchy, or else became prominent in British government service. Changes in community and caste identity and social interaction after baptism, are examined by looking at opposition to baptism among immediate family and the wider *baradari*, at the extent to which relations subsequently became Christians, and at marriage patterns after baptism. The post-baptismal occupational status of converts will also be examined. Evaluation of the extent to which conversion also prompted a change of external identity has been assisted by reference to photographic and portrait material which helps to indicate the ways the converts wished to present themselves physically after baptism.

My concern with conversion processes in this particular time and place arises out of earlier work on the socio-religious history of the region. In a previous study[2], I examined the pattern of 'contact and controversy' which resulted when evangelical missionaries first started to target *ashraf* ('well-born') Muslims in the 1830s. While converts from Islam to Christianity played an important part in this dynamic, the 'processes' of conversion received only the briefest of attention. In an article, 'Artful apostasy? A Mughal Mansabdar among the Jesuits', I was able to pay more attention both to 'process' and to transfer of 'identity' in examining cases of conversion to Christianity from the seventeenth to the nineteenth centuries.[3] The object of the present paper is both to examine some of the unanswered questions raised in that article, and to consider some converts from various Hindu castes as well as the converts from Islam to which my attention had previously been restricted. The data used here concerns, in the main, missionaries and converts connected with Protestant Anglican missions in north India. Particularly useful for comparative purposes are John Webster's examination of the impact of American Presbyterian activity in the same region, and Antony Copley's study of some cases of conversion among the religious elites in some other regions of India.[4]

INDIVIDUAL CONVERSIONS AMONG EDUCATED ELITES

To the constant despair of the various missionary societies, the incidence of conversion to Christianity was relatively low in this region at a time when equal emphasis was still being placed on the evangelism of illiterate villagers and educated elites. The number of Protestant 'Native Christians' in the North-Western Provinces (NWP) and Punjab was registered as barely two thousand in 1852, a figure which rose only to just over five thousand by 1862, in spite of increased evangelical activity in the Punjab after its annexation.[5] Not until the last decades of the nineteenth century did 'mass conversions' of adults, usually in village or small-town environments, begin to occur in the NWP and Punjab, with the result that 'Native Christians' in the Punjab alone numbered over forty thousand by 1901. Only in times of famine, such as 1837 and 1860, had baptisms been suddenly boosted in the mid-century period, the new converts being mainly small children who were unable to make a conscious decision for a change of religious identity. In this situation, the few cases of conversion from among the educated elites which did occur were regarded as symbolically highly significant, as indications of a breakthrough which would precede 'rich harvests' in the decades to come, both by 'downward filtration' to the village masses and by lateral influence on other high caste and *ashraf* individuals. Four such cases will be examined in detail here, two from Hindu and two from Muslim backgrounds. While this particular sample partly reflects the availability of sufficiently detailed first-hand accounts, it also reflects the comparative incidence of such conversions more accurately than might be supposed. For although Muslims comprised only about fourteen per cent of the population of the NWP, (compared with over fifty per cent in the Punjab) the converts from Islam within the Presbyterian missions in the whole region comprised more than a third of the total. While similar statistics for the Anglican missions are not available, anecdotal evidence would suggest that the Muslim proportion, especially among the elites, was probably at least as high for these missions

17

too. Certainly one of the converts from Islam commented in the 1890s that although 'compared with converts from amongst Hindus, converts from amongst Mohammedans are fewer far', he nevertheless pointed out that 'learned Mohammedans are coming in larger numbers into the fold of Christ than the unlearned'.[6] To support his case, he appended a list of more than one hundred 'Christian converts of some distinction from Mohammedanism in India', who were now 'holding honourable positions' either as clergy or in government service.[7]

Converts from Hinduism:[8]

Nilakantha/Nehemiah Goreh (1825–1885, Baptized 1848, ordained deacon 1868, priest 1870)

While Nehemiah Goreh is one of the most well known of the 'native Christians' who converted in this region, attention has mainly centred somewhat eulogistically on his post-baptismal role and writings, with little attention paid to his initial contacts with the missionaries, during which he wrote tracts in defence of Vaishnavism, and in criticism of Christianity.[9] The balance has been ably redressed by Richard Fox Young's critical study of Goreh in his book *Resistant Hinduism*.[10] While much of what follows is based on Fox Young's work, particularly on his translations of Goreh's Sanskrit writings, I have also used the records of the missionaries and government servants with whom Goreh came into contact, notably the Rev. William Smith and Dr John Muir, in order to raise some questions about this particular conversion process which will then be addressed to the accounts of some other conversions during the same period.[11]

Although Goreh spent his boyhood in Benares, his family were Chitpavan Brahmins originally from Poona in Maharashtra. They had accumulated wealth earned in the service of various Deccan rulers, some of which they then used for charitable works in Benares, where Goreh's father chose to settle in order to devote himself to meditation. His father's younger brother managed the family affairs, and it is clear that the Goreh family was regarded with considerable respect in the city. At the time, in the late 1830s, when Goreh reached his teens, various Protestant missionary societies, notably the Church Missionary (CMS) and the London Missionary (LMS) Societies were concentrating their evangelistic activities on Benares, building churches, schools and orphanages, and preaching in the city bazaars with the aim of attracting a brahmin audience. Interest in the local religious elites was reflected also in the plans being made by the East India Company to turn the Benares Sanskrit College into an Anglo-Oriental College. Like most wealthy brahmin families, Goreh's relations could afford to ignore the British administered College, for he was taught privately by various pandits in the city. He later said, 'Of English I did not know so much as the *a b c* until a short time before my conversion'.[12] The aggressive bazaar preaching of the missionaries in the vernacular languages he could not ignore so easily, his biographers relating that it was with the aim of silencing them, that he first visited their compound. In several other cases which will be examined, the initiative in coming into face-to-face contact would also be taken by the would-be remonstrator or 'enquirer', thereby initiating a sequence of meetings and exchanges of letters or tracts, sometimes broken up by long intervals of silence, and of seeming complete retreat, which nevertheless finally resulted in 'conversion'. In Goreh's case, the first meeting in 1844 with a local, and long experienced CMS missionary, the Rev. William Smith, took the form of 'a few questions on the nature of Christianity'.[13] In a brief note written in Hindi, Goreh queried Smith's explanation of sin and salvation, arguing that if God is omniscient there is no point in allowing 'poor helpless creatures', particularly children, to suffer as a form of 'probation'.[14] This theme was to pre-occupy him for the rest of his life. Smith then gave him a copy of a book which had been specifically written in Sanskrit by a British government official to persuade brahmins, like Goreh, that they should abandon the various Hindu paths in favour of Christianity. This was the *Matapariksa: a sketch of the argument for Christianity and against Hinduism* (Calcutta, 1839), which had been written by John Muir, who as principal of the Benares Sanskrit College was currently engaged in overseeing its amalgamation with an English medium school, against the express wishes of the local pandits.[15] In a letter received the following day by Smith, Goreh objected to Muir's evangelical treatment of the problem of 'evil'. The encounter was then seemingly abandoned for nearly a year, during which time, however, Goreh studied Muir's book in greater depth, and prepared a counterblast in Sanskrit in the form of the *Sastratattvavinirnaya*, which amounted to a defence of Vaishnavism against Christianity.[16] For more immediate purposes of face-to-face rebuttal, he also prepared a Hindi tract outlining some 'Doubts Concerning Christianity', which he presented to Smith, and circulated widely in Benares. As in his initial letter, objections to Christian ideas of sin and salvation, and the nature of evil, featured prominently in the six 'Doubts', together with denials of missionary misunderstanding of the function of images, and the transmigration of souls.[17] While the 'Doubts' might be seen as Goreh's answer to bazaar preaching, his much longer Sanskrit work, the *Sastratattvavinirnaya*, was designed to ward off the effects of John Muir's erudite and aggressive challenge in Sanskrit. Some of the other converts too, would first set pen to paper in rebuttal not of the Bible itself, but of missionary and evangelical attacks on their inherited belief systems. Significantly, a simultaneous response was being masterminded the very same year, 1844–5, by some learned Muslim objectors to missionary bazaar preaching in nearby cities such as Lucknow and Agra.[18]

Yet within a relatively short time after this second meeting with the missionaries, Goreh had secretly presented himself for baptism as a Christian. What had happened between April 1845 and March 1848? It seems clear that regular dialogue with the CMS missionary, William Smith, had prepared the way, even though Smith was on leave in England when Goreh finally 'converted'. He also renewed his contact with the evangelical Sanskritist, John Muir, whose anti-Hindu writings he had initially decried, confiding to Muir's pandit that, 'in consequence of my having had of late much intercourse with the Reve, Mr S[mith], and my attention engaged with the subject of Christianity, many doubts have arisen in my mind with regard to Hinduism'.[19] Significantly the pandit so addressed considered that Goreh 'was gone mad', an indication of the response the news of his eventual conversion would receive in Benares. The exact nature and extent of Muir's influence upon him has not as yet been ascertained, but it is known that they met several times, and that Muir gave him a copy of his recently published Sanskrit 'Life of Christ'.[20]

In later years, particularly when lecturing to Brahmo Samaj audiences, Goreh would stress that conversion to Christianity cannot be the product either of human reasoning or of intuitive processes, for, 'how came I to entertain these notions? Certainly not by own reasoning or intuition, for I know that while I was a

Hindoo, and unacquainted with Christianity, I never dreamed of them'.[21] Rather, he concludes, 'Christianity is a supernatural revelation from God', indicating that it was his own encounter with Christian notions of revelation, first in evangelical tracts which he initially rejected, and then through constant dialogue with the Benares missionaries and with John Muir, that he finally accepted the 'now very different notions about God from what I had before.' Muir had indeed urged him, it seems, not to 'dive too deep or I shall be drowned, nor seek to fathom things for which God has not given man the line'.[22] Yet, in spite of his subsequent disclaimers, letters written subsequently during his frequent periods of renewed 'doubts' suggest that Goreh was in fact distinctive among other converts of this period in attaching more importance to 'arguments from reason' rather than to those from 'revelation'. Certainly his preoccupation with the question of God's foreknowledge and man's freewill, and his constant requests to Smith for 'evidences' of the 'truth of Christianity' suggest this. It seems that his insistence to the Brahmos more than twenty years later on 'revelationary' criteria may have been a rationalization in retrospect of the process as he had actually experienced it. This is not to say that study of the Bible did not play an increasingly important part in the preparatory process, but that in Fox Young's words, he required 'rationally based assurance about religious truths.'[23]

Evidence abounds that he suffered a deep, prolonged and multi-faceted 'crisis', spiritual, intellectual and social, before accepting baptism, lasting from 1845 until 1848, and recurring intermittently even afterwards. Several times he was on the point of baptism, on one occasion agreeing to meet Smith in Calcutta, and then failing to turn up. Doubts continued to depress him for the rest of his life, in spite of the active missionary role he immediately adopted after baptism on behalf of his Christian mentors. For accounts of the final decision to accept Christian baptism, and the change in social as well as religious community which followed, we are dependent on the diaries of other missionaries in Benares, for neither Smith nor Muir, his earlier confidants, was near at hand. Fearing the reaction in his caste, and in the city generally, Goreh sought assistance from Christians in nearby Jaunpur, where he was baptized in secrecy on 12th March 1848, taking the 'Christian' name, Nehemiah. The news was nevertheless soon broadcast in Benares, where an Urdu newspaper announced, 'The son of a most respectable man, Nilakantha, went from here on the 12th to Jaunpur, and there through error wandered into a ruinous path, and has come to eat and drink with the Christians'.[24]

What is certain is that once he had accepted baptism, and in spite of continuing doubts, Goreh very rapidly adopted a dual identity, marked by a readiness to assist the Benares missionaries in their efforts to persuade not only the local brahmans but also the bazaar crowds of the truth of Christianity, by using his traditional status as 'pandit' or religious scholar to enhance his claim to inner knowledge and authority. Within a few months he helped to revise Smith's *Sat-mat-nirupana*, or 'inquiry into the true religion', for a second edition, and risked his life in some injudicious bazaar preaching. In 1853 the anonymous publication, in Hindi, of his *Vedantmat ka bicar aur khristiyamat ka sar*, by 'a Benares pandit' showed the use to which he was prepared to put his erstwhile scholarly and religious identity.[25] Symbolic too of a seemingly complete volte face was his willingness after baptism to serve as pandit to J. R. Ballantyne, John Muir's successor as principal of the Benares Sanskrit College, an institution which he had avoided in his boyhood. He subsequently became tutor to the Sikh prince, Dilip Singh, also a convert to Christianity, and accompanied him to Britain, where he met Queen Victoria, and was introduced to Max Müller by John Muir, the Sanskritist who had earlier played a crucial part in his own conversion process.[26] Indeed the process came full circle when in 1860 he published his *Saddarsanadarpana*, (translated the next year into English as *A Rational Refutation of the Hindu Philosophical Systems*), a work which marked the mirror image of the *Sastratattvavinirnaya*, his first counterblast, in 1844, against Muir's aggressive evangelical tract. Fox Young considers that it was in this later work, rather than at the point of conversion, that Goreh rejected the claims of reason for the surety of revelation, arguing however, that even so he never really found the complete equilibrium and spiritual certainty which he sought.

Goreh's struggles both before and after baptism also reflect the social ostracism faced by most high caste converts to Christianity. His uncle, a former diwan to a minor Muslim ruler, the Nawab of Banda, had vainly used all his powers of persuasion to prevent the baptism, after which Goreh was rejected from his caste.[27] Even more influential had been his father's pleas not to take the final step. Indeed it was partly the closeness of his bond with his unworldly father which caused his vacillation so many times during the three years after his initial move towards Christianity. Yet it was his widowed father alone among his relatives and caste who accepted the baptism, once he was assured that his son would still visit him, seemingly on the ground that it was better to have converted to another faith, than to have become an atheist. His younger brother, still a child at the time of the baptism, was not allowed to meet Goreh again for four years, but in later life the brothers established a close relationship in spite of the seeming incompatibility of their roles as Christian pastor and Hindu pandit, and in spite of Goreh's unremitting attempts to persuade his brother to accept baptism. Goreh's young wife, who had been sent back to her father on his baptism, was later retrieved by force, with the connivance of the local British magistrate, and accepted baptism on her deathbed shortly afterwards. The Christian accounts of this event miss altogether the irony of missionary criticism of Goreh's uncle for his forceful attempts to dissuade him from baptism, yet fulsome praise of the local British community for equally forcefully 'rescuing' his wife from her relatives.

From 1848 until his death in 1895, Goreh was one of the leading 'native Christians' in India, seemingly an archetypal convert from Brahminism, a 'Christian pandit', and symbol of a hoped for future missionary impact on the higher castes. But how typical was he? In two or three ways he was completely his own man. First, although he remained a Christian, and was ordained in 1868, he continued to be beset by doubts, moving over course of time from a 'Low Church' Anglican to a 'High Church' stance, but even then admitting to doubts about some of the most fundamental doctrines of Christianity. Partly for this reason he refused to accept any high profile position, feeling more at ease as an itinerant lecturer, who would help out where needed but would not 'represent' any particular sectarian or theological stance. After twenty years he was, however, prevailed on to accept ordination. In the 1870s he seemed to find a more congenial life style with the Anglo-Catholic Cowley Fathers, belonging to the Oxford Mission, whose asceticism and celibacy might seem redolent of the *sannyasi* stage of the Hindu life cycle. If so, he nevertheless found the obligation to perform such menial tasks as cleaning his own cell repugnant in practice, and in the end he left the order. His difficulty in defining and acting out an appropriate social role is even reflected in a certain ambivalence about his appearance. Reluctant to adopt European dress, he adopted for his first pastorate, a robe-like garment of his own invention, as a compromise between the garb of a brahmin pandit and a priest. When a local British officer 'laughingly told him that he looked more like a *maulvi* than a clergyman', he exchanged it for the white cassock, commonly worn by Christian pastors in India. He later apologized for donning what to 'some people' seemed a 'Romish' garb, writing that 'the Church has doubtless some wise reason for prescribing it'.[28]

While the time span between Nehemiah Goreh's first encounter with Christianity and his acceptance of baptism was relatively short, the process of enquiry and doubt continued in his case for most of the rest of his life. Whereas some converts lapsed in the face of continuing doubts, sometimes returning to the community of origin, but sometimes remaining in the limbo of an 'outcaste', Goreh remained a Christian until his death, yet modified his allegiance within the Anglican community. If his identity was actually quite shaky, his missionary colleagues nevertheless chose to portray him as the archetype of·a learned convert from the ranks of the Brahmin caste, a pandit, or religious teacher, and even on occasion a *shastri*, or particularly respected authority on sacred texts, whose conversion proved their ability to penetrate the learned Hindu elites. Thus his birth-name, Nilakantha, or 'blue-necked', which associated him with the Hindu deities, was retained on the frontispieces of many of his publications on religion, in tandem with the baptismal name, Nehemiah, which linked him to the Judaeo-Christian prophetic tradition he had chosen to adopt.

Master Ram Chandra/Yesudas (1821–1880, Baptized 1852)

A second very prominent convert from Hinduism was Ram Chandra, Goreh's contemporary, who was baptized four years later, in 1852, following more than a decade of close contact with Europeans then engaged in administration and education in the city of Delhi. He was one of a number of converts around that date from the Kayasth caste, whose ancestors typically had served the Mughals and their successors, and who now sought employment for their sons with the recently established East India

Company's bureaucracy. Ram Chandra's father had served the British as a *tahsildar* (revenue collector) in Delhi district, but he died suddenly in 1832 when his eldest son, who had been born in Panipat, was about eleven. Ram Chandra, who had five younger brothers, had been studying in a privately-run vernacular school, but his widowed mother had no resources to allow him to continue. Further schooling was made possible by a marriage to the deaf-and-dumb daughter of a wealthier Kayasth family, thus enabling him to enter the English Department of the Company's recently re-established Delhi Anglo-Oriental College. He soon attracted the attention of his teachers for his abilities, particularly in mathematics and languages, and in 1844 was given a post as a science lecturer in the Oriental Department. The contributions he made to the fame of Delhi College in the 'renaissance' era of the 1840s I have detailed elsewhere.[29] I intend here to follow more closely than was appropriate in that context, the process of Ram Chandra's conversion to Christianity. As in the case of Goreh and most of the other high caste converts of this period, Ram Chandra wrote letters and diaries at the time, and also subsequently published an account called 'Why I became a Christian', from which, with the help of some 'observer' accounts, the process can be reconstructed in some detail.[30]

There are many similarities to Nilakantha Goreh's case, but also some significant differences. Unlike Goreh, who deliberately sought out the missionaries in order to refute them, Ram Chandra was studying and working alongside Europeans, in a secular context, for several years before Christianity made any impact on him. Compared to Benares, the city of Delhi had hardly yet felt the effects of evangelical pressure, and the Delhi College was particularly immune from missionary influence. Ram Chandra later recounted that one of the lecturers did give him Christian literature while he was a student, but when he rejected it, there was no follow-up. His own account suggests he passed through a phase of agnostic theism similar to several high caste Hindus in the English medium colleges of Calcutta a decade earlier. He was clearly a leader of sceptical opinion in the college, recounting:

> I with the assistance of the higher students of the English and Oriental Departments, formed a society for the diffusion of knowledge among our countrymen. . . . We

25

first commenced a monthly . . . in which not only were the dogmas of the Mahomedan and Hindu philosophy exposed, but also many of the Hindu superstitions and idolatries were openly attacked. The result of this was that many of our countrymen, the Hindus, condemned us as infidels and irreligious; but as we did not advocate Christianity, but only recommended a kind of deism, and as we never lost our caste publicly, by eating and drinking, all our free discussions did not much alarm our Hindu friends.[31]

He and his friends scoffed at the idea that the missionaries, whose intellects they despised, could have any influence upon them, and as for the Company officials, 'it was then my conscientious belief that educated Englishmen were too much enlightened to believe in any bookish religion except that of reason and conscience, or deism. . . . for my part, I considered all bookish religions, as absurd and false.'[32] He meanwhile became well known in Delhi as something of a free-thinking 'philosopher', taking an active part in a number of intellectual controversies among both Hindus and Muslims, and concentrating his own efforts on the writing of a mathematical textbook. He later attributed the sudden change in his attitude to Christianity to a chance exposure to the observance of Europeans at prayer. When the college headmaster who, to no avail, had earlier suggested Bible-reading to him, asked him to escort a Brahmin visitor to a service in St James's Church:

out of mere curiosity we went there, and saw several English gentlemen whom I respected as well informed and enlightened persons. Many of them kneeled down, and appeared to pray most devoutly. I was thus undeceived of my first erroneous notion, and felt a desire to read the Bible.[33]

While this explanation may seem simplistic, especially in contrast to Goreh's tortuous intellectual questioning, it was repeated by Ram Chandra in various subsequent writings. There followed, he recounted, a period of intense study of the New Testament, which had been thrown in a corner unread many years before, with the result that, 'I became aware that salvation is not merely in knowing that there is one God, and that polytheism and idolatry are false, but that it is in the Name of our most blessed Saviour, the Lord Jesus Christ.'[34] In contrast to Goreh he seemed to

experience sudden and comp...
realization struck him. In Ram...
carried out on his own seems to ...
process than it was for Goreh, and in ...
he turned to Hindu and Muslim schol...
Christians, of whom there were anywa...
Delhi. He seems to have been indebted ...
later became his godmother, for enco...
period of crisis rather than to any prominen...
missionary. He recounted that, 'I read ma...
together with some treatises of Hinduism an...
and had frequent discussions with the Professors ...
but particularly with the latter.'[35] Significantly, a ...
appears to have encountered Brahmo reformist ...
after his own baptism, Ram Chandra recorded that '...
thought of following the Bengal reformers'. Neverthele...
contacts seem to have been with Muslim scholars, ra...
either Hindu scholars or with prominent Christians, ...
Chandra continued right up to his baptism to challenge ...
tenets, notably on the question of miracles, even thoug...
'argument from miracles' was much more central to Chris...
than to Islamic apologetics. The reasons for this oblique approa...
are difficult to reconstruct, for although it was later reported tha...
Mughal circles hoped to draw wavering Hindus to Islam rather
than to Christianity, there is little other evidence for such
competition for converts as early as the 1850s. Significantly,
however, his post-baptismal contribution to Christian evangelism
would continue to be among Muslims, rather than among fellow
Hindus. There is some evidence for unease among Muslims in
Delhi, for at the exact juncture that Ram Chandra was coming to
his decision for baptism, a government official, one 'Abd-Allah
Athim, was also challenging the Delhi '*ulama* to defend the 'truth'
of their revelation. Ram Chandra, therefore was both cause and
symptom of the beginning of public confrontation over religious
identity among Delhi's elites, whereas Goreh's stance vis à vis the
Benares missionaries, had taken the form of a much more
personal and introverted crisis.

In contrast indeed, to Goreh's furtive baptism, was the
deliberately public character of Ram Chandra's reception into
the Anglican Church. It seems that he felt spiritually ready for
baptism by 1850, but financial worries made him hesitate, as did

f losing caste. Questions of inheritance were probably of
ern in his case than uncertainties about the success of his
published mathematics textbook, which after bad reviews
utta had been sent to England for scrutiny. He openly
ledged the 'economic factor' as an obstacle to baptism, for
ifficulties of debts and of marrying my daughters in Delhi
coming an open Christian troubled me greatly'.[36] This diary
was made a month before his baptism, yet in spite of 'great
ess of mind', he finally went ahead with the ceremony without
ting for the verdict of the London mathematicians on his
ok. As it happened the response was favourable, and orders for
e book for use in government schools did help to relieve his
mmediate financial worries. This was unresolved, however, when
n 11 July 1852 he was baptized with the name, 'Yesu Das', in St
James' Church, near Delhi's Kashmiri Gate. Although fear of an
outcry among Delhi's Hindus was just as strong as in Benares, it
was decided to go ahead regardless of any possible reaction.
There are a number of possible reasons for the difference. Ram
Chandra, though a well known, high caste Hindu, was not a
Brahmin of a respected local family as was Nilakantha Goreh.
Also, his agnosticism, and disrespect for Hindu rituals had been
widely publicized for a decade. Although he was respected as a
teacher, and a scientist, he was already despised among orthodox
Hindu circles; his formal transfer of identity was hardly a gain to
Christianity in their eyes. On the other hand, he was baptized
along with another well known Kayasth, a sub-assistant surgeon
named Chimman Lall, who after education in the local Delhi and
Agra government colleges, had studied medicine in Calcutta.[37]
The association of these two converts with western and secular
education was strong enough to arouse fears of a more widespread 'movement' towards Christianity in the government
schools and colleges of the region. In these circumstances, the
conclusion can only be drawn that there was no physical
opposition mainly because the local British officials not only
honoured the occasion with their presence, but also provided an
armed guard to prevent any disturbance at the church. As a result,
although, according to one newspaper, 'the news ran like wildfire
through the place', rousing horror and speculation among the
Hindus, Delhi rapidly recovered from the shock. As I have shown
elsewhere, the reaction among learned Muslims was actually
deeper than among the converts' co-religionists.[38] A Muslim

28

poet encapsulated the popular mood of anathema in a Persian couplet:

> July the eleventh, fifty two,
> Master was baptised, Doctor too;
> Enraged at this the people cried,
> To hell the damned couple has hied.[39]

Although it seems that the Hindu community in general may not have felt much loss from the baptism of a self-proclaimed sceptic, Ram Chandra did, of course, lose caste, and some of the Kayasth community collected signatures from the local *baradari* condemning him. He was obliged to leave his home, and a long nine-year interval elapsed before he was able to retrieve his wife after she had agreed to accept baptism. Although he was baptized 'Yesu Das', he continued to be known by his Hindu name, and he maintained the outward physical appearance appropriate to his caste and occupation. Indeed, missionary circles later claimed that he fully recovered his influence within his *baradari*, even though he never regained caste. They also said that one of his brothers, who held a relatively high position in district government, was a secret convert, but feared to accept baptism. Certainly both teacher and surgeon were able to resume their normal occupations immediately after baptism, and although there were unlooked for repercussions among Muslim learned circles, concern among the wider Hindu community seemingly rapidly abated, at least, that is, until the rebellion of 1857 convulsed the city.

For 'Master' Ram Chandra continued in his lecturing role at Delhi College from 1852 until 1857, his scholarly reputation now enhanced by the success of his mathematics book, and seemingly suffering no adverse effects from his baptism. He was increasingly made use of as a go-between and informant by the Agra missionaries in their new plans to evangelize Delhi, because of his close relations with both Hindu and Muslim scholars in the city. However, in May 1857 he only narrowly escaped death at the hands of the sepoy rebels, and his partner-in-baptism, Dr Chimman Lall, was killed with many of the 'native' as well as European Christians who had the misfortune to encounter the sepoys in the first flush of the uprising. The baptisms had, in spite of the seeming cooling off after the initial reaction, later interacted in various quarters with other reasons for an upsurge of resentment against the newly intensive missionary concentration on this city. His identity in the eyes of his fellow citizens nevertheless remains somewhat ambiguous. For there was some suggestion that apart from receiving help from his brothers, some nameless Hindus and Muslims in the bazaars also helped to save his life in 1857, and that in turn, Ram Chandra later intervened to save some of the anti-Christian *'ulama* from British charges of raising *jihad*. Whatever his exact role in 1857, Ram Chandra suffered considerable demotion when the British recovered the city, mainly because Delhi College, where he had taught so long, and the only prestigious higher education institution in the locality, was not reopened. Consequently he had to take a series of lower level posts in schools and colleges outside Delhi. Only when religious controversy re-erupted in north India in the late 1860s did he come into his own again as a debater and writer in defence of Christianity, and in attack on Islam, the target of his earlier debates with the city's scholars.

His partner in debate from 1867 onwards was a third convert from Hinduism, Tara Chand, one of the first high caste Indians to be baptized by the new mission established in Delhi by the Society for the Propagation of the Gospel. Together these two converts started an Urdu religious monthly called *Muwaiz-i Uqba*, which soon aroused the ire of some local *'ulama* who retaliated in the same style.[40] Ram Chandra's two major controversial works in criticism of Islam were the *I'jaz-i Qur'an*, and the *Tahrif-i Qur'an*, published in Delhi, respectively in 1870 and 1877. It is significant that he chose to resurrect two of the stock themes of pre-Mutiny debate between Muslims and Christians, the questions of miracles and of textual reliability, in answer to the widely circulated books of various north Indian *'ulama*. He wrote in Urdu, following the medieval formulae of Muslim religious debate, thus adopting the scholarly mode of a by-gone era in order to remedy the errors which European missionaries had made before 1857 in failing to take on sufficiently convincingly the roles considered appropriate for religious debaters in an Indo-Muslim context.

He was successful in this role in so far as he was responsible for drawing some other high caste and *ashraf* Delhi citizens to Christianity, notably one of King Bahadur Shah's sufi disciples, one Mirza Ghulam Nazir. Yet missionary colleagues found him too aggressive in his approach to Muslims, regretting in particular, a tract in which he identified the Prophet Muhammad with the

Anti-Christ.[41] Certainly his position as a 'native convert' remained ambiguous. Although, unlike Goreh, he suffered from no personal doubts about his adopted faith, both his former community and his new missionary colleagues had some misgivings about his activities.

Converts from Islam:

Shaikh Salih/'Abd al-Masih (c. 1769–1827, baptized 1811; ordained Lutheran c. 1820, Anglican 1826)

It is usually assumed that Christian missionaries were less successful in securing conversions from Islam than they were from Hinduism. Yet 'Abd al-Masih, the first significant Muslim convert to Protestant Christianity in this region, was baptized as early as 1811, shortly before the Company raised its ban on missionary activity within its Bengal territories. The event might be seen as initiating the conversion phenomenon presently being studied, both because his European mentors, the Company chaplains, Henry Martyn and Daniel Corrie, were themselves the first evangelical missionaries to preach in this region, and because he, in turn, was responsible for some fifty high caste and *ashraf* baptisms in the years after 1813. When he commenced his own preaching in 1812 he started a diary in Urdu, which was immediately translated and published, in an abridged form in the CMS journal, the *Missionary Register.* Although this diary does not cover the period of his conversion, he made retrospective comments about it in later entries, which together with the observations of his European contacts, permit some reconstruction of the process.

'Shaikh Salih' was born in Delhi in the 1760s, in a Muslim family which claimed *ashraf* origins, on the grounds of its descent from Turkish immigrants into India. Whatever, its high social origins, it seems clear that by the mid eighteenth century, when Salih was born, the family was only of marginal social status within the *ashraf* category. His immediate forefathers seem to have been minor scholars, his father and an uncle having served as tutors in various aristocratic families. He was taught Arabic and Persian by his own father, but does not appear to have had any higher learning. This is perhaps not surprising, given the instability of late Mughal Delhi. Indeed, the family's migration to Lucknow in the 1790s, when Salih was about twenty-one, was probably occasioned by problems of employment in Maratha-occupied Delhi. Missionary records state that,

> his connexions were among the most respectable people in the Dooab, though, from the changes in the Government of late years, they had fallen into comparative poverty.[42]

At the time he first came into contact with evangelicals he had already been briefly employed by various Europeans in Lucknow, mainly in clerical capacities. He had also taken military service with a Muslim chief against the Marathas, and was currently engaged in the menial employment of the manufacture of 'green paint'. Although missionary sources describe this as 'a more than mere livelihood', employment more suited to his class and educational background was clearly hard to come by in the circumstances of the recent British take-over of the region. Little is known, however, about his spiritual state before his contact with Christianity, although missionary accounts stress, as they were wont to do when recording other conversion cases, the 'zeal' hitherto shown by the convert for the religion of his birth, for 'at this time Abdool was so zealous a Mussulman, that he induced a Hindoo servant . . . to become a Mahometan'.[43] There is also an allusion to the revulsion he had allegedly felt at witnessing gratuitous violence while serving against the Marathas, a state of mind his biographer construed, which 'prepared' him for Christianity.[44]

The context of Salih's first encounter with Christianity was the effort made by Henry Martyn, one of the first evangelical Company chaplains, to preach to the Indians living in the vicinity of his cantonment postings. This was frowned on by his Company superiors, and in all but the one case of Shaikh Salih, seems to have proved utterly fruitless. What was different in his case? The encounter occurred in the city of Cawnpore, where Martyn had adopted the practice of preaching in his own courtyard on Sunday mornings to an audience mainly of beggars. Co-incidentally, Salih's father was at that time 'engaged as private tutor in the house of a rich native', which happened to adjoin Martyn's compound. Salih later recounted that he overheard Martyn's sermons from the next-door house, and feeling curious, wanted 'to see the sport'.[45] Although his initial motive was a wish to make fun of Martyn's 'enthusiastic' soul-searchings, he claims he was immediately struck by the 'reasonableness' of the first sermon he heard, which was an exposition of the Ten Commandments. It was recorded that he relished the clarity of these rules, for, 'he had previously been perplexed about the contradictions maintained by the different Mahometan sects'.[46] When he asked his father for assistance to obtain a post which would gain him access to Martyn's household, it seems that he co-operated by asking friends to secure his son a post copying Persian manuscripts. He thus lived clandestinely in Martyn's house, not yet declaring his real interest, but using his position to make enquiries about Christian doctrine. The crisis came when Martyn, having completed his translation of the New Testament into Urdu, asked Salih to bind it. According to Daniel Corrie,

> On reading the word of God, he discovered his state, and perceived therein a true description of his own heart.[47]

Unfortunately there is no record of the particular parts of the New Testament which are held to have affected him, especially as he kept his own counsel, even now, about his attraction towards Christianity. Not until Martyn was on the point of leaving India did he speak out, begging to be accepted for baptism. Partly because he had experienced earlier disappointments, and partly because Salih had hidden this gradual 'process' from him. Martyn remained sceptical about the genuineness of his conversion. He allowed him, however, to accompany him to Calcutta, where he remained 'not entirely convinced of this man's real change of heart'.[48] In the end he refused to baptize him, recommending him, on his own departure from India, to the care of the other chaplains in Calcutta, who, after an interval of five months during which they 'made full investigation' until 'thoroughly satisfied with the Shekh's account of his conversion', they baptized him on Whit Sunday 1811.

Like several other converts from this region of northern India, Salih was baptized at a considerable distance from his family home, though in his case the reason was connected less with his own fear of repercussions than with missionary caution in thoroughly 'screening' the convert. David Brown, the chaplain who baptized him, giving him the name 'Abd al-Masih ('servant of Christ'), characterized the occasion as a 'public' baptism, yet one to which 'private notice' had been given, presumably in a successful effort to screen the audience equally thoroughly. For about a year afterwards he remained in Calcutta, his future sphere of activity something of a puzzle both to himself and his mentors. For the newly baptized 'Abd al-Masih seems to have felt some understandable reserve about immediately throwing himself into evangelistic activity without a fuller study of the Bible, an attitude which was seemingly misunderstood by some of his mentors as 'a proof of aversion to labour'.[49] A compromise was arrived at by requiring him to preach in a private house in Calcultta, but even this appears to have so aroused the ire of some local Muslims that they 'made him many offers of money etc, if he would renounce Christianity or leave the place.'[50] False charges were also made which brought him into the public courts. In July 1812, it was decided that he should accompany one of the chaplains Daniel Corrie, to his new posting in Agra. At that time Corrie, though cautious because, 'so often have I been deceived by these people, that I almost fear to speak decidedly of any of them', nevertheless felt so much confidence in 'Abd al-Masih that he could record, 'judging from present appearances, I should be more disposed to fear for myself than for Abdool'.[51]

The presence of 'Abd al-Masih and Daniel Corrie in Agra in 1813–4 resulted in the first crop of Protestant baptisms in the north-west, which if falling somewhat short of a 'mass conversion' phenomenon, nevertheless reached a total of at least fifty, including a number from high caste and *ashraf* backgrounds, as well as some peasants and craftsmen of various religious affiliations.[52] There seems no doubt that 'Abd al-Masih possessed some particular qualities of personality which allowed him to make a breakthrough of this order. He seemed to attribute some of his own success to his maintenance of the physical appearance and the aura of a sufi Muslim. Like Goreh, he was reluctant to join the formal clerical hierarchy, preferring the unassuming role of a catechist. Pressure finally induced him to take first Lutheran, and later Anglican orders, but he clung to his familiar appearance and life-style. Indeed, when criticized in later years for having turned 'firangi', 'Abd al-Masih was always quick to deny any acculturation, priding himself that the curiosity he aroused among Muslims was partly because in retaining his 'turban, Arabian dress, and Turkish horse', he was often mistaken for a Persian traveller.[53] If this suggests, far from 'native simplicity', a very cultivated exoticism, it is well supported by a striking oil portrait which reflects the 'truly venerable personal appearance' which was commented on in contemporary accounts.[54]

He had been joined in Agra by one of his nephews who also accepted baptism, as did one of his brothers. Unusually, it seems, he did not experience opposition from any of his immediate family members, even though the rest of his relations remained Muslim. His father, it has already been suggested, had been instrumental in introducing him to Henry Martyn in the first place. His mother, to whom he was particularly close, always welcomed him to the family home in Lucknow, and he recorded the holding of Christian worship in the family house whenever he visited the city.[55] He remained unmarried, and this seems to be an unusual, if not unique, case of a baptism occurring without causing any deep ruptures within the family and the immediate community. Reactions to his conversion in the vicinity of both Agra and Lucknow were more pronounced. His own success as a proselytizer of course aroused the curiosity, and sometimes the anger, of fellow Muslims, '*Ulama* passing through Agra stopped to enquire about him, and sometimes to dispute with him. On his frequent visits to his family in Lucknow he was sometimes spat upon, and he himself attributed his physical safety only to British protection, recording that, 'were it not for fear of the Resident, they would cut my throat'.[56] He also claimed to receive protection from the formidable sister of the ruling nawab, and her bodyguard of armed slavegirls.[57] Certainly he had friends at court, for he was also received in audience by the king of Awadh's wazir. Although he failed to secure similar royal attention in Delhi, he was at least allowed to deliver gospels to the palace. No conversions seem to have followed from these aristocratic and *ashraf* connections which probably reflected political rivalries and mere curiosity, rather than any intrinsic interest in the apostate Muslim's new Christian identity and message. His direct influence seems to have been restricted to the hinterland of Agra, where apart from preaching he prepared Urdu commentaries on parts of the New Testament, and assisted Daniel Corrie, the evangelical chaplain who had all but adopted him after Henry Martyn's departure, with the translation of sermons and biblical passages for the use of the growing flock of converts. Yet, after 'Abd al-Masih left this region in the mid-1820s most of his converts lapsed, some of the *ashraf* Muslims having returned to Islam much earlier. Although his impact was therefore both short-lived and restricted, and he failed to set up a permanent mission station in either Agra or Lucknow, it seems that his conversion and subsequent activities were more significant than those of any other Indian convert during the early years of evangelical activity in this region. Certainly the Urdu scriptures were first widely disseminated in north-western India by 'Abd al-Masih. In Lucknow, in particular, he seems to have sown the seeds of a curiosity about Christianity which would have repercussions in court circles a few years after his death. His daily journal detailing his encounters and his conversations on religion and other matters provides one of the earliest and fullest sources for studying both his own 'conversion process' and the attempts of an Indian convert to produce the same effect on others.

Imad ud-din (1830–1899, baptized 1866, ordained deacon 1868, priest 1872, D.D. 1884)

Imad ud-din's history fits the purposes of this paper more fully than any other, mainly because he wrote and published several accounts of the spiritual struggles he experienced before conversion, the first of these written almost immediately after his baptism, and the last only a few years before his death some thirty years later. While the first of these accounts, 'A Mohammedan brought to Christ', subtitled the 'Autobiography of a Native clergyman in India', will be drawn on extensively in what follows, the retrospective accounts will also be referred to, in order to show new stresses, and subsequent modifications, in the years when Imad ud-din had become very well known, even notorious, in the region.[58] For a second reason to focus on him is that he played an extremely active role in the life of the Christian community in north India, reflected in his participation in controversy with Muslim scholars, and in his invitation to the Parliament of Religions in Chicago in 1893, for which occasion he wrote a final account of his life, although he was by then too unwell to make the journey.[59]

The 'Reverend Imad ud-din' can be compared to 'Father Goreh' in several significant ways. Much is made in his autobiographical accounts of the strength of his *ashraf* credentials. For he was descended through thirty generations, from a family of religious note which had settled in Hansi, not far from Delhi, 'in which city', he recorded, 'there were twelve religious chiefs'.

The name of one of these religious chiefs was Jalaluddeen; whose son was Shekh Fateh Mohammed; whose son was

36

Moulwie Mohammed Sirdar; whose son was Moulwie Mohammed Fazil; whose son was Moulwie Mohammed Siraj-uddeen, my father; whose children are my brothers and sisters and myself.[60]

Thus, like Nehemiah Goreh, Imad ud-din would be perceived by the Evangelicals as well as by himself, as having been captured for Christianity from among the strongholds of north Indian religious tradition, in this case from a Sunni and sufi stronghold. Significantly, in an abbreviated version of his autobiography which was published after his death, a missionary editor attributed to him longstanding Christian credentials by claiming a link between Imad ud-din's family and a Sasanian king of Persia, one Mushzad, who, it was here alleged,

> was a Christian, and it was a favourite reply of Imad-ud-din, when reproached for abandoning the faith of his fathers, to say, 'Nay, verily, we have but returned from wandering in error to the faith of our father, for at the head of our family there stands a Christian, and by God's grace a good Christian too'.[61]

This was but a particularly strong and imaginative articulation of a common tendency to put forward mythical pedigrees as part of the process of creating appropriate genealogies and 'histories' in support of newly adopted convert identities.

Like Nehemiah Goreh's family too, Imad ud-din's immediate forefathers were certainly men who were revered for their spirituality in the immediate locality. His grandfather, Maulawi Muhammad Sirdar, had been called to nearby Panipat to minister to the Afghan chief, Ghulam Muhammad Khan, and his father, Maulawi Muhammad Siraj ud-din, received similar esteem from the local chiefs for his learning and piety, Imad ud-din recording that 'he is ever occupied, as before, in acts of worship by day and in vigils at night'.[62] However, unlike Goreh's family, but like Shaikh Salih's and Ram Chandra's, Imad ud-din's family was, by the 1840s, feeling the economic consequences of Company infiltration into the region. He later explained,

> In the time of Shahjahan my ancestors were in fairly prosperous circumstances, and had ample revenues and estates. Their lands and possessions remained in our family

during the time of the Mahrattas; but in the days of my grandfather, when the English Government came into the country, my grandfather mistook his own interests, and our property was all conviscated, and we then directed our attention to study and to giving instruction.[63]

The implication of the euphimistic reference to 'mistaken interests' would appear to be support for the Marathas against the Company when the British conquered the old Mughal heartlands in the north-west, necessitating a 'turning inwards' to private study and teaching.

There is no doubt that, like all the other elite converts of this period, Imad ud-din experienced a deep spiritual crisis before accepting Christian baptism. In his case the process can be reconstructed in graphic detail from his own first-hand accounts. From his early teens he recounts that he began searching for spiritual fulfilment within his own Sunni-sufi tradition. At fifteen he joined the Anglo-Oriental College in Agra, where his elder brother, Maulwi Karim ud-din, was a lecturer in the Oriental Department. While he spent all his free time with the *'ulama*, sufis and other Muslim scholars of the city, it seems clear that it was 'intercourse I had had with some Christians' attached to the college that initiated 'some doubts in my mind respecting Mohammedanism'.[64] Relations, class-fellows and the local *'ulama* combined to drive such doubts away temporarily. Significantly, a class-fellow named Safdar 'Ali (who was later to accept baptism shortly before Imad ud-din, and then to influence his own decision) was foremost among those who took active steps to help him to reinforce his Muslim identity, taking him to seek advice from the learned Maulawi 'Abd al-Halim, who was in the service of the Nawab of Banda, coincidentally the same ruler whom Nehemiah Goreh's uncle had earlier served.

Finding no satisfaction from others, Imad ud-din then embarked on a lonely quest, involving a deep study of all available 'Mohammedan works', to 'thus find out what is true', side by side with experiments with various sufi austerities.[65] This search seems to have lasted for a period of more than ten years, dating from some point in his student years (1846–51), until the early 1860s. He was, at first, it seems, at the heart of an active *'ulama* group which centred on the Jama masjid in Agra, and as a sign of his deep involvement with their concerns, he later recorded that he was often asked to preach in that mosque against the local evangelical missionaries, who had just begun to target the local '*ulama*. 'I remained there preaching and expounding the Commentaries and Traditions etc, for three years'.[66] He attended inter-religious debates as an observer, but was seemingly unmoved by what he heard from either side. It was, however, through one of the Muslim protagonists, one Dr Wazir Khan, a local surgeon, that Imad ud-din claims he was influenced to seek spiritual satisfaction on the path of sufi austerities, recording that, 'the person who entangled me in this calamity, and thus deceived me, was Doctor Wuzeer Khan, who had come to Agra as sub-assistant surgeon.'[67] In a later account, nearly half a century distant from the pains he had then experienced, he expressed the experiment rather less bitterly, as 'I dived also into the waters of Sufism and tested it'.[68] At some point in the 1850s he despaired of finding his goal in the British provincial capital of Agra, and proceeded to wander the whole middle Ganges region, sometimes accepting invitations to preach in mosques, but really seeking a way out of the impasse he had reached through further experiments with sufi austerities. He records of this period:

> As soon as I was entangled in this subtle science I began to practise speaking little, eating little, living apart from men, afflicting my body, and keeping awake at nights. ... I constantly sat on the graves of holy men, in hopes that, by contemplation, I might receive some revelation from the tombs. ... whatever afflictions or pain it is in the power of man to endure, I submitted to them all, and suffered them to the last degree; but nothing became manifest to me after all, except that it was all deceit.[69]

At this stage he renounced his former companions, and retired to the jungles, covered in red ochre in the garb of a fakir, with the intention of 'utterly renouncing the world'.[70] In one town he passed through he was treated as a saint, and disciples began to flock to him. Knowing the hypocrisy of this situation, he became even more despairing, convinced by now 'that there was no true religion in the world at all.'[71] At the centre of his despair was the realization that all known forms of Islamic mediation had failed to show him a way out of his predicament. This long period of uncertainty and irresolution can be compared with the crisis Goreh was simultaneously undergoing, which had commenced at about the same date, in the mid 1840s, but which was resolved in favour of Christianity within a period of three or four years, although doubts recurred for the rest of his life. Imad ud-din's spiritual crisis lasted at least ten years, during which time he had no direct contact with Christians, and continued to seek a resolution within the parameters of Sunni and sufi Islam.

> But still my soul found no rest; and in consequence of the experience I had had I only felt daily in my mind a growing abhorrence of the law of Mohammed.[72]

The next and final stage, in the early 1860s, was to return home to Panipat, from where he went to Lahore, the difference now being that he abandoned any pretence of upholding the *shariat*. Consequently, the once revered saintly figure was now criticized by the local *'ulama*, at which point his despair led him to the point of suicide. Lahore, however, was to be the scene of his conversion to Christianity.

His own accounts differ in the details emphasized in the subsequent process. In the earliest account, written in Urdu in the year of his baptism, and published in English shortly afterwards, he emphasized the role of the headmaster of the Lahore Normal School, a Mr Mackintosh, who gave him a teaching post.[73] While there he heard about the baptism at Jabalpur, of an old school friend, from their Agra College days, Maulawi Safdar 'Ali, whose own 'conversion process' had been initiated through contact with the convert from Hinduism, now Christian proseletiser, Nehemiah Goreh.[74] This news was a great shock, particularly as Safdar 'Ali had been in the forefront of those in Agra who ten years earlier had tried to reinforce Imad ud-din's own Islamic faith. In this account Imad ud-din explains his own subsequent move towards Christianity in terms of his fervent attempts, through correspondence, to restore Safdar 'Ali to Islam, to which end, he says, he read for the first time the Old and New Testaments, together with all the controversial literature which had been generated in north India in recent years. Mr Mackintosh then undertook to explain the New Testament to him. The precise moment of transition he described as follows:

> When I had read as far as the seventh chapter of St. Matthew, doubts fixed themselves upon my mind respecting the truth of Mohammedanism. I became so agitated that I spent

whole days, and often also whole nights, in reading and considering the books; and I began to speak about them, both with Missionaries and Mohammedans.[75]

He then spent a further year studying the Bible, mainly at night, coming to the final conclusion that, 'the religion of Mohammed is not of God . . . and that salvation is assuredly to be found in the Christian religion.'[76] The Muslims in whom he confided tried to dissuade him, urging him to dissimulate, rather than 'make my faith public'. He refused to listen, and shortly afterwards went to Amritsar, the centre of Anglican missionary activity in the Punjab, to ask for baptism.

Thirty years later he wrote a slightly different account, which omitted any reference to Safdar 'Ali as the initial stimulant, putting the emphasis instead on an unnamed 'aged, God-fearing, honourable English layman who was in Government service', who in 1864 urged him to read the Bible. This, most probably, was his colleague, Mr Mackintosh. His 'words so pierced my heart that from that moment I gave myself up whole-heartedly to examine into the Christian faith.'[77] Two years' Bible study followed, after which, 'having come to the conclusion that the religion of Christ is the true faith, I was baptized on April 29, 1866.' He explained elsewhere that the reason he went to Amritsar for baptism was because Robert Clark, a leading CMS missionary there, had been the first to exhort him by letter to turn to Christianity.[78] While there is some inconsistency in the details of these accounts, all confirm a long-drawn out and often despairing process during which Imad ud-din first tried to find satisfaction within the parameters of Islam, at the end of which, after reading the New Testament, and aided by various Europeans, he decided for baptism.

Initially, he said, most of his relatives and friends 'turned away from me'.[79] Yet, far from rejecting him, most of his family joined him in baptism. His revered eldest brother, Maulawi Karim-ud-din, who had so much influence upon him in his student days, never came to terms with his baptism, yet seems to have resumed contact with him afterwards. Two years after his own baptism one of his other brothers, Maulawi Khair-ud-din, and their father, Maulawi Siraj-ud-din, reputedly aged one hundred, and in a state of semi-consciousness, also received baptism. By 1873, Imad ud-din recorded that his wife who had initially been 'very displeased with me', had accepted baptism, along with their nine children. Like Ram Chandra, he had thus succeeded in creating around himself a new 'Christian family', to the dismay, no doubt, of those Punjabi Muslims who had regarded this family as spiritual mentors in their own community. Resentment was compounded by the aggressive part he was to play for the rest of his life in attacking Islam through tracts and debates.

For like Nehemiah Goreh and 'Abd al-Masih, and also several other converts from both Islam and Hinduism, Imad ud-din was ordained as a Christian minister, and subsequently became the agent for further conversions in the region. But unlike Goreh, though he suffered the same depths of depression during the fifteen or so years before his conversion, once the baptism had been performed, Imad ud-din seems to have had no further doubts, recording soon afterwards that, 'the agitation of mind and restlessness of which I have spoken has entirely left me'.[80] Shortly before his death he wrote that from the day of his baptism, 'for nearly twenty-seven years, it has been my thought night and day how to rescue Mohammedans from the errors in which they are plunged'.[81] So great was his own certainty that he had proceeded to write twenty-four books, mostly on controversial issues, and he took part in debates not only with the Sunni *ulama* of his own previous acquaintance, but also with the followers of other competing religious reform movements, such as the Ahmadis and the Arya Samajists. He wrote and debated in Urdu, and never fully mastered English. Like most other converts from both major religious traditions, he maintained his accustomed dress and life-style, rejecting Western dress. He also continued to use the name Imad ud-din, which though Muslim in origin, seemed transferable in meaning ('Pillar of the faith') to his new religious identity. He ended his life, in 1900, as one of the most well-known Christian ministers in the Punjab and north India.

CONCLUSIONS: CONVERSION CASE STUDIES IN THE CONTEXT OF 'CONVERSION THEORY'

Some attempt will now be made to relate these four case studies, and others from the same period and region, to theories about conversion processes in Africa and the Middle East, as well as in other contexts in India. Scholars from various disciplines have concerned themselves with the factors at work in movements towards both Islam and Christianity in sub-Saharan Africa, and the contribution of Robin Horton, in particular, in comparing responses to Islam and Christianity in terms of intellectual/cognitive factors, has been challenged and modified by other African specialists.[82] Conversion to Islam within an 'Islamic world' context has also received considerable attention recently, following the editing by Nehemia Levtzion of some seminar papers which introduced a comparative regional approach to the evaluation.[83] This volume included a paper on South Asia, since when there have been a number of further studies on Islamization in various parts of the subcontinent.[84] Particular mention should be made of the contribution of Richard Eaton, not only his studies of the medieval Deccan, but also his recently published study of Islamization in Bengal, in which he includes a chapter on 'Mass conversion to Islam: Theories and Protagonists', which evaluates some theoretical approaches, past and present, to the understanding of conversion in various parts of South Asia.[85] A useful bibliographical article by Lewis Rambo, although now rather dated, attempted to categorize and evaluate various disciplinary 'perspectives' he had identified within recent studies of conversion.[86] While some of this theoretical work, in relation both to conversion in Africa and to the Islamization of South Asia, may not seem directly relevant to nineteenth century Christian conversion in India, I have nevertheless drawn upon it to provide a context for the processes observable in these detailed case studies in north-western India. For comparatively little attention has so far been paid to setting conversion to Christianity in India in a theoretical context. Robert Frykenberg has, however, suggested ways in which appropriate questions might be posited.[87] Significantly, among the few case studies so far published on the Christianization of South Asia, are some earlier contributions by some of the members of the Toulouse workshop, notably Geoffrey Oddie's edited collection of articles, and Antony Copley's recent article on conversions among India's elites.[88]

What generalizations, then, can be made on the basis of the conversion processes identified and examined here in mid nineteenth century north-western India beyond confirming that it was amongst the religious elite groups that conversion was significant in this particular period. In all the four cases examined, and also in several others which have not received detailed attention here (for example a government official, 'Abd

Allah Athim, and a Delhi schoolmaster, Tara Chand), the sources indicate a long drawn-out 'spiritual crisis' in which conversion was a 'process' rather than an 'event'. Such cases might be examined both in terms of the 'intellectual/cognitive' process, first developed by Horton in relation to conversion in Africa, into which Nilakhanta Goreh's struggle might be placed, and in terms of the 'ecstatic' convert syndrome, developed by Richard Bulliet in relation to Islamization, the context, perhaps, of 'Abd al-Masih or Ram Chandra's sudden 'illumination' at the end of a long-drawn out process.[89] In terms of older, but still much debated theories, all the cases discussed in this paper, whatever their particular characteristics, undoubtedly exhibit features of the 'spiritual re-orientation of the soul', discussed in Arthur Nock's, *Conversion: the old and the new in religion*, very recently re-evaluated in relation to African conversion by Humphrey Fisher.[90] Significant in all these studies of individual conversions is the recognition that although 'road to Emmaus' sudden illuminations occasionally occur, much more usual is

> not a single event, but an ongoing process in which the totality of a person's life is transformed . . . while there may be an immediate ontological change in a person's spiritual life, the consequences of that change often emerge only slowly and painfully in the life experience of the individual.[91]

The conversion experiences of Nehemiah Goreh, Ram Chandra, and above all, Imad ud-din, all suggest long drawn out 'ordeals', in which the 'intellectual' and 'spiritual' elements are separately identifiable, yet intertwined. In trying to separate the elements, psychoanalytical theory, rightly suspect to cautious empirical historians, may nevertheless, 'offer some new insights into conversion'.[92] Efforts to 'go behind' the autobiographical data supplied by the converts themselves, in order to examine the reasons for recurring 'depressive' and 'ecstatic' states both before and after baptism, might be assisted by such perspectives and techniques in, for example, the tortuous cases of Nehemiah Goreh and Imad ud-din.

But before such approaches are given the aura of exact sciences, it should be remembered that the 'testimonies' relied upon so heavily in these case studies are anyway somewhat suspect. Apart from the consideration that most of them were translated and edited by missionary mentors with an 'interest' in the outcome, the editor of 'Current research', citing the work of sociologists in this field, reminds us that,

> the 'testimony' or conversion autobiography is not merely the raw report of one's personal experience but the creation of the convert which combines personal experience with the expectations, theology, and symbolism of the group which the person wants to join. They do not imply that the person is consciously deceitful, but, rather, is subtly influenced by the group to interpret his/her life in terms compatible with the needs of the group.[93]

Conversion accounts should not therefore be taken at 'face value', but 'as the active transformation of one's self-understanding and relationship to the particular community which has become the person's reference group'. This is, of course, well known, but easily forgotten in the excitement of discovering a first hand account from the pen of a recently baptized convert. Distinctions should therefore be made between the reliability of the various accounts cited above. Imad ud-din's many versions of his conversion experience perhaps constitute the most satisfactory reconstruction of such a process, not only because the first was written immediately after baptism, but also because the many subsequent 'various readings' allow for some diagnosis of some likely reasons for his altering the script. No doubt, in recounting, for example, the spiritual crisis of his middle years on the eve of his death, time had mellowed his memory of the trauma.[94] There is the advantage, too, that his earliest account also exists in the original Urdu, with which a recent new translation into English tallies very closely. Even with several first-hand accounts over time, it is still impossible to ascertain how far the convert has been influenced by his new Christian 'group' to 'reinterpret his life in terms compatible with the needs of the group', its 'theology and symbolism', in this particular case the 'needs' of the readers of the *Church Missionary Intelligencer* in the shires of England, as well as the missionaries on the spot. However, the availability of several similar 'cases' from within both major religious groups, who were converted at about the same time and place, may outweigh some necessary scepticism about the usefulness of the source materials in the formulation of generalizations about the processes experienced.

These painfully detailed accounts of pre-conversion 'crises' certainly permit some generalizations about 'agency'. While the preaching of particularly charismatic evangelists may have initially drawn attention to Christianity (for example, 'Abd al-Masih to Henry Martyn), the aggressive attacks on Islam and Hinduism, engaged in by some missionaries in the bazaars, were just as likely to generate rebuttal (in the case of Goreh), or scepticism (in the case of Ram Chandra). Significantly, once baptized and ordained, several of these converts, notably Ram Chandra and Imad ud-din, then engaged themselves in similar aggressive preaching and writing tactics. Why such men had eventually been drawn to Christianity was, their own accounts suggest, the result of a complex sequence of encounters, debates, and study, sometimes self-directed, and sometimes directed by European Christians, both missionary and lay, or by Indians, not necessarily of their own community, who had already converted. Study of the Bible, always held by missionary organizations to be the key to successful evangelism, was recorded by most of these converts as instrumental in their final conversion, although, as in Ram Chandra's case, sometimes only taken up after a period of total rejection. The gospels, particularly St Matthew, were said to have been particularly influential, although 'Abd al-Masih recorded that he was first attracted by a sermon on the Ten Commandments. Goreh, in contrast, seemed initially to have needed not scriptural, but intellectual reassurance, though in trying to convert other Hindus he subsequently put the emphasis on the Bible as a 'supernatural revelation', whose 'truth' could not be tested by 'reason'. Observance of the behaviour of Christians, particularly Europeans, was also claimed as an influence, especially in the case of Ram Chandra, who recounted being suddenly 'transformed', by the sight of Christians at prayer. Further study of the conversations and debates they engaged in, the letters written, and the texts read, is necessary before anything more conclusive can be said on the 'agencies' at work in the 'spiritual reorientation of the soul' characteristic of these conversions, but the data certainly exists to make this a viable undertaking, in spite of the caveats mentioned above.

Those who are sceptical of 'spiritual' motivations for changes of religious identity, in this or other contexts, prefer to emphasize social and economic incentives. Thus commentators on conversion to Islam in South Asia have preferred to pay attention to various definitions of 'social conversion' as explanations both of 'individual' and of 'mass conversions' in the medieval era. Various formulations of a 'Religion of Social Liberation thesis', and of a 'Religion of Patronage theory' (Richard Eaton's coinage) have been pressed into service to account for conversions considered to have taken place to gain either socio-religious equality or socio-economic mobility. Both have been discredited as explanations of mass conversions to Islam in India, although their relevance may still be argued in some particular circumstances.[95] Peter Hardy has nevertheless argued that both the process and the end result should be viewed in social rather than in interiorized religious terms for 'in Indian life "conversion" means more a change of fellowship than of conduct or inner life – although the latter may in time occur.'[96] Do such theories which emphasize the 'shifting of camps' rather than the adoption of new, intrinsically religious identities have any relevance to Christian conversion hundreds of years later? While the first (social liberation) clearly has some relevance for some earlier and later movements in other parts of India, for example the mass conversion of fisher castes in south India, it is the second (patronage) which has been put forward in Muslim and Hindu communities at the time, and intermittently ever since, to explain conversion to Christianity from amongst their own members. Converts to Christianity, it is said, benefited socially and economically, receiving, in Eaton's terms, 'some non-religious favor from the ruling class'.[97] Examination of these four cases of conversions from high çaste, elite backgrounds has shown that some of the converts might indeed be perceived as suffering economic disadvantages in the early stages of British rule, and may have been influenced by their own perceptions of their enhanced life chances as converts, though there is no evidence that this was indeed their own thinking. The missionaries, for example, perceived 'Abd al-Masih as suffering social and economic demotion under the new British regime, but there is no evidence for his own perception of his lot. On the other hand, there is some positive evidence that Nehemiah Goreh, born in a wealthy family, lost out economically by conversion, and that Ram Chandra hung back from baptism, after acknowledging inner 'conversion', because of financial concerns about his family. Yet, in none of these cases does it seem likely that hope either of economic betterment or of improved occupational patronage was anyway an overarching factor in their final decisions. What then were the actual occupational shifts? Interestingly, two out of the four converts who have been studied here became 'religious leaders' within their new communities, as they had been in their old (Pandit Nehemiah Goreh and Maulawi Imad ud-din were ordained.) Missionary records suggest that although Imad ud-din was offered, after baptism, a more lucrative post in the educational service, which would have led to 'influence and competence', he nevertheless chose ordination of his own accord because of the spiritual fulfilment he believed it would offer him.[98] There are also several other examples of converts who were ordained in this period, for example the Reverends Thakur Dass, Tara Chand and Ahsan Allah. Among those who had secular professions, Ram Chandra continued in the same occupation of college teacher, Maulawi Safdar 'Ali was promoted from deputy to District Inspector of Schools, while 'Abdullah Athim, also already in government service before baptism, rose to be Extra Assistant Commissioner in the Punjab. Did the new occupational status, and financial rewards, represent upward or downward mobility? While pandit (or alim) to pastor might be seen as a continuum, the connotations would differ when viewed from within, or without, the various communities in question. While Abd al-Masih may seem to have gained status as a result of baptism (paint dealer to pastor), much depends on whether he was really, in the first place, in the predicament of genteel poverty that his missionary mentors liked to think. Ram Chandra, having pulled himself up from poverty by his own efforts, continued to teach after baptism, yet never regained his former status as a Delhi College lecturer. However, the cause here was not baptism *per se*, but wider changes connected with the 1857 risings. The sources seem too loaded, and the criteria too community-bound, to yield any useful conclusions on occupational grounds alone. In the eyes of all other communities, Christian converts, of whatever former background, or present occupation, continued to be perceived as of low social status, even though individuals might earn personal respect or friendship. Imad ud-din might respond to this by listing, and publishing, the names of over one hundred 'Christian Converts of some distinction from Mohammedanism in India', who had maintained 'honourable' positions after baptism, but the very fact that he felt the need to do so, reinforces the perceptions of other communities about them.[99]

In terms of Peter Hardy's rather wider usage of the concept of 'social conversion', a more easily measurable 'change of fellowship' certainly did occur after baptism, although the former fellowship was not always entirely lost for ever. As we have seen, many of those who accepted baptism thereby lost the 'fellowship' of their immediate family and *baradari*, among them, Nehemiah Goreh, Ram Chandra and Imad ud-din. Yet 'Abd al-Masih, according to his own account, retained the goodwill of his family, and although only one nephew followed him in baptism, he was always welcome in his Lucknow home. Family relationships usually improved over time. One of Ram Chandra's brothers, and his father, allegedly already senile, were eventually baptized, and even Goreh was able to visit his elderly father, though the rest of the family ostracized him. Towards the end of his life, however, he re-established close relations with his younger brother, a traditional pandit. In most cases wives were recovered and baptized after an interval, for example, Imad ud-din's after some five years, Ram Chandra's after nine, and Nehemiah Goreh's only after the forceful intervention of a British magistrate. There is insufficient evidence at the moment to take any further the important and interesting question of the processes through which wives either followed their husbands into baptism, were restrained from doing so by their kin, or made a voluntary decision in one direction or the other. Claims were certainly made in the case of Ram Chandra that he was able to exercise a strong influence in his *baradari* in spite of being an outcaste Christian, and that Imad ud-din too, recovered some influence among his kin. Although the number of these high caste and *ashraf* converts was very small, their social status, previous reputations for religiosity, and in some cases, teaching roles, within their own communities, made their baptisms a matter of concern to a wider public beyond kin and caste. Furthermore, a degree of 'networking' followed, not only when some of their own close family members eventually accepted baptism, but when the baptism (and sometimes ordination) of one such 'enquirer' then influenced the conversion of another, sometimes across Hindu/Muslim divisions. 'Pandit' Nehemiah Goreh, for example, influenced 'Maulawi' Safdar 'Ali, who in turn played a part in 'Maulawi' Imad ud-din's conversion. The cross-community implications of baptism were also demonstrated when the baptism of two Kayasths in Delhi, caused more overt concern among elite Muslims than it did, at the time at least, among local Hindus. The ramifications of seemingly isolated examples of baptisms among the elites and across caste and community boundaries have thus been shown to be very significant.

Certainly such converts all gained a new community, in both a physical and a spiritual sense, even when they did not entirely lose or renounce the old. A newspaper report that the 'respectable' Nilakantha had gone 'to eat and drink with the Christians' exemplifies the significance attached to social taboos in determining the boundaries between religious identities and communities. Even before baptism a change of residence had often been necessary in order to avoid family and caste pressures directed to the preservation of these boundaries. After baptism, sanctuary was often taken with local missionary families, as in Nehemiah Goreh's case, or through a complete change of environment in a centre of Christian activity and community exemplified by 'Abd al-Masih's prolonged stay in Calcutta, and Imad ud-din's move to Amritsar. Subsequent employment as pastors and teachers anyway often necessitated a Christian institutional 'home', although those such as Safdar 'Ali and Abdallah Athim, who worked in government service were able to maintain more diverse and closer links with other non-Christian strata of the population. The extreme case of social isolation was perhaps experienced in the 'Christian villages', established for the protection of groups such as Christianized famine orphans, which aimed to socialize children of various caste backgrounds according to a new and foreign, as well as a Christian ethos. The little attention which has so far been paid to the new Christian communities which thus evolved in north-western India in the late nineteenth century has concentrated on the mass movement phenomenon of the late nineteenth century. It is apparent, however, from the evidence of these four case studies that new communities, often somewhat ambivalent in identity, had come into being earlier in the century as a consequence of the adhesion of branches of families following the initial baptism of one strong-minded male member, and a subsequent process of inter-marriage with other newly Christianized individuals and families.

It was, of course, a consequence of the difficult process through which they had gradually come to the momentous decision to change their religious identities through baptism, that the learned converts from Islam and Hinduism should then seek to proclaim their new identities and beliefs. Most of them as we have seen, became Christian evangelists in their leisure hours, if not actually by profession. Yet, most of them also sought, in an era not yet influenced by conscious nationalism, to publicly maintain their 'Indianness', in ways which sometimes involved bitter conflict with the missionary hierarchy. This was reflected too, in continuities in their style of living, including dress and dietary habits, use of the vernaculars in publishing and preaching, and was symbolized initially, in the adoption of baptismal names which while indicating their new religious identities, usually nevertheless retained the name bestowed in the community of their birth. Ram Chandra, significantly, was scarcely ever known by his 'Christian' name of 'Yesu Das', nor Tara Chand as 'Moses'. 'Pen names', used for evangelistic publications often incorporated the 'old' name and title with the 'new', for example, 'Reverend Nehemiah Nilakantha Sastri Goreh'. Most, as their photographs and portraits indicate, preserved the physical and outward appearance of learned scholars within the traditions of their birth, or as in Nehemiah's case, contrived a style of dress which homogenised Christian 'clerical' dress with conventions deemed appropriate for the particular religious elite in which they had been born. While adopting the belief system of the Europeans, there was a reciprocal awareness of cultural and social boundaries, which was partly a reflection of the popular bazaari identification of Europeans as '*firangis*' or '*bara sahibs*', while the convert clergy were scorned as '*kala sahibs*' or '*kala padres*'. The consequent ambiguity of their identities, in their own eyes, as well as those of their former co-religionists, is perhaps best summed up in a remonstrance of the Reverend 'Abd al-Masih, the only one to fully renounce his birth name, Shaikh Salih, in refutation of an accusation that he had, through change of life style, as well as belief system, apparently become a 'Feringee':

> I was born in Hindoostan: my colour is black, my dress different from that of the Sahibs, and I have a beard like yourselves; how then can you call me a Feringee? If you call me a Christian you will call me right.[100]

NOTES

1 The region is the old 'North-Western Provinces' (NWP) of the Company's Bengal Presidency, (today's U.P.) There is some reference also to the Punjab Province where some of the converts were either born or employed.

2 *Muslims and Missionaries in Pre-Mutiny India* (London, 1993).

3 In P.G. Robb (ed.) *Society and Ideology: Essays in South Asian History presented to Professor K.A. Ballhatchet* (Delhi, 1993), pp. 72–96.

4 John C.B. Webster, *The Christian Community and Change in Nineteenth Century North India* (Meerut, 1976); Antony Copley, 'The Conversion Experience of India's Christian Elite in the Mid-Nineteenth Century', *Journal of Religious History,* Vol. 18, No. 1, (June 1994).

5 Joseph Mullens, *The Results of Missionary Labour in India* (London, 1856); *A Brief Review of Ten Years' Missionary Labour in India between 1852 and 1861* (London, 1863).

6 Rev. Imad-ud-din, D.D., *Mohammedan Converts to Christianity in India* (London, n.d.), p. 9.

7 *ibid*, pp. 13–16.

8 Full biographical details will be given about the four converts whose experiences form the core of this study. Reference will also be made to a handful of others from similar backgrounds, but about whom insufficient information is at present available to consider them in detail. They include Chimman Lal, Tara Chand, and Safdar Ali. 'Abd Allah Athim, an important convert from Islam, has already been the subject of a separate article. See Powell, 'Contested Gods and Prophets: Discourse among Minorities in late Nineteenth Century Punjab', *Renaissance and Modern Studies* (Dec. 1995 pp. 38–59).

9 The classic account from the Christian perspective is by a fellow member of the Anglo-Catholic order which Goreh finally joined. C.E. Gardner, *Life of Father Goreh* (London, 1900).

10 Richard Fox Young, *Resistant Hinduism: Sanskrit Sources on Anti-Christian Apologetics in Early nineteenth-century India* (Vienna, 1981).

11 Particularly useful as a 'participator-observer' account of this conversion process is Rev. W. Smith's *Dwij: the Conversion of a Brahman to the Faith of Christ* (London, 1850), supplemented by Smith's reports and letters to the Church Missionary Society deposited in the CMS archive at Birmingham University (CI1/0265/1–99).

12 *A Letter to the Brahmos, from a converted Brahman of Benares,* (Calcutta, 1867), p. 32.

13 Smith, *Dwij,* p. 38.

14 *ibid*, pp. 38–9.

15 John Muir (1810–1882). A civilian who occupied various judicial, revenue and educational posts in north India from 1830 to 1853. He retired early to Scotland to pursue his interest in Sanskrit studies. His most well known work is *Original Sanskrit Texts on the Origin and History of the People of India* (5 vols, London and Edinburgh, 1858–70). See *DNB*, XIII, pp. 1164–5.

16 *Sastratattvavinirnaya*, A Verdict on the Truth of the Sastra, (1844–5); it was republished, edited by S.L.Katre, at Ujjain, 1951 (not seen).

17 For Smith's synopsis of Goreh's 'Doubts' see *Dwij*, pp. 59–70. For Fox Young's commentary, *Resistant Hinduism*, pp. 104–5.

18 Powell, *Muslims and Missionaries in Pre-Mutiny India*, pp. 158–91.

19 *Dwij*, p. 94.

20 *Sriyesukhrstamahatmya: the Glory of Jesus Christ* (Calcutta, 1848).

21 *A Letter to the Brahmos from a converted Brahman of Benares* (Calcutta, 1867), pp. 32–4. 'Christianity does not come from the reasoning and speculation of men, like other religious systems, but is a revelation from God', *The Brahmos: their idea of Sin, its Nature and Punishment* (Poona, 1882), p. 1.

22 *Dwij*, pp. 106–7.

23 *Resistant Hinduism*, p. 169. Smith's reports to the CMS detailing their conversations show many examples both of the reading of Biblical passages which seemed at least temporarily to quell Goreh's doubts, and of his initial need to receive intellectual satisfaction, confirming Fox Young's conclusion that the 'tension between faith and reason . . . dogged him to the end of his career'. p. 169.

24 *Dwij*, p. 142.

25 Or, *Vedantism and the essence of Christianity* (1853).

26 *Resistant Hinduism*, pp. 170–1.

27 *Dwij*, pp. 109–12.

28 *Do I Truly and Honestly Believe in the Doctrine of the Church of England . . .* (Poona, 1884).

29 Powell, *Muslims*, pp. 207–9.

30 For biographical details see A. de Morgan, editor's preface to Ram Chandra. *A Treatise on Problems of Maxima and Minima solved by Algebra* (London, 1859); Sadiq al-Rahman Qidwa'i, *Master Ram Chandra, qadim Dihli Kalij ki ek ahm shakhsiyat* (Delhi, 1961); E. Jacob, *A Memoir of Professor Yesudas Ramchandra of Delhi*, Vol. 1 (Cawnpore, 1902); 'Abd al-Haqq, *Marhum Dihli Kalij* (2nd ed. Delhi, 1945).

31 Jacob, *Memoir*, p. 11.

32 *ibid*.

33 *ibid*, pp. 43–4.

34 *ibid*, pp. 44–5.

35 *ibid*, p. 45.

36 *ibid*, p. 59.

37 Chimman Lall was baptized as 'Masih Sahar' ('supported by Christ'), Rev. M.J. Jennings to Mr Hawkins, Delhi, 15 July 1852, USPG archive, Rhodes House, Oxford: Series X 1283.

38 Powell, *Muslims*, pp. 212–19.

39 Jacob, *Memoir*, p. 84.

40 *ibid*, pp. 125–7; see Rev. Tara Chand's reports to the SPG in USPG archive: Series E 17/40.

41 This book, *Masih-ud-Dajjal* was withdrawn after the first edition as likely to arouse the 'fiercest antagonism of the followers of Islam', E.M. Wherry, *The Muslim Controversy*, (London, Madras and Colombo, 1905), p. 78.

42 *Missionary Register* (henceforward *MR*) (Oct. 1827), p. 262.

43 Daniel Corrie, 'Memoir of Abdool Messee, 17 Dec. 1812, in *MR* (July, 1813), p. 261.

44 *ibid*, p. 262.

45 *ibid*, p. 263.

46 Corrie's paraphrase of Abdal Masih's explanation, *ibid*, p. 263.

47 *ibid*.

48 *ibid*, p. 264.
49 'Memoir and Obituary', *MR* (Oct. 1827), p. 450.
50 'Memoir', *MR* (July, 1813), p. 265.
51 *ibid*, p. 266.
52 Abd al-Masih's journal, published in *MR*, 1814–1816.
53 ibid, *MR* (Oct. 1826), p. 393.
54 'Memoir and Obituary', *MR* (Oct. 1827), pp. 450–1. The portrait hangs in the CMS headquarters in London.
55 e.g. 'returned home and had prayers with the family', 11 Feb. 1821, Lucknow, Journal, CMS archive, Birmingham University: CII/0194/6.
56 *MR* (Aug. 1826), p. 394.
57 Journal, 13 Feb. 1821, Lucknow, CMS archive: CI1/0194/6.
58 Imad ud-din, *Waqi'at-i 'Imadiyya*, Urdu, 1866, translated as *A Mohammedan brought to Christ; being the Autobiography of a Native Clergyman in India*, (2nd ed. Lahore, 1870). A second English translation was published more recently by Ernest Hahn as *The Life of the Rev. Mawlawi Dr.'Imad ud-din Lahiz* (Vaniyambadi, 1978), pp. 1–17. This edition contains an appendix added in 1873.
59 *Mohammedan Converts to Christianity in India* (London, n.d. but originally written 1893).
60 *Mohammedan Brought to Christ*, p. 5.
61 Preface to *Mohammedan Converts*.
62 *Mohammedan Brought to Christ*, p. 6.
63 *ibid*, pp. 5–6.
64 *ibid*, p. 8.
65 *ibid*, p. 9.
66 *ibid*, p. 11.
67 *ibid*, p. 10.
68 *Mohammedan Converts*, p. 4.
69 *Mohammedan Brought to Christ*, p. 11.
70 *ibid*, p. 12–13.
71 *ibid*, p. 14.
72 *ibid*.
73 *ibid*, pp. 16–17.
74 Safdar 'Ali explained the reasons for his conversion in *Niyaz-namah* (Allahabad, 1867).
75 *Mohammedan Brought to Christ*, p. 17.
76 *ibid*.
77 *Mohammedan Converts*, pp. 5–6.
78 *Mohammedan Brought to Christ*, p. 18.
79 *ibid*, p. 19.
80 *ibid*.
81 *Mohammedan Converts*, p. 6.
82 R. Horton, 'African conversion', *Africa*, XLI (1971), pp. 85–108; 'On the rationality of conversion', *Africa*, XLV (1975), pp. 219–35; 373–339; H.J. Fisher, 'Conversion reconsidered: some historical aspects of religious conversion in Black Africa', *Africa*, XLIII (1973), pp. 27–40; J.D.Y. Peel, 'Conversion and tradition in two African societies', *Past and Present*, 77 (1977), pp. 108–141.

83 N. Levtzion (ed.) *Conversion to Islam* (New York, 1979). See, in particular, Levtzion, 'Towards a Comparative Study of Islamization', pp. 1–23, and bibliography, pp. 247ff.
84 P. Hardy, 'Modern European & Muslim Explanations of Conversion to Islam in South Asia: a Preliminary Survey of the Literature in Leutzian, *Conversion*, pp. 68–99.
85 Richard M. Eaton, *The Rise of Islam and the Bengal Frontier*, 1204–1760 (Berkeley, Los Angeles, London, 1993), espec. pp. 113–19.
86 L.R. Rambo, 'Current Research on Religious Conversion', *Religious Studies Review*, VIII, 2 (April, 1982), pp. 146–59.
87 R. Frykenberg, 'On the study of Conversion Movements: a review article and a theoretical note', *Indian Economic and Social History Review*, XVII, 1 (1980).
88 G.A. Oddie (ed.), *Religion in South Asia: Religious Conversion and Revival Movements in South Asia in Medieval and Modern Times* (2nd rev. & enl. ed, New Delhi, 1991); Copley, 'Conversion Experience'. Copley suggests a 'push-pull' model as a means of examining factors of attraction and hostility between Christian and Hindu culture.
89 Richard W. Bulliet, *Conversion to Islam in the Medieval Period: an Essay in Quantative History* (Cambridge, Mass. and London, 1979), p. 35.
90 A.D. Nock, *Conversion: the Old and the New in Religion from Alexander the Great to Augustine of Hippo* (Oxford, 1933); H.J. Fisher, 'Many deep baptisms: reflections on religious, chiefly Muslim, conversion in Black Africa, BOAS, 1994, pp. 68–81.
91 Rambo, 'Current research', p. 156.
92 *ibid*, p. 155.
93 *ibid*, p. 149.
94 Compare *Mohammedan Brought to Christ* with *Mohammedan Converts*.
95 Eaton, *Rise of Islam*, pp. 113–19.
96 Peter Hardy, *The Muslims of British India* (Cambridge, 1972), p. 8.
97 Eaton, 'Mass Conversion', p. 116.
98 Rev. R. Clark, annual report for 1867, CMS archive: CI1/069/93.
99 *Mohammedan Converts*, appendix.
100 'Abdul Masih's journal, *Missionary Register* (Aug. 1826), p. 393.

Chapter 2

Old Wine in New Bottles?

Kartabhaja (Vaishnava) Converts to Evangelical Christianity in Bengal, 1835–1845

Geoffrey A. Oddie

This paper owes a great deal to the anthropologist, Robin Horton. In the 1970s, he produced several important articles on the role of indigenous or pre-conversion ideas in the spreading of Islam and Christianity in Africa.[1] While his specific arguments about the African situation are still a matter of debate, there can be no doubt that his work has had a considerable impact on studies of conversion and religious change, not only in Africa, but in other countries as well.[2]

Of special relevance in what follows are three of Horton's more general and interrelated points – ideas and assumptions which have influenced much of our discussion of Kartabhaja conversion. Firstly, Horton joins with many other scholars in calling for a return to 'the intellectualist approach' – an approach 'which takes systems of belief at their face value – i.e. as theoretical systems intended for the explanation, prediction and control of space-time events'. Secondly, and in line with this, he underlines the role of reason and endorses Weber's concept of 'rationalization'. To 'rationalize', in Weber's view, is 'to reorder one's religious belief in a new and more coherent way to be more in line with what one knows and experiences'. Thirdly, when discussing ways in which 'rationalization' or change takes place, Horton stresses the importance of continuities and links between old and new systems of belief. As he writes in the second of his articles on African conversion, 'One does not treat any human group as a *tabula rasa* automatically registering the imprint of external cultural influence. Rather one treats it as the locus of thought-patterns and values that determine rather closely which of these influences will be accepted and which rejected.'

In 1972, one year after Horton published the first of his articles on African conversion, Dennis Hudson published an analysis of Hindu and Christian theological parallels in the conversion of H. A. Krsna Pillai – a nineteenth century Tamil convert.[3] This might be rated as another example of 'the intellectualist approach'. Furthermore, although it is a study of the intellectual development and process of adaptation involved in the conversion of *an individual,* it does provide some clues as to how the dynamics might work in a Hindu and more general 'mass movement' context – the term 'mass movement' being used in this and in the following discussion to indicate both 'quantity and connectedness' in low caste and tribal conversion.

In 1984 Richard M. Eaton published a study of pre-Christian cosmology and the role of indigenous ideas in the conversion of large numbers of tribals in north-eastern India (1876–1971)[4] and there has also been some attempt to explore the relationship between south Indian religious ideas about famine and subsequent mass conversions to Christianity in Travancore in the nineteenth century.[5]

However, apart from the latter somewhat restricted investigation, there has been no serious study of the role of pre-conversion ideas in the rise and growth of Christian group or mass movements which originated within the framework of Hindu caste society. How important were religious ideas or assumptions in these movements? How far did pre-existing beliefs and attitudes either inhibit or facilitate the conversion process? What parallels were there in Hindu and Christian thought and how important were these parallels in conversion? This paper is an attempt to explore these issues with reference to Kartabhaja conversion in the first half of the nineteenth century.

THE SOCIAL CONTEXT AND RISE OF THE KARTABHAJA MOVEMENT

The Kartabhaja sect is commonly regarded as an offshoot of the Bengali Vaishnava movement.[6] The sect, together with many other movements, arose in the flux and turmoil of rapid political, social and economic change in Bengal in the mid-eighteenth century. The first in a succession of hereditary leaders of the sect, Ram Saran Pal, who died in about 1783, was a *Sadgop* (milkman) by caste, but cultivator by profession.[7] In the early nineteenth century the community also included brahmans and some well placed Western-educated members of the burgeoning middle class.[8] For the most part, however, members of the sect were low caste, poor and illiterate people engaged in a variety of agricultural operations.

In districts like Krishnagar, where they remained integrated within the existing caste system, they appeared to be much the same as their Hindu and Muslim neighbours among whom they continued to live. But while generally speaking they continued to conform to the customs and practice of their low caste neighbours, they were strongly influenced by a spirit of restlessness and spiritual discontent. As we shall see, they attended their own secret or semi-secret religious meetings and were already showing signs of wanting change and revolution.

'Change', to echo one of Horton's remarks, was 'in the air'. In this case, it was not so much because of alterations in the basic structure of Hindu society, but because of chronic rural indebtedness, landlord oppression, floods and famine.[9] These events meant that tens of thousands of the poor low caste people were driven from their homes, unsettled in mind and spirit and were in the process of seeking for something better. Some, including Kartabhajas, who had only recently settled on the banks of the Jellinghy river,[10] were searching for a new Messiah who would deliver them from all their woes. Many more, perhaps most, were open to new teachings including the competing claims of gurus, *fakirs* and other religious leaders.[11] It was in this atmosphere of economic hardship, social disruption and crisis that the Kartabhaja movement grew and flourished in the late eighteenth and early nineteenth centuries.

EARLY CONTACTS WITH EVANGELICAL CHRISTIANITY AND THE CHRISTIAN MOVEMENT AMONG THEM

Before discussing Kartabhaja teachings in detail it is important to say something about the origin of Kartabhaja contact with Evangelical Christianity and the spread of the Christian movement among the Kartabhajas in the Krishnagar district in the 1830s and 40s.

The Christian movement among Kartabhajas was centered in villages near the town of Krishnagar (the district headquarters) which is about 100 miles north of Calcutta. This was and still is in the heart of the picturesque rice- growing region well watered by the Jellinghy River and its tributaries.

Like many other Christian movements in India it was preceded by a fairly long period of exposure to Christian teaching and preaching. The Serampore Baptists, Carey, Marshman and others, were actively preaching in the area in the late eighteenth and early nineteenth centuries[12] and the Church Missionary Society (CMS) began missionary operations in the district in the early 1830s.

In 1832 the CMS opened schools in the district headquarters and in Nadia (Nabadwip), an ancient cultural and religious centre (the birthplace of Chaitanya), on the opposite side of the Jellinghy. Christian scriptures were introduced and read. In 1835 the Rev. William Deerr, a man fluent in Bengali[13] who had spent thirteen years in neighbouring districts, returned from Europe. Leading a team comprising himself, a Bengali school teacher and two Bengali catechists ('native' co-workers), he commenced preaching in the town of Krishnagar and surrounding villages.[14] In 1835, in the course of their preaching, the two catechists, Paul and Ramathon, visited the village of Dipchandrapore about six miles west of Krishnagar. The people most interested in what the catechists had to say were Kartabhajas led by an educated village blacksmith called Chandy. In this case, the Kartabhajas had already publicly renounced idol worship and were suffering some degree of annoyance and persecution from Hindu neighbours. The catechists presented them with a portion of Christian scripture and left. This visit was followed up by the Rev. Deerr who had further discussions with Chandy and others on several occasions.[15]

The Christian movement among the Kartabhajas began at Dipchandrapore, or as one missionary put it, Dipchandrapore was the '1st and moving point' of conversion to Christianity in the Krishnagar district.[16] Many of the Christian 'mass' movements elsewhere in India began with local initiative, indigenous leaders seeking out the Christian missionaries.[17] In this case, however, it was Bengali Christian preachers who stumbled across a village where the people were especially willing and anxious to listen, and it was Chandy, the Kartabhaja leader, who played a key role in discussion with the missionaries.

In 1836 about 30 persons, including Chandy, were baptized.[18] This event created a great deal of interest especially among the converts' relatives. Persecution increased, but so too did interest in the Christian movement. Visitors came to the village and news spread among relatives in other villages nearby.[19]

In 1838 leading men in 10 villages belonging to the Kartabhaja sect, along with their families (400–500 people) embraced Christianity.[20] By this time the movement had spread extensively among Kartabhajas – at least 50 miles north-east of Dipchandrapore and in and around centres such as Solo, Joginda and Ranaband.[21]

It was at this point that the whole character and tone of the movement was suddenly transformed and came to include not only Kartabhajas, but many other Hindus as well. Towards the end of 1838, as a result of unusually heavy rain, all the flats alongside the Jellinghy river were seriously flooded. Everyone, Hindus, Muslims and Christians alike, lost almost all their crops and faced starvation. Deerr and other missionaries who had limited resources concentrated almost all their efforts on providing relief for Christians. The message was crystal clear. If you are starving and need food and other assistance join the Christians. The next few months saw an unprecedented upsurge of interest in joining the CMS mission. By October 1839, when the Bishop of Calcutta visited the area, there were more than 4,000 enquirers and baptized Christians.[22]

The Christian movement in the Krishnagar district therefore began with the Kartabhajas and continued to include a high proportion of Kartabhajas right up to the end of 1838. A few more were swept into the fold along with thousands of other Hindu converts after the floods and subsequent relief measures. Among the latter-day Kartabhaja enquirers were at least seven gurus who commanded the allegiance of numerous disciples scattered in villages throughout the district.[23] The great majority of those who embraced Christianity in this the second phase of the movement were, however, ordinary Hindus and not Kartabhajas.[24]

As we have seen, it was the Kartabhajas who first responded to missionary preaching and it was these people who persevered in spite of the suffering and persecution which occurred in the early stages of the Christian movement.[25] Furthermore, as the missionaries most closely associated with the movement declared, it was the Kartabhajas who were 'the most consistent Christians', the 'best and steadiest', or those who gave them 'the greatest satisfaction'.[26] When asked to give an account of why they were involved in the new religion it was they who constantly pointed to the nature of their religious journey and the way in which Christianity seemed to satisfy long felt religious needs and make sense *in the light of their own Kartabhaja system of beliefs*. Indeed, it is through the Kartabhaja movement that we can see more clearly than in many other cases of Christian conversion in India, the way in which pre-conversion ideas predisposed indigenous groups in favour of Christianity.

KARTABHAJA AND EVANGELICAL CHRISTIAN BELIEF

The Kartabhaja movement was from the beginning a fairly open, fluid and eclectic movement – absorbing and reflecting a wide variety of influences as it developed in the late eighteenth and early nineteenth centuries. Its somewhat amorphous and hetero-geneous character, reflected in a variety of sub-divisions, was partly a consequence of the fact that for much of the nineteenth century the Kartabhajas had no written scripture which they could call their own. There was an oral tradition that began to develop under Dulalcand (1775–1832). This comprised songs, including theological comment, noted down by four of his disciples, but not finally sanctioned and published by one of his successors as the *Bhaver Gita* until the 1880s.[27] The Baptist missionaries met members of the sect in the early nineteenth century, and the editor of the Baptist journal, *Friend of India*, who was in a position to know, wrote in January 1836 that

> the sect have not yet produced any account of their doctrines. Indeed they hold pens, ink and paper in contempt. They are too material for them. Their doctrine is therefore wholly traditional, and is propagated by initiated disciples, in correspondence with the chief at Ghospara.[28]

In spite of this lack of a written tradition the teachings and sayings of the Kartabhaja leaders (further illuminated by the publication of the *Bhaver Gita*) are now fairly well known. What are less well known are the teachings of the lesser Kartabhaja gurus and the beliefs and attitudes of ordinary disciples who operated at the grass-roots level. Here, however, scholars are fortunate in having access to an abundance of missionary comment which reveals a great deal about the variations in belief and practice among ordinary followers of the Kartabhaja way.

KARTABHAJA LINKS WITH THE VAISHNAVA TRADITION

The Kartabhajas have always claimed that they are part of the Vaishnava tradition and that the roots of the sect lie in Chaitanya's *bhakti* or devotional movement of the sixteenth century.[29]

(a) *Avatara.* Like Vaishnavas or followers of Vishnu in other parts of India they therefore have a theology which has some important parallels with Christianity, perhaps the most obvious point of similarity being a belief that God has become incarnate in human form. According to the Vaishnava and Kartabhaja tradition Vishnu or God, the Creator and Maker of all things, was and is generally seen as a beneficent deity who, whenever the world is out of joint, takes the form of a creature, usually an animal or human, to visit the world and save humankind. As the *Bhagavadgita* has Krishna (an incarnation of Vishnu) say 'In every age I come back to deliver the holy, to destroy the sin of the sinner, to establish righteousness' (Chapter 4, Stanza 8).

(b) *Bhakti.* Chaitanya (1485–1533) who was born at Nawabdip only a few miles from Krishnagar where the Christian movement took place, was a devotee of Lord Krishna, one of Vishnu's most popular incarnations. He not only propounded Krishna as the one God and object of worship, but through his highly emotional movement of song and dance conveyed the simple message that *moksha* or salvation could be obtained through devotion or love of God. Priestly rituals, learning or logic were all unnecessary. As in Evangelical Christianity his stress appears to have been on the *accessibility of salvation* which was open to all irrespective of religion, social status or background. And as was the case in all forms of Christianity he or, at least some of his followers, appear to have adopted some form of *congregational worship*.

SPECIFIC KARTABHAJA TEACHINGS

The Kartabhajas not only shared with other branches of the Bengali Vaishnava movement some basic theological ideas and teachings which, at least to some extent, paralleled ideas in Evangelical Christianity; there were also parallels between some of their more distinctive doctrines and Christian views.

As already mentioned, one of the most striking features of the Kartabhaja movement was the openness of Kartabhajas to the possibility of further truth. They were, therefore, more open and less certain or settled in their views than the followers of many other religious groups. Their very background speaks of a long term quest. While some of them were Hindus who became Kartabhajas and then Christians, others had an even longer history of changing religious affiliation. Their forebears had been Hindus converted to Islam.[30] They were therefore born as Muslims with a Hindu background, they joined the Kartabhaja movement and were finally baptized as Christians.

For some of the Kartabhajas the long search was a search for truth. The leaders of the movement seem to have placed some emphasis not only on being truthful,[31] but also on seeking truth through discussion. In the *Bhaver Gita* there are, for example, passages which encourage a questioning approach towards scripture and religious propositions.[32] The idea of seeking truth was also prominent among the converts to Christianity. When asked why he had become a Christian one old man at Solo replied that 'the habit of Kurta Bhojas was to enquire after truth, and search and examine different religions.'[33] The quest was not, however, always put in terms of seeking some kind of intellectual truth or understanding. For Gokool, the Baptist convert, the search was for a way of happiness through the performance of Hindu rituals;[34] for Kangali, another Baptist convert who had spent many years as a wandering ascetic with begging bowl and matted hair, the search was a desperate attempt to find 'the true guru',[35] and, for those who became Christians at Dipchandrapore, their greatest longing was to have a vision of God – to see God with their own eyes.

The Kartabhajas' familiarity with Vaishnavite notions of *bhakti* and incarnation and their somewhat tentative views and lack of a rigid commitment to any one particular religious position were all factors which made it easier for them to understand and respond in a favourable way to Christian teaching. But perhaps of even greater significance were specific Kartabhaja ideas which provided further parallels and linkages with Christian doctrine. Like Christians, they placed emphasis on the worship of one God. They also rejected idol worship, questioned concepts of hierarchy implicit in the caste system and practised congregational and inter-caste forms of worship. As the Baptist missionary, the Rev. J. Marshman, pointed out, for Kartabhajas, caste was nothing, idols were nothing and brahmins were nothing.[36]

Followers, drawn from different caste backgrounds met perhaps weekly or once a month but in the strictest secrecy. The Rev.

Weitbrecht who had several discussions with the leader and other members of the sect in Burdwan, wrote that:

> they meet every Thursday in certain villages, after sunset, two or three hundred together, sitting cross-legged in a circle, on the ground, They sing hymns in praise of their Creator. Every distinction of caste ceases at these nightly meetings, the Brahmin is sitting in brotherly fellowship by the side of a Sudra and the Mahomedan. They break bread together and a cup passed round the circle, from which all are drinking.[37]

The Rev. Deerr, who had considerable knowledge of Kartabhaja ideas and practice in the Krishnagar district, explained that there, after the hymn, they 'admonish each other to be virtuous, and inculcate the doctrine that God is pure, Merciful & Holy'.[38] Referring to the love feast which he argued 'seems to form the principal part of their Worship', he described the ignoring of caste distinctions, the atmosphere of mutual love and support and the fact that during the feast they not only took food from each other's hands, but frequently put rice in each other's mouth.

Any refusal to perform image worship or observe the usual caste distinctions and taboos in public was extremely dangerous as it invited ostracism and outright persecution. In practice, therefore, most Kartabhajas (like the Bahais converted from Hinduism at a later date) lived a double life. Once the meeting was over they reverted to the practices which operated in ordinary everday life. As Deerr pointed out, the brahmin once more became the brahmin and the Muslim resumed his life as a Muslim.[39] Except for the few occasions when they joined in secret with other members of the sect, Kartabhajas therefore continued to observe the rules of social behaviour, rituals and forms of worship which they had always practised prior to their involvement in the movement – the women of Hindu background, for example, continuing to play a prominent role in keeping up Hindu rituals within the home.[40] The Protestant missionaries tended to regard this type of behaviour as hypocrisy, and Kartabhaja converts who had not already been made outcastes were expected to publicly and openly renounce caste and all forms of idolatrous worship.[41]

Notwithstanding disappointment that the Kartabhajas had not come further in their rejection of the caste system, many of the missionaries underlined the extent to which Kartabhaja teachings and life style were already in accordance with Protestant Christianity. As the *Friend of India* remarked, the Kartabhajas recognized two of the main principles of true religion 'the spirituality of divine worship and the obligation of mutual good will and love.'[42]

As already implied, parallels in Kartabhaja and Christian thought were not confined to ideas about the spiritual nature and oneness of God, social equality and congregational forms of worship. The notion of God becoming incarnate (of his being present in the life of a person on earth) was a part of Vaishnava tradition. This idea, further refined and re-expressed in Kartabhaja theology, provided yet another fundamental link and parallel with Christian belief – in this instance with Christian teachings about the nature of Jesus.

GOD'S REVELATION AND ACTIVITY THROUGH THE *KARTA* OR GURU

After his death, Chaitanya was regarded by his followers as an incarnation of Krishna and therefore God.[43] During the early years of the Kartabhaja movement Ram Saran, who was viewed by many as the first *Karta* or guru of the sect, was believed to be an incarnation of Chaitanya, and hence he too was regarded as Krishna or God on earth.

Referring to the attitude of devotees of the Ghospara *Karta* or guru after conversations with members of the sect at Burdwan in 1839, the Rev. Weitbrecht wrote that

> The Kurta bhojas have peculiar ideas about the divine presence. While they acknowledge it to pervade over the universe, they believe at the same time, that there is a divine incarnation continued in the world, one particular person being the representative of God. The leader of the sect is considered as bearing that exalted character. He resides in a village near Hooghly river, called Khasbara.[44]

When disciples were initiated into the sect they were given a special *mantra* or incantation. There are references in a variety of sources to at least three different *mantras* which were used by Kartabhaja gurus on various occasions. In at least some cases, the conversation which took place immediately prior to the disciple's initiation, placed some emphasis on the notion of the guru himself being 'the truth'. The claims attributed to Jesus in St. John's Gospel that 'I am the Truth' are echoed in the words of the Kartabhaja guru who asked the disciple to say to him that 'You are truth. Whatever you say is true'[45]. The *mantras* themselves convey an idea of what was expected of the relationship between guru and disciple – a view which was also similar to Christian notions of the appropriate relationship between Jesus and his followers. They emphasize the power of the guru who can bestow salvation and blessings on the disciple, the unworthiness and insignificance of the disciple and thirdly, the need for the disciple to serve and obey.[46] Indeed, for those devotees who swapped the *Karta* for Jesus there must have been a certain *déjà vu* about the 'new' discipleship.

Like Jesus, and as an incarnation of God, the *Karta* was also believed to possess supernatural powers. It was said of Iswar Chandra, who met Marshman in 1802, that he could, for example, heal incurable diseases and give speech to the dumb.[47] Ram Saran's wife, Sati Ma, who succeeded him for a short period, was buried under a pomegranate tree at Ghospara. Pilgrims who resorted there in great numbers, including some of those who subsequently became Christian, considered the dust of the place especially sacred, so much so that a touch or taste of it would help them in attaining their objective.[48]

CONTRASTS AND DIFFERENCES WITH CHRISTIAN TEACHING

One of the key factors in Kartabhaja conversion was not just parallels in thought and teaching, but also differences. The parallels facilitated understanding, but it was the perception of difference which seemed to make the transfer of faith worthwhile. The Kartabhaja debates with the Bengali and European Evangelicals took place within a framework of thinking which both parties appear to have had little difficulty in understanding. For Kartabhajas the most persuasive arguments appear to have related to Christian claims about Jesus – his moral qualities, advent and second coming – all of them ideas which had an appeal in the early nineteenth century climate of disillusionment and dissatisfaction.

JESUS AS THE TRUE GURU

The familiar concept of the guru could be linked with the image of Jesus. But what sort of guru was Jesus ? Was he like the *Karta* or subordinate gurus in the Kartabhaja sect, or was he different?

Notwithstanding their possession of a *mantra* and formal allegiance to the *Karta*, some of those involved in the movement had doubts about whether they really had found the true guru, without whom no one could hope 'to cross the river of life.' [49]

According to much in Kartabhaja teaching, gurus were not supposed to be caught up in worldliness or immoral behaviour. The *Bhaver Gita* declared, for example, that 'one must practise both modesty and poverty if one really wishes to realise God.' [50] There can be little doubt, however, that Dulalchand, the third leader of the sect, lived in considerable luxury. Describing a visit to his residence in 1802, J. C. Marshman wrote that 'Dulal's handsome and stately house, exceeding that of many Rajahs, and his garners around filled with grain, all the gifts of his deluded followers, convinced us of the profitability of his trade.'[51]

Dulalchand's sons (Iswarchandra and Indra Narayan) were singled out and especially condemned by Bengali writers as not living up to the highest of moral standards. And this was precisely at the time the largest number of Kartabhajas were converted to Christianity.[52] Even if allegations of greed, corruption and sexual immorality levelled against them were largely untrue, these allegations must have created · further unease among more ordinary members of the Kartabhaja sect.

What is very clear is that some of those Kartabhajas who began to think about adopting Christianity, already had doubts about the integrity or moral standing of the Kartabhaja gurus. For them there was a contrast between what they knew of contemporary gurus and the Jesus of the Gospels. Two of these converts were Krishna Pal, the Baptist convert, and Peter Chandy the first, best known and most highly respected convert of the Krishnagar district.

Krishna Pal was especially struck by Jesus' humility and by his teachings in the Sermon on the Mount. According to the writer of his memoir, when Krishna preached,

> he would contrast, with wonderful effect, Christ washing the
> feet of his disciples, with the Hindoo spiritual guide, having

his foot on the disciple prostrate at his feet. He would dwell
with delight on the divine properties of the Redeemer,
proving from thence that he only was the true Gooroo, and
would confirm these descriptions by reading to his heathen
auditors the Redeemer's sermon on the mount.[53]

Peter Chandy was also convinced that the true guru would be a
man of great love and humility. When in the 1830s a certain fakir
proclaimed himself as the true heir of the Rajah of Burdwan and
deliverer of the people, many Kartabhajas rallied in support of the
rising ruler. However, after giving him his initial support, Chandy
decided that the fakir could not be the expected messiah, as he
was quite clearly 'subject to hatred and pride'.[54]

Having developed some idea of what the true guru should be
Chandy found these ideas and expectations fulfilled in teachings
about the person of Christ.

MESSIANIC EXPECTATION

Messianic expectation, such as that reflected in Chandy's comment, was widespread in Bengal in the eighteenth and early
nineteenth century.[55] As we have noted, it was a period of great
instability, turbulence and change, not to mention the economic
hardship and suffering of ordinary people who naturally longed for
some kind of leader who would deliver them from all their trouble.

Messianic ideas were quite explicit in the Vaishnava tradition.
They are reflected in the imagery of Kalkin who like Krishna was
recognized as an *avatar* of Vishnu. God Himself would one day
reappear as Kalkin riding on a white horse and carrying a blazing
sword in his hands, to punish the wicked, comfort the virtuous
and re-establish a golden age. Nor were messianic ideas unknown
in Islam especially in Shiah and Sufi circles, including among Sufi
preachers in the Krishnagar district in the early nineteenth
century.[56]

Among Kartabhajas messianic expectation reflected disillusionment with contemporary gurus and a recognition that they were
not able to satisfy long-felt needs. A commonly held view was that
God would appear in human flesh – perhaps through some
extraordinary public intervention, or perhaps in a more personal
way whereby the individual would 'see' God through the inner eye
and through that encounter achieve salvation.

When Deerr first visited the Kartabhajas of Dipchandrapore they said, at least twice, that 'unless you can show us God as plain as we can see your body we cannot believe'[57]. Chandy was however in the habit of opposing the missionaries in order to elicit information,[58] and in a subsequent conversation with Kruckeberg, he revealed that he and his party were somewhat less concerned with God's physical or bodily manifestation. 'On their first visit to Kishnaghur they found me walking under a tree', wrote Kruckeberg:

> Chandy asked me to show them God. I replied, 'Do you want to see him with your outward eyes?' It had been one of their rules, before they came in contact with Christ, that an inward eye was necessary to see God. My reply led to a confirmation of that rule, and gratified them. [59]

This latter interpretation of Dipchandrapore Kartabhaja belief was subsequently confirmed by Deerr when in 1839 he declared that the Dipchandrapore Kartabhajas' 'chief principle' was that 'by devotion God will give them eyes, and they will obtain a sight of Him, and through that sight salvation.'[60]

The Kartabhajas of Dipchandrapore were of Hindu origin.[61] Those of Muslim origin scattered in villages elsewhere in the region were possibly influenced less by the idea described above (that the individual would see God through an inner eye) than by the local Islamic preaching that God himself would take the initiative and intervene. While on a preaching tour in 1838, Deerr met with a 'learned Mahomedan', a 'Terpish', who was preaching the message that 'God was to appear in the form of a human body',[62]_ and this appears to have been the view of a Muslim Kartabhaja convert interviewed in Ranaband who declared that his people had been looking for 'a visible appearance of the Deity', by a sight of whom they hoped for salvation.[63]

THE BENGALI AND EUROPEAN CHRISTIAN RESPONSE

No matter what the questions were about God's activity, the Bengali catechists and European missionaries were faced with the task of convincing persistent enquirers and also critics that Christian scripture and Christianity were relevant to their situation and provided at least some of the answers. It certainly does not appear that either Deerr or Kruckeberg believed in an immediate Second Coming or that God would act in the near future in some unusual way.[64] But what is clear is that the missionaries and their assistants were able to point to three of the basic claims in Christian scripture in order to attempt to satisfy messianic hopes and expectation. In the Old Testament there was the prediction that God would appear as a Messiah in human form, in the New Testament there was the claim that this had already happened through the advent, life and death of Jesus Christ and in the latter part of the Bible there was the promise that He (the risen Christ) would come again. All of these themes were exploited in missionary preaching among the Kartabhajas. For example, when preaching to Christians and non-Christians alike at Dipchandrapore in August 1837, Kruckeberg read and explained Isaiah, Chapter 9 'by which they seemed to be much edified.'[65] This includes the well-known verses where God is described as being on the side of the oppressed and where the prophet predicts God's coming as the Messiah who will rule in justice for evermore. The message one can safely assume was that this promised Messiah had already come, that Kartabhaja longing could be satisfied through worship of Him and that His rule was (as verses 4 and 5 so clearly state) associated with justice for oppressed and exploited people. In developing the Christian idea of the incarnation, Deerr honed in on the Kartabhaja quest for a sight of God by referring to the passage in St. John's Gospel Chapter 14, verse 9, where Jesus says 'he that hath seen me hath seen the Father'. According to Deerr, Jesus was God 'manifest in the flesh' and all that the Kartabhajas were seeking was 'in the Gospel'.[66] Nor did the missionaries ignore the doctrine of the Second Coming. The Rev. Weitbrecht, referring to his conversation with a Kartabhaja leader, noted that the latter 'was exceedingly pleased to hear that Christ was to appear a second time, and that all true believers in him, wait for his advent.'[67] There is clear evidence then that missionaries who played a key part in the Kartabhaja Christian movement made a deliberate attempt to link pre-existing beliefs with the presentation of the Christian Gospel.

CONCLUSION

It is the argument of this paper that Kartabhaja interest in Christianity was somewhat different from that of most other groups who joined the Protestant churches in large numbers in

Bengal in the first half of the nineteenth century. Unlike the other mass movement converts who joined the churches later (1839–1840) after the floods and handouts, the Kartabhajas were especially interested in the theological and other ideas associated with Christian teaching and the Christian way of life.

In common with many other oppressed and low caste peoples the Krishnagar Kartabhajas had been uprooted and forced to move. They had been searching for a new and better place in which to live and, like many of their fellow-travellers, their physical journey was not unrelated to an open-mindedness and spiritual quest. As the Christian missionaries might well have said, their search was for 'a new heaven and a new earth'. Amongst other things they were seeking for 'the true guru', a messiah, or a saving vision of God, a more accepting, less hierarchical fellowship, and rituals and forms of worship more expressive of their changing views of God and the world around. Though many of them found what they wanted in the Kartabhaja religion, others were less strongly committed, and, for them, participation in the movement was only one stage in an ongoing journey somewhere else. For those who found in Christianity greater religious and ideational satisfaction, the Kartabhaja experience was, nevertheless, an important stage in their religious and conceptual journey. It was at least one of the factors which predisposed them more in favour of Christian teaching. As we have seen, Kartabhaja belief and doctrine provided striking parallels with Christian belief. And because they already shared many of the same basic assumptions, values and beliefs, the Kartabhajas were in a better position than most of their Hindu and Muslim neighbours to be able to understand and respond to evangelical claims about God and the Christian message of salvation.

In conclusion there are three points one might keep in mind.

First, it is not our contention that belief or intellectual conviction was the only factor in Kartabhaja conversion. But what we are saying is that, at least in this case, pre-Christian ideas played an important part in the conversion process. Furthermore, there is some evidence that pre-conversion ideas also played a part in the conversion of other groups, if not in Bengal, then elsewhere. The best known case is that of the madiga (untouchable) followers of the Rajayoga sect who joined the American mission in Andra Pradesh, in South India, in the 1860s and 70s.[68] According to missionary and other accounts the Rajayoga gurus taught many ideas which were similar to those in Christianity. Like Chandy and other Kartabhajas they and their followers were influenced by ideas of incarnation and were looking for a messiah which they eventually discovered in Jesus Christ.

Second, while Horton in his theory of African conversion stresses the over-riding importance of one particular teaching, namely monotheism, we cannot point to the over-riding importance of any one idea in Kartabhaja conversion. Different Christian ideas appealed strongly to different individuals – though, as we have noted, some teachings had a greater impact and were more influential than others.

And third, as Horton himself points out with reference to the situation in Africa, it is not always possible to clearly distinguish between ideas of Christian and non-Christian origin. Some Christian commentators argued that similarities in Kartabhaja and Christian belief were not accidental; that Kartabhaja practices, such as the communal meal, were the result of earlier contact with Christian teaching. However, there is no way of establishing whether this was the case. What one can say is that Bengal had a long history of indirect and direct contact with the Christian movement. As is well known, Jesus is mentioned and respected in the Koran – a text which had been important in the life of some Kartabhaja converts. Dominican, Augustinian and Jesuit missionaries were active in Bengal in the seventeenth and eighteenth centuries,[69] and lastly, there is specific evidence that some of the Krishnagar converts had been influenced by earlier Protestant preaching.[70] There can be no doubt, therefore, that missionaries were building on earlier Christian foundations. Nevertheless, the point remains that some of the basic concepts and practices which were important in Kartabhaja conversion, such as the institution of the guru, concepts of incarnation and the practice of *bhakti*, were a part of Bengali culture well before the rise of the Christian movement. Kartabhaja conversion, like the conversion of the *madigas* in the American mission, may have been encouraged by long term and very gradualistic Christian influence, but older pre-Christian systems of belief also played a part in creating conditions which fostered and facilitated the adoption of Evangelical Christianity.

NOTES

1 'African Conversion', *Africa*, Vol. XLI, No. I, April 1971, pp. 85–106; 'On the Rationality of Conversion', Part 1, *ibid*, Vol. 45, No. 3, 1975, pp. 219–235 and Part 2, *ibid*, pp. 373–99.
2 For further discussion of Horton's work see D.M. Schreuder and G.A. Oddie, 'What is "Conversion"? History, Christianity and Religious Change in Colonial Africa and South Asia', *Journal of Religious History*, Vol. 15, No. 4, December 1989.
3 D.D.Hudson, 'Hindu and Christian Theological Parallels in the Conversion of H.A. Krsna Pillai, 1857–1859,' *Journal of the American Academy of Religion*, Vol. X1, No. 2 June 1972.
4 R.M.Eaton, 'Conversion to Christianity among the Nagas, 1876–1971,' *Indian Economic and Social History Review*, Vol. XX1, No. 1, January–March 1984.
5 Dick Kooiman, *Conversion and Social Equality in India*, (Delhi, 1989), pp. 81–82, 188–189.
6 Ramakanta Chakrabarty, *Vaisnavism in Bengal 1486–1900*, (Calcutta, 1985), pp. 354–356, 359; Aparna Bhattacharya, *Religious Movements in Bengal and their Socio-Economic Ideas (1800–1850)*, (Patna, 1981), pp. 45–46.
7 J.H.E. Garrett, *Nadia*, (Calcutta, 1910), p. 47.
8 CMS archives Birmingham, CI1/0 306/71, J Weitbrecht, Journal, 3 May 1839 and CI1/0 306/71 Dealtry's Journal of a Visit to Krishnaghur, July 1840 (Deerr's answer no.1).
9 For social and economic conditions in Bengal during this period see especially Dharma Kumar (ed.) *Cambridge Economic History of India*, Vol. 2, pp. 86–176, 270–331 and for conditions in Krishnagar, Garrett, *op.cit.*
10 *Church Missionary Register,* June 1839, p. 305.
11 Chakrabarty, pp. 346–348; Steven Fuchs, *Rebellious Prophets*, (Bombay, 1965), pp. 108–124.
12 *Church Missionary Register,* October 1839, p. 461; *Periodical Accounts Relative to the B.M.S.*, No. X1, pp. 262–266.
13 CMS CI1/M18, 1839–43, Bishop of Calcutta to Earl of Chichester, 14 April 1841.
14 *Christian Intelligencer,* 1839, p. 548.
15 For an account of the origins of the movement see especially Deerr's account in CMS CI1/088/8, Deerr to Jowett, 15 October 1835 and Deerr's answers to Dealtry's questions in CMS CI1/087/7 'Account of an Extraordinary Work which it is hoped is a work of Grace amongst the Heathen in some Villages North of Kishnaghur', 15 February 1839. See also CMS Kruckeberg's Journal, 20 May 1843 which includes important details on Chandy's life.
16 CMS CI1/0167/19 Kruckeberg to Sec. 4 March 1850.
17 John C.B.Webster, *The Dalit Christians. A History*, (Delhi, 1992), pp. 55–57.
18 *Christian Intelligencer,* 1839, p. 549.

19 *Church Missionary Register,* June 1839, p. 304.
20 CMS CI1/087/7 Deerr's reply in Dealtry, 15 February 1839.
21 *Christian Intelligencer,* 1839, pp. 545–547; *Church Missionary Register,* March 1840, pp. 166–167. November 1841, pp. 501.
22 For these dramatic events see especially CMS CI1/08/4/26, Bishop Wilson to Earl of Chichester, 30 October 1839 and CI1/M8, 1839–43,14 April 1839; J. Long, Handbook of *Bengal Missions,* London, 1848, pp. 183–184 and *Friend of India,* 11 April 1839.
23 CMS CI1/087/6, Archdeacon Dealtry's Journal of a Visit to Krishnagar, July 1840, with answers of missionaries to Queries by the Archdeacon in 1840 (Deerr's reply); *Bishop Wilson's Journal Letters addressed to his family,* London, 1863, pp. 309,314 and 317.
24 G. T. Spencer (Bishop of Madras), *A Brief Account of the Church Missionary Society's Mission in the District of Krishnagur in the Diocese of Calcutta,* (London, 1846), p. 16.
25 For references to the persecution of Kartabhaja Christians see especially CMS CI1/087/7, Deerr's reply in Dealtry, 15 February 1839; CI1/087/6, Deerr's reply to question no.9 in Dealtry's Journal,1840; CMS CI1/0167/19, Kruckeberg to Sec., 4 March 1850; CMS CI1/0 306/72, J. Weitbrecht, Journal, 7 December 1840 and CI1/0306/73, Journal, 9 February 1845; CMS CI1/0 19/3, Journal of a Native Catechist (Paul Chakrabarty)11 April 1839; *Christian Intelligencer,* 1839, p. 91 and September 1844, pp. 370–371.
26 CMS CI1/M10, J.Pratt, 'Minute on the Necessity of Strengthening the Missionary Establishment . . .', 20 October 1845 (Section 19); Kruckeberg, Journal, 2 January 1843; J.Weitbrecht, *Protestant Missions in Bengal,* 2nd. edition, London, 1844, p. 324.
27 Chakrabarty, p. 367.
28 *Friend of India,* 14 January 1836 (vol. 2, p.11.) According to the Rev. Weitbrecht, who met members of the sect in Burdwan, 'they read different works, and quote largely from any shasters which favour their views' (CMS CI1/0 306/71, Journal, 3 May 1839) and, according to Deerr, they had no special 'written account' of their faith, 'but they teach their tenets, by verbal communication' (CMS CI1/087/6, reply to Dealtry,1840).
29 Chakrabarty, pp. 354–356, 359; Bhattacharya, pp. 45–46.
30 On Kartabhaja converts of Muslim background see CMS CI1/087/6. Deerr's reply to question no. 2. in Dealtry's Journal,1840; *Bishop Wilson's Journal Letters,* pp. 293, 311, 317; *Christian Intelligencer,* 1839, p. 546; G.T.Spencer, *op.cit.,* p. 19.
31 One of the main teachings of Aulcand, the founder, was 'Speak the truth and follow one God', and, because of its emphasis on truth, the movement was sometimes known as *Satyadharma* or *Sahajdharma,* (Bhattacharya p. 44).
32 According to Chakrabarty (p. 374) the *Bhaver Gita* stated that 'an unquestioning attitude is deplorable. One must determine the truth and untruth of propositions before they are accepted or rejected. The supporters of the scriptures very wrongly deplore the questioning attitude'.

33 *Christian Intelligencer,* 1839, p. 546 (J.H. Pratt).
34 *Periodical Accounts Relative to the B.M.S.,* Vol. 2, No. Vlll, p. 124 (22 December 1800).
35 B.M.S. archives Oxford, Folder IN/7 ('Kangali Mahant' – c. 1795 – 1864).
36 See extract from his Journal (15 April 1802) in *Periodical Accounts Relative to the B.M.S.* No. Xl, p. 263.
37 J.J. Weitbrecht, *Protestant Missions in Bengal,* pp. 323–324.
38 CMS CI1/087/6 Deerr's reply to question no.3 in Dealtry's Journal, 1840.
39 *Ibid.* Deerr's reply to question nos. 3–6.
40 *Ibid.* Deerr's reply to question no. 5.
41 The early Baptist Kartabhaja converts, Krishna Pal and Gookool, publicly 'threw away' their caste by eating with the missionaries. The Dipchandrapore enquirers, who were 'more respectable' than the converts who came later, were outcasted prior to their baptism on the grounds that they had prayed with the missionaries and were therefore already Christians (the implication being that all Christians were polluted). Converts at an Anglican service in Ananda Bas (N.N-W of Krishnagar) some years later were asked immediately prior to baptism if they would ' give up caste'? and they replied 'yes we have already' (*Periodical Accounts,* vol. 2, no. xi, pp. 123; CMS CI1/087/7 Dealtry,' Account of an Extraordinary Work . . .', 15 February 1839; *Church Missionary Register,* February 1840, p. 107.)
42 *Friend of India,* 11 April 1839.
43 Bhattacharya, p. 12.
44 CMS CI1/0 306/71 J.J. Weitbrecht, Journal,3 May 1839.
45 Chakrabarty, pp. 365–366.
46 See, for example, Ward's translation of the Ghospara guru's mantra, which is as follows: 'O Sinless Lord, O great Lord; at thy pleasure I go and return : not a moment am I without thee. I am ever with thee; save, O great Lord,' (William Ward, *View of the History, Literature and Mythology of the Hindoos,*Vol. 3, London, 1822, p. 176.) Variations of this mantra given by Krishna Pal (himself a disciple) and also by Deerr omit the reference to the 'sinlessness' of the Karta, but otherwise they are much the same.(Krishna Pal, Memoir, pp. 10–11 and CMS CI1/087/6, Deerr's reply in Dealtry, 1840) According to Kruckeberg, Chandy was often told by 'a mantra in his ears' to join himself to 'the righteous one' (CMS Journal, 20 May 1843.)
47 *Periodical Accounts Relative to the B.M.S.,* No. Xl, Extracts from Marshman's Journal, p. 262; Bhattacharya, pp. 47, 50–51.
48 CMS CI1/086/6 Deerr's reply to question no.1 in Dealtry's Journal of a Visit to Krishnaghur, July 1840.
49 Chakrabarty, p. 374.
50 *Ibid.* p. 375.
51 Periodical Accounts, No.Xl, Extracts from Marshman's Journal, p. 266.
52 Bhattacharya, p. 47.
53 *Memoir of Krishna Pal,* p. 28.

54 CMS Kruckeberg, Journal, 20 May 1843.
55 Fuchs, *op.cit.*
56 *Church Missionary Register,* November 1840, p. 505; *Christian Intelligencer,* 1839, p. 91.
57 *Christian Intelligencer,*Vol. 5, no. 2, December 1835, p. 577.
58 CMS Kruckeberg's Journal, 20 May 1843.
59 *Ibid.*
60 Christian Intelligencer, 1839, p. 549.
61 CMS CI1/0167/19 Kruckeberg to Sec. 4 March 1850.
62 *Christian Intelligencer,* 1839, p. 92.
63 *Ibid.* p. 547.
64 In this sense their views reflect main-line Evangelical teaching . See S.Piggin, *Making Evangelical Missionaries,* (Oxford,1984), pp. 70,146.
65 CMS CI1/M7, Kruckeberg's Journal, 6 August 1837.
66 *Bishop Wilson's Journal Letters,* p. 317.
67 CMS CI1/0 306/71 Weitbrecht, Journal,June 1840.
68 See especially Emma Rauchenbush-Clough, *While Sewing Sandals. Tales of a Telugu Pariah Tribe,* (New York etc., 1899), pp. 113–201.
69 K.S.Latourette, *A History of the Expansion of Christianity,* Vol. 3, (New York, 1971), pp. 258–259,263,273.
70 *Christian Intelligencer,* 1839, p. 546.

Chapter 3

Strength of Tradition and Weakness of Communication – Central Kerala Dalit Conversion

George Oommen

INTRODUCTION

This paper focuses on the nature of gospel communication and the role of ideas during and in the follow-up of the dalit conversion movements in central Kerala, when Pulayas joined the former Anglican Church in large numbers. It happened in the middle of the nineteenth century.

Most other studies tend to stress the social factors contributing to conversions.[1] This paper seeks more to pose certain questions than to reach definite conclusions on the transmission of religious teachings, for the simple reason that the data available is not by any means plentiful. While acknowledging that diverse influences were at work, the question still remains whether in fact communication had been as effective as the missionaries claimed.

Pulayas or *Cheramar (Cherumas)*, the agricultural labour outcastes, and one of the lowest status groups in old Kerala, rate themselves a rung above the Parayas. They are numerically the larger of the two. Missionary work aimed at bringing them into the Anglican Communion reached its peak in the latter half of the ninteenth century. They constituted more than half of the membership of the Diocese of Travancore and Cochin in 1947 when it became the Madhya Kerala Diocese of the Church of South India. In the midland region of Travancore and in highlands to the east, they worked as farm hands raising paddy, tapioca and cash crops while in the paddy fields of the west coast they were ploughers of the soil, sowers of seeds, transplanters of seedlings, removers of weeds, irrigators, harvesters, dryers of grain and loaders into the wooden storage space. Both men and women participated in all farm operations.

DALIT RELIGION/RELIGIOUS ACTIVITIES

Religion was an integral part of Pulaya social existence. George Mathen, a Church Missionary Society (CMS) Syrian Christian missionary stated, 'with regard to their religious notions and practices, they admit the existence of a Supreme Being but are unable to comprehend how the government of this vast world can be carried without the assistance of subordinate agents'.[2] Thus popular conceptions of the deity were mainly confined to 'subordinate agents', (in step with or parallel to their own status in this world) and spirits of the deceased ancestors which held a major position in their worship. These spirits were called *Chavars, Madans, Parakutty* and *Chathan.* Describing the spirit worship a CMS Missionary with many years of ministry among Pulayas observed, 'Their notions of a Deity are very crude; of a God who loves them they know nothing. All their religious ceremonies turn upon keeping off the wrath of malignant spirits: for this purpose they sacrifice cocks whose blood they sprinkle upon their altar'.[3] These altars were situated in the midst of groves in certain consecrated raised squares called *Yakshi Ampalam* and *Pey Koil*, as they have no temples.[4]

Pulayas, squeezed at the bottom of the most repressive socioreligious structure known to human beings, were not incapable of striking discordant notes through their ritual activities. Pulaya medicine men and witch doctors claimed secret and close communion with the spirits of the dead and performed *mantravadam* or sorcery. *Mantravadis* were believed to possess the powers of bringing malaise and misfortune on wrong-doers, especially the cruel landlords and wicked bossmen. Pulayas believed in the all pervasive dominion of the spirits on human affairs and held the sorcerers in awe and esteem. The upper castes dreaded these agents of the demons and the ghosts. Some social control over the excesses of the high caste landlords was exercised through the threat of Pulaya black magic in Travancore.[5]

In spite of the prominent role played by the primordial worldview in the worship of the Pulayas, their assimilation into higher sanskritic forms of worship was also evident. *Thevaratampuran*, meaning god whom high castes worship (literally meaning master's god) figured in the Pulaya concept of polytheism or pantheism. *Bhagavati* and *Kali* were the goddesses to be appeased in times of danger and illness.[6]

Festivals were the most obvious institutional expression of social and religious life in the feudal set-up of yesterday's Travancore and Cochin. In festivals and ceremonies connected to the agricultural operations and harvests, Pulayas had a significant level of participation, although some activities in which they participated were rather oppressive like the sham fights in northern Travancore.[7] In some regions Pulayas joined the festival processions. *Vittu Iduka,* a celebration on the day of *Bharani* during the months of February–March was an occasion to bring the paddy seeds to the Bhagavati temples. Pulayas had to stand at an assigned distance while offering the paddy grains. In *Mandalam Vilakku,* a forty-one day celebration in honour of Bhagavati, Pulayas were allowed participation at the culmination of the festivals.[8] During the harvesting and threshing seasons Pulayas' ritual participation was an essential requirement and obligation. The Pulaya headman performed ceremonies along with the landowner. Their religious activities reflected and reinforced the hierarchy and fulfilled obligations connected with the caste system in the economic and the social life of the village. The divine hierarchy also was modelled by the earthly hierarchy.

In brief we may note that: (1) Pulayas shared in a multi-tiered religious system; (2) their accessibility was mainly to subordinate gods reflecting their social status; (3) they seem to have been caught up in a kind of 'sanskritization' process as far as their obligatory ritual participation was concerned. With these observations about the religion of the Pulayas let us move on to look at the communication of the Gospel by the missionaries.

COMMUNICATION OF THE GOSPEL

Formalities and Means of Christian Instruction:

Christian instruction which preceded baptism and continued within the new Anglican congregations of the Pulayas constituted an important aspect of CMS missionary work. It is not an easy task to assess the effectiveness of even explicit instruction in building up a modicum of comprehension of the Gospel. Information on the content and methods is not as exhaustive as one might have liked. However, it is possible to obtain some idea of the process from the nature of the Christian instruction imparted by the missionaries, the people involved, and the way in which Pulayas responded to particular aspects of Christian teaching.

Christian instruction involved a considerable amount of teaching in what the missionaries called 'the fundamental doctrines of the Gospel'. This included, among other things, teachings on the 'only means of salvation provided for mankind in Christ', and 'the distinct offices of the Father, the Son and the Holy Ghost'. The Creed, the Lord's Prayer, the Ten Commandments and 'the explanation of them as contained in the Church catechism' were also invariably included in missionary instructions.[9]

The period between a Pulaya candidate's acceptance of Anglican instruction and actual baptism, which usually extended to about two years, was considered a time of 'probation' during which the candidate had to sufficiently demonstrate 'strictly consistent Christian conduct' revealing a proper understanding of Christian fundamentals. A strict examination of the candidate's 'knowledge' of these teachings was conducted by missionaries immediately prior to baptism. To the CMS missionaries, successful completion of probation and evidence of 'sincere' motivation on the part of the Pulaya candidates were sufficient to be eligible for membership of the invisible church of Christ. Baptism was an external recognition thereof. After attending a group baptism ceremony along with many other missionary colleagues, Hawksworth gives the following description of the occasion:

> We had the first baptism of slave converts in the Velloor school; between fifty and sixty were present, and (from) the numerous candidates for baptism nineteen were admitted into the visible Church of Christ . . . Their hearty responses and decided, brief and pointed answers as to motives . . . [and] strictly consistent Christian conduct for many months past, . . . left no doubts on our minds that many of these, I hope all, were already members of the invisible Church of Christ.[10]

As is apparent from the above remarks most of the candidates for baptism were considered unsuitable. Indeed, this was a typical situation.

Successful completion of what must have often been a difficult period of learning and probation ended in baptism. Both converts and missionaries considered baptism to be an event of great importance. 'The necessity of being thoroughly prepared' for such an occasion seems to have been taken quite seriously by Pulaya candidates.[11] In most of these ceremonies, one or more missionaries personally examined the candidates. It is evident from missionary descriptions that the ability to repeat certain teachings and to give set answers was seen as further proof that the candidates understood Christ's way of salvation as preached by the missionaries. A typical baptism is described by Hawksworth as follows:

> There were sixty-five candidates for baptism, all neatly clad (so different from former appearance) and their faces beamed with delight . . . They were questioned, not only to ascertain their knowledge of scriptural truth, but also to ascertain, as far as possible, their apprehension of Christ as a living and a present saviour. Their answers were prompt, correct, and at times, thrilling. To the question, 'Why is Christ gone to heaven', the reply, instant, unanimous, and self-interested was, 'He is gone to prepare a place for us!'. Doubtful cases were carefully canvassed, especially by one who had visited them from hut to hut, and does so regularly, who knows them individually.[12]

Communicators of the Gospel

(a) English missionaries and the Syrian Christian priests prominent in the Anglican hierarchy were the first groups to convey the Christian message to the Pulayas. Instruction mainly took place during routine, but rather infrequent, visits to the congregations. In most cases the English missionaries seem to have taught and preached in the vernacular, although occasionally they relied on translators.

From the comment and evaluation of the missionaries, it can be assumed that the preaching and verbal communication of the Gospel were largely a one-way process, and not much of what they preached was actually understood. In fact language itself was one of the main barriers. Andrews, who was well versed in Malayalam, observed, 'How earnestly I long to preach Christ to these poor jungle slaves. Their language or dialect, is very peculiar. But they understood you much better than you can understand them'.[13] Apparently the colloquial of Pulaya speech and language was vastly different from that of other caste groups like Syrian

Christians and Nairs, with whom the missionaries communicated on a regular basis. English missionaries were unable to truly enter into the spirit and style of Pulaya verbal communication. This is how Andrews commented on the translation by Peet, a Malayalam scholar among the Travancore missionaries, on another missionary's lesson to a group of Pulayas: 'I am afraid not much of the good advice has been understood. Few among them can make a long grammatical sentence. Their own colloquial is peculiarly short and categorical, almost every other sentence being in the form of a question'.[14]

Syrian Christian missionaries were also somewhat dissatisfied with the quality of their own communication with the Pulayas during Christian instruction. Koshi Koshi and I. Eapen who earnestly tried to enter into dialogue with the converts did not meet with much success because the Pulayas' conversational style and skill were different from what they expected. In fact, the new Christian vocabulary introduced by the missionaries was somewhat alien to them.[15] While teaching the Pulaya candidates of Mepra, Koshi Koshi found many responses from the candidates did 'not fully correspond' to Anglican Christian instruction. It was apparent that several Christian concepts and terms as taught by them had not always survived the journey into Pulaya minds unscathed. Koshi Koshi observed, 'It is indeed a hard struggle for them to get at some of the terms necessarily employed in their instruction such as 'repentance', 'faithfulness' etc. so that they often said one thing while [they] meant quite another . . . .'.[16]

The assessment that the explicit message of the Gospel and some of the concepts and terms employed by the missionaries were not fully understood by many Pulayas is further strengthened by the experience of Andrews. He went to great lengths to 'draw out their minds and make them see' by careful questioning and long dialogues with them. Andrews' journals and diaries contain valuable information on his evaluation of the situation. He wrote 'It is rather difficult to get an idea clearly into a slave's mind. It reminds me of driving a nail into hard wood, and one often finds that the blow thought to be most effectual has only be[en] cut not driven in . . .'[17] However, significantly enough, Andrews' frustration arose not merely from language difficulties, but also from resistance to ideas and concepts which did not correspond to the Pulayas' preconceived notions about God and

His divine attributes. For instance, the concept of a loving God, and of easy accessibility to a supreme being were not altogether understood. In fact, certain concepts were rejected by Pulaya candidates however much missionaries tried to convey them. Andrews may have been thinking of these barriers to communication during the final years of his missionary work in Travancore when he wrote:

> . . . the slaves, naturally, can understand scarcely anything, and have exercised only their lowest and most animal propensities . . . they present a state of mental stultification united to a high degree of animal craftiness that I can scarcely describe. I have now come into close contact with their mind and words of thought for some years, and I feel that till the Spirit of God moves over the face thereof, and commands 'let there be light', . . . the darkness that broods in them is as deep or deeper than that of any other natural minds that I am brought into contact with.[18]

(b) Another group involved in the instruction programmes were the teacher-evangelists of the CMS mission referred to as 'Readers' and 'Assistant Readers'. The ongoing teaching of the candidates and converts was the responsibility of this group. The missionaries relied heavily on the work of teacher-evangelists for the successful Christianization of the Pulaya congregations.

An assessment of the teacher-evangelists' communication with the Pulaya is constrained by the fact that they were not required to send reports or diaries of their work to the CMS office in London, and any reports which they may have compiled appear to have disappeared. However, occasional evaluation of the evangelists, particularly by English missionaries, can be used to draw certain indirect conclusions about their role as communicators of the Gospel.

With few exceptions, almost all these 'Readers' were Syrian Christians in origin. CMS missionaries generally agreed that they were efficient and diligent teachers, but were limited in their ability to communicate the Anglican version of the Christian message. Firstly, for most of them, teaching Pulayas was a form of employment and a source of increased income rather than an evangelistic opportunity. Their joining or leaving the mission invariably followed their getting or losing employment', observed Koshi Koshi, a Syrian Christian missionary.[19]

Secondly, the CMS missionaries also believed that many of these Syrian Christian 'Readers' were ill-equipped as conveyers of fundamental Christian teachings and that they were 'very backward in the knowledge of saving truth'. Edmund Johnson felt 'some of them were most shamefully ignorant of Gospel History'.[20] It is apparent that the missionaries were dissatisfied because these teachers did not fall in line with Anglican aims of evangelism and Christian instruction.

The end result of such strong and widespread dissatisfaction with Syrian Christian Readers can only be imagined. However, it is apparent that the aims of Anglican missionaries as distinct from the Syrian Christian evangelist-cum-teachers in communicating the fundamentals of the Gospel were incompatible. We can therefore safely assume that such a disjunction limited the effectiveness of these teachers as conveyers of the Anglican perception of the Christian message of salvation.

(c) A careful analysis of the missionary reports and correspondence reveals another significant group which was part of the communication network of the Anglican mission, but did not belong to the Church hierarchy. They were the Pulayas themselves. Given the limitations of the missionaries and the evangelists in communicating the message, the role played by the Pulayas was indeed significant. In fact the most important and effective interpretations of Anglican teaching took place when Pulayas articulated and discussed among themselves. This is how Andrews describes the learning pattern in a 'slave school' in Kottayam:

> In general, the first man who clearly understands the teachers' meaning, immediately [turns] to the others and explains it, another and another takes it up, so that shortly it is perfectly understood by all. This, I think, goes far to account for the greater progress made by slaves in learning . . .[21]

CMS missionaries made extensive use of the services of the 'leading Pulayas' in already well-developed congregations who evidently were more articulate and comparatively more literate. Andrews, who was aware of the missionary monologues, observed that often 'the conversations carried on between the teacher and some of the headmen' among Pulayas were the most effective way of interpreting the Gospel.[22] There is sufficient evidence to suggest that the traditional 'headman' (Moopen) in many localities emerged as the real leader, playing a significant role interpreting the fundamentals of Christianity and preparing Pulayas for baptism. This also showed that the pre-Christian status of 'headmen' as teachers, whom missionaries referred to as 'leading men', saw no decline due to the change of religion.

All the same, only three of the 'headmen' were appointed to the position of 'slave school master', which was almost equivalent to the Syrian Christian teacher's position. These were Pooven Paul, Joshua and Xavier, who played a significant role in the spread of Christianity among the Pulayas of central Travancore. The use of such 'headmen' increased later though none of them seems to have been appointed as 'Reader' initially. Unfortunately we have no records, except one, of their preaching. W. J. Richards translated a journal written by Joshua and sent it to London. Although it is brief, it indicates that he used day-to-day illustrations familiar to his people in order to interpret Christian teaching.[23]

The significance of the Pulayas' role in the teaching and interpretation network of the Anglican Church has to be seen in the light of the fact that they themselves were the best and most effective communicators. Although they were not officially teachers, the Pulayas were successful, the 'headmen' in particular. One of the reasons they did so well may be attributed to their own interpretation of the Gospel linking it comprehensibly to pre-existing Pulaya beliefs, traditional practices and real life situations.

Ideas

'One must not suppose these slaves do not exercise their reason' observed Andrews, despite the extreme frustration he felt in his struggle to teach the Pulayas.[24] Notwithstanding the limitations in the explicit communication of the Christian message, certain ideas appear to have made a stronger appeal to the Pulayas than to anyone else.

The notion of a God or a supreme being who is accessible and approachable was not easy to comprehend for many Pulaya converts. Indeed, such a notion of God was in complete contradiction to their traditional religious experience. A. F. Painter while discussing the Pulaya belief system observed, 'The existence of a Supreme Being is acknowledged by them, but they have been taught to believe that they are too degraded to approach Him'.[25] Before their conversion to Christianity the Pulayas only worshipped the regional and local deities as distinct from other deities which were accessible only to higher castes. Moreover, this practice corresponded with their caste position in society. Andrews attempted at one point to explain his understanding of a supreme God drawing a parallel between the untouchables' accessibility to the Raja and to God. However, this analogy made no sense as the Pulayas had no access to the Rajas in the first place, and would have been killed if they made a move in that direction. To them God was associated with 'evil' and was mostly inaccessible. They did not want to be near him.[26] Thus Christian concepts which did not correspond to the Pulayas' experience were not readily accepted by the candidates.

At the same time, Pulaya candidates seem to have been attracted by certain attributes of God as portrayed by Anglican missionaries. Several missionaries note that the concept of a loving God found receptive ears among the Pulayas. Andrews observes: 'It was indeed good news to them to hear that God loved them, and would have them to be saved. They seemed to have gained juster ideas of the deity, and the love of Christ has been accepted without hesitation.'[27] The idea of a loving God was in direct contrast to the Pulayas' established beliefs about the deity. Indeed, their religious activities were directed towards containing the negative power, particularly the wrath of the gods. So, why did these Pulaya candidates respond so positively to the idea of a loving God? Apparently, the practical implications of such an attribute of God as portrayed by the missionaries encouraged a positive response. Some missionaries linked their sermons and lessons to Pulaya aspirations for better treatment in society. The following description of how Koshi Koshi preached to Pulayas reveals how certain Christian ideas affected them:

> I spoke to them about the only one God the creator of all things, about the nothingness of idols, the sin of idolatry, sin in general, and its terrible consequences after death and of the only means of salvation provided for all mankind in Christ. They appeared pleased that all men of both high castes and low castes were alike in the sight of God and all descended from the same common parents and that our

holy religion recognized no distinction of caste but Christians are taught to regard all classes as brothers and sisters.[28]

The very fact that Pulayas were accepted into a religion of their masters and were able to have access to the religious privileges which came with it was sufficient demonstration of the missionary message of love and equality. Andrews, the most popular missionary among the Pulayas, linked salvation through Christianity among other things to the privileges which 'had now come to the slaves'. The right of Pulaya Christians 'to assemble for learning, or to take Sabbath for a rest' were shown as evidence of such privileges.[29] Similarly, George Mathan, the pioneer of the anti-slavery movement, preached to the Pulayas about their wretched condition and of the benefits they would derive, temporally as well as spiritually, by embracing Christianity.[30] Such messages linking Christianity to certain privileges that the Pulayas might enjoy definitely caught their imagination.

The image of the Christian God as a powerful guarantee against 'Satan's special attacks and hatred' seems to have found ready acceptance. In fact, the use of such images by the missionaries to get across the Christian message obviously reinforced some of the Pulayas' pre-existing notions of God. One missionary observed that Christianity offered Pulayas 'deliverance from the fear of the devil, whom they stand in the greatest terror'. A Nair reported to the missionaries that after the arrival of Christianity among the Pulayas the 'evil spirits were obliged to run away from the places' and there was 'scarcely any instance of demonical possession' among them.[31] Some of the priests of the Pulayas who converted to Christianity demolished the images of their deities in the presence of the missionaries, thereby suggesting belief in the power of the new God which they had found in Christianity.

'Slaves believe that persons attacked with any disease if prayed over in their Church will get cured,' observed Oommen Mammen.[32] Epidemics particularly put such belief to the test. In Tiruvalla during a cholera outbreak Pulaya converts brought the sick for the prayer. When patients died, it brought ridicule from non-Christian Pulayas. Indeed, missionaries feared that 'enquirers might backslide' when it was seen that Christian prayer had failed. Moreover there were incidents which indicate that some Pulayas saw baptism as a guarantee against disease and calamity.

From the available sources it is not entirely clear how widespread these beliefs were. However, it is clear that Christian teachings which could be demonstrated in practical everyday life were better received than others.

Cultural Continuities

'A host of baptized heathens . . . a mass of Pulayas calling themselves Christians who are impure and heathen in their lives.'[33] This is how Caley, an Anglican missionary who greatly influenced the attitudes and the policies of the CMS mission in Travancore until the end of the nineteenth century, referred to Pulaya Christians. These remarks were made precisely 20 years after the first Pulaya baptism. Significantly, the Bishop of the diocese used similar words to express his dissatisfaction with the Pulaya Christians within the Anglican Church. He said, they were 'degenerating into a state of heathenism'.[34]

From the initial stages of the conversion movement, CMS missionaries were determined to implement rigid Christianization and as far as possible prevent any contact between Christian and non-Christian Pulayas. Adult baptism did not take place until converts had demonstrated sufficient evidence of strict separation. The structures established for Christian instruction, examination of Christian motives, and finally baptism itself were developed to guard against any form of accommodation and weed out any remaining non-Christian practice.

Despite the strict Christianization and its apparent success, it did not take long for the missionaries to discover the persistence of non-Christian religious and cultural practices among Pulaya converts. Responding to this problem, Koshi Koshi, a Syrian Christian priest, wrote: 'The facts and doctrines of Christianity appeared to have fared much like the contents of a leaky vessel'.[35] Indeed, CMS missionaries were conceding the failure of Christianization at least in certain Pulaya moves.

Both English and Syrian Christian missionaries felt disappointed at the continuation of pre-Christian religio-cultural practices among the converts.[36] The Provincial Council of the CMS in Travancore, which consisted of both missionaries and Syrian Christian priests, formally discussed this issue and concluded that the Pulaya Christians were 'not well established

90

in the faith'. It is evident that this comment was made in direct reference to continued pre-Christian religious practices.

Referring to the tendency of converts to resort to non-Christian practices to ward off the 'evil' effects of 'former gods', Bishop Hodges wrote, 'The Pulayas are often found to be uncertain and foolish as children, and easily led away'.[37] Several references to the continued practice of non-Christian ceremonies can also be found in missionary letters. 'Superstitious dread of the corpse of a person' who died of smallpox was common among Pulaya Christians and missionaries found it difficult to secure a 'Christian burial' for victims of smallpox. The failure of Western medicine easily led some converts to promise offerings or sacrifices to temples. Having analysed this practice, C. A. Neve observed,

> At times of epidemics, especially smallpox, . . . some of our converts are exposed to great temptation to fall away from their Christian faith, and join their old heathen associates in offering to the Demon who is supposed to be the author of the disease.[38]

Thus for at least some Pulaya converts the distinctions between Christians and non-Christians were not as sharp as the missionaries expected.

CONCLUSION

This brief historical review suggests that during the conversion movements in Travancore, the transference of Christian ideas was limited. Missionaries do not seem to have been especially effective in communicating the Gospel due to language limitations and barriers, and their inadequate understanding of the converts' pre-Christian religious concepts and notions. The converts however were inspired and motivated by the message of equality preached by missionaries which had relevance to their oppressive social existence.

Available data suggests that the most effective communicators of Christian teaching (even if not adequately understood) were Pulayas themselves, their headmen, who spread these new ideas through their own idiom. However, by using their traditional vocabulary they may have given room for converts to continue to interpret Christian teachings in a traditional Pulaya way.

Before concluding, theories on the role of ideas in African conversion advanced by a well-known anthropologist, Robin Horton, may not be out of place.[39]

According to Horton, pre-existent worldviews played a vital role in African conversion. Africans, who were living in a period of rapid social change gradually came to feel that their traditional worldview was no longer adequate as a method of 'explanation prediction and control'. They were, therefore, predisposed towards the development of some other and more satisfactory cosmology; and this they discovered in Islam and Christianity – options already present in the African situation. But though experienced as increasingly inadequate, traditional cosmology nevertheless continued to play an important part in the conversion process. According to Horton, 'the locus of traditional thought patterns' determined rather closely which external cultural influence (i.e., which aspects of Islam or Christianity) would be accepted and which rejected.

For Horton, the African cosmology has a two-tier structure: lesser spirits concerned with events in the microcosm and the supreme being concerned with events in the macrocosm. As the social relationships and the boundaries are redefined due to social change, less attention is paid to lesser spirits, and the supreme being takes over as an important reality which helps them (the converts) to understand, predict and control events.

Horton's theory in general challenges one to look at pre-conversion cosmology and the intellectual process involved in any conversion. His arguments are a timely reminder that scholars should not only be aware of the dangers of regarding conversion as a purely social phenomenon, but should also take into account the possibility that, in certain circumstances, cosmology facilitates the process.

However, in applying this to the Travancore situation one runs into difficulties.

Firstly, the two-tier structure of African cosmology does not fit the Pulayas' pre-existing belief system which was multi-tiered, incorporating an hierarchy of gods. Spirits of the deceased ancestors had a significant role and position in their religious activities. On the next level were 'subordinate agents' or malignant and malevolent spirits. *Thevaratampuran* (master's god), *Bhagavati* and *Kali*, comparatively high forms of deity, also figured in the Pulaya religious activities.

Secondly, the preaching of the CMS missionaries was in direct contradiction to the Pulayas' previously-held thought patterns and perceptions of God although certain concepts such as protection from evil spirits and the concept of equality were part of their pre-Christian cosmology. Especially important in contradicting missionary teaching was the traditional conviction about the wrath of gods. Missionaries largely admitted failure in conveying this message.

Thus missionary communication cleared the path not for a fulfilment but for a contradiction or a confrontation of two opposites – Gods of wrath and Gods of love. Consequently in the transference of ideas they confronted obstacles and failures.

Lastly, I would like to observe that pre-existing ideas were not conducive to Pulaya conversion to Christianity. They may have converted inspite of the pre-existing belief system. Possibly the most effective communications were those related to sociological aspects like equality of castes. In fact this only confirms the overall proposition of historians of Christian conversion in India that the sociological rather than cosmological factors were of primary importance in the conversion process.

NOTES

1 D.B. Forrester, *Caste and Christianity: Attitudes and Policies on Caste of Anglo-Saxon Protestant Missions in India*, (London, 1970).

J.W. Gladstone, *Protestant Christianity and People's Movement in Kerala: A Study of Christian Mass Movement in Relation to Neo-Hindu Socio-Religious Movements in Kerala 1850–1936*, (Trivandrum, 1984).

D. Kooiman, *Conversion and Social Equality in India: The London Missionary Society in South Travancore in the 19th Century*, (New Delhi, 1989).

G.A. Oddie, 'Christian Conversion in Telugu Country, 1860–1900: A Case Study of One Protestant Movement in the Godavary-Krishna Delta', *Indian Economic and Social History Review*, Vol., No. 1, Jan–March, 1975.

John C.B. Webster, *The Christian Community and Change in Nineteenth Century North India*, (Delhi, 1976).

2 Journal of George Mathen, 31 Dec. 1850, CI O/161/21 CMS Archives at Birmingham University. Hereafter CMS. London. CMS.

3 'Travancore and Its Population', *CM Intelligencer*, Vol. XIII, 1862, Sept. p. 215.

4 Edgar Thurston, *Castes and Tribes of Southern India*, Vol. II, (Madras, 1909), p. 86.

5 See Kathleen Gough, 'Cults of the Dead Among the Nayars,' in Milton Singer (ed.) *Traditional India*, (Philadelphia, 1959), p. 264.

6 *The Missionary Register,* 1852, p. 443; Thurston, *Castes and Tribes,* Vol. II, pp. 83, 86.

7 Thurston, *Castes and Tribes,* Vol. II, pp.59f.

8 L.A. Krishna Iyer, *The Cochin Tribes and Castes,* Vol. I, (Madras, 1909), pp.113–115.

9 See Annual Letter, Koshi Koshi, July–Sept. 1857, CI2/0147/3 CMS., George Mathan, Journal, Quarter ending 31 March 1851, CI2/0161/23 CMS, *Proceedings of the CMS 1861–62,* p. 165.

10 *CMS Report,* 1859–60, p. 148.

11 Annual Letter of Koshi Koshi, July to Sept. 1857, CI2/0417/3 CMS.

12 *Proceedings of the CMS 1862–63,* p. 150.

13 Andrews, Diary 6 Sept. 1856, CI/023/9, p. 8, CMS.

14 Andrews, Journal 11 Dec. 1857, CI/023/13, p. 12, CMS.

15 Annual Letter of Koshi Koshi, July to Sept. 1857, CI/10147/3 CMS., *CMS Record,* Vol. XII, 1867, p. 310.

16 Annual Letter of Koshi Koshi, July to Sept. 1857, CI/0417/3 CMS.

17 Andrews, Diary 21 July 1857, CI/023/12, p. 5, CMS.

18 Annual Letter of Andrews, 1 Jan. 1863, CI2/023/27 CMS.

19 Annual Letter of Koshi Koshi, Sept. 1861, CI2/0147/10 CMS.

20 *CMS Report,* 1856–57, p. 137.

21 Andrews, Journal 20 June 1858, p. 14, CI2/023/15, CMS.

22 Andrews, Journal 11 Dec. 1857, p. 12, CI2/023/13 CMS.

23 'Journal of Joshua, A Slave Teacher' G2I5/01885/56, pp.56–57, CMS.

24 Andrews, Journal 2 Aug. 1857, p. 10, CI2/023/12 CMS.

25 A.F. Painter, 'The Pulayas of Travancore', *The Diocesan Gazette,* April 1882, p. 192.

26 Andrews, Diary 2 Aug. 1857, p. 19, CI2/023/12 CMS, Andrews, Diary 21 July 1857, p. 5, C12/23/12 CMS.

27 Andrews, Journal 1 Feb. 1858, p. 8, CI2/023/14, CMS., See also Andrews, Journal 19 July 1856., p. 2, CMS., Andrews, Diary 23 Nov. 1856, p. 26, C12/023/9 CMS.

28 Koshi Koshi, Journal July to Sept. 1857, CI2/0247/3 CMS.

29 Andrews, Journal 12 Sept. 1858, p. 17, CI2/028/16 CMS.

30 Letter of George Mathen, 14 Nov. 1866, *CMS Record,* Vol. XII, 1867, p. 309.

31 *CMS Report,* 1856–57, p. 138.

32 Letter of Oommen Mammen to Venn, 24 Aug. 1859, CI2/0157/2 CMS.

33 Annual letter of Caley, 29 Dec. 1874, CI2/055/13 CMS.

34 Letter of Bishop J.M. Travancore and Cochin to Gray, 22 May 1880, G21/5/0 CMS.

35 Annual Letter of Koshi Koshi, 3 Dec. 1874, CI2/0147/14 CMS.

36 Annual Letter of Caley, 29 Dec. 1874, CI2/055/13 CMS.

37 Bishop Hodges, 30 Jan. 1892, *Extracts of Annual Letter 1891–92,* p. 196, CMS Office.

38 C.A. Neve 'Outcastes and Their Attitudes to the Gospel and Some of the Hindrances to Their Ingatherings' *The Travancore and Cochin Diocesan Record,* Vol. XVIII, No. 4, Aug. 1908, p. 54.

39 Robin Horton, 'African Conversion', *Africa,* Vol. XLI, April, 1971, No. 2, pp.85–108; 'On the Rationality of Conversion', Part I, *Africa,* Vol.

XLV, 1975, No. 3. See for a discussion of Horton's theory's application to South Asia, D. Schreuder and Geoffrey Oddie, 'What is "Conversion"? History, Christianity, and Religious Change in Colonial Africa and South Asia', *The Journal of Religious History*, Vol. 15, No. 4, Dec. 1989.

Chapter 4

The French Mission and the Mass Movements

Henriette Bugge

'Mass movement' is a term traditionally applied to large-scale conversion movements towards Christianity which took place above all in the Telugu and Tamil areas of South India from the 1870s and well into the first decades of the twentieth century.[1] One of the most significant aspects of the mass movements was that they occurred as group movements. Large groups of people, family by family, caste-group by caste-group or village by village flocked to the mission compounds and demanded to be baptized as Christians. The number of Protestant Christians in the Madras Presidency rose from a little less than 75,000 in 1851 to about 300,000 in 1891.[2] Even though the mass movements have traditionally been viewed as a predominantly Protestant phenomenon[3] it should be stressed that the Roman Catholic missions witnessed a similar increase. The congregations of the French *Société des Missions Étrangères* (MEP) in South India increased from 192,000 in 1880 to 295,400 in 1901, and the Jesuit Madurai mission increased in the same period from 169,000 to 260,000.[4]

This situation was new and quite unexpected for most missionaries, Roman Catholic as well as Protestant. For the first time, a significant number of conversions occurred not in response to any change in missionary strategy or effort, but spontaneously. What was the background of these mass movements, and how did the missionaries handle them?

THE BACKGROUND OF THE MASS MOVEMENTS

Looking at one Roman Catholic mission, the MEP in South India, we find that the arguments usually put forth do not apply in this case, even though they may be of relevance when discussing the Protestant missions. Dr. Duncan Forrester argues that the main impetus behind the mass conversion was a growing restlessness and dissatisfaction among the lower castes. This restlessness, coupled with the gradual erosion of traditional social ties within the village communities, made the lower and untouchable castes more receptive to the missionaries and especially to their criticism of the caste system. The Protestant missions had from the beginning argued against the caste system and had done everything in their power to eradicate all attitudes and actions based on caste in the Christian communities.[5]

How, then, do we explain that the Roman Catholic missions, which had no qualms about accepting caste in their congregations, also witnessed mass conversions on a considerable scale? Partly the answer lies in the too ready acceptance of the explanations offered in the available sources. The Protestant missionaries, who with the exception of the Leipziger Mission and the Church of Sweden Mission were heavily influenced by English Evangelical revivalism, viewed Indian society and in particular the institution of caste as the primary obstacle to conversion. For decades they had debated among themselves, in missionary journals, as well as publicly, agreeing that caste was what characterized Indian *vis-à-vis* European society,[6] and that eradication of caste had to be the primary objective for missionaries and administrators alike in modernizing Indian society. They therefore often found it difficult to ascribe the actions of the mass movement-converts to anything else than what they had been teaching and preaching for so long: the dissatisfaction with the caste system.

In another part of India, Rosalind O'Hanlon has shown how groups of low caste Marathas listened to what the missionaries preached about the equality of all men, about the freedom to move upwards on the social scale, and about the Christian Bible being available to all believers not only to high-caste priests. However, they drew another lesson from these teachings than what the missionaries expected: they organized a Hindu-reform movement, among other things emphasizing the free entry right to Hindu temples for all castes and the right for every man, irrespective of caste, to study the Puranas.[7]

In the same way, it is entirely possible that the mass movements were not primarily a movement towards the freedom, equality and social justice promised by the Protestant missionaries, even though that is the way the missionaries themselves saw it.

Rather than being a direct answer to the preachings of the missionaries the mass movements were one of several movements of the time, attempting to find a new social and religious identity, in a period of profound social change. Active proselytism was not unique for the Christian missions, and the tradition for religious protest movements was strong.[8]

THE DIFFERENT VIEWS ON INDIAN SOCIETY

The Roman Catholic missions had never been as eager as the Protestants to change Indian society. Indeed, the Catholic missionaries had since their arrival in India in the sixteenth century strived to conform with Indian society as much as possible. In the seventeenth century there was a fierce debate going on in France concerning the so-called Chinese rites. The Jesuit missionaries – who stood close to the Sorbonne University – argued that all Chinese rites could be accepted in the Church with only slight modifications, and that it even was possible to use prayers like 'Blessed Confucius, pray for us in heaven'.[9] The MEP missionaries, who saw themselves as allies of the Pope, accepted this only to a certain degree, but agreed with the Jesuits that Chinese and Indian religions were entities separate from society, and that one could accept social customs in the Church, even if one could not accept purely religious ones.[10]

A similar debate occurred in the eighteenth century concerning the Malabar rites; i.e. the rites of the Indian Christians which were accepted in the Roman Catholic missions.[11] In the 1820s the Abbé Dubois, perhaps the most well known of the MEP missionaries, wrote a pamphlet where he argued that it would never do to translate the Bible into the vernacular, because only few missionaries could achieve the necessary high and flowing style of classical Tamil, so necessary if the missionaries wanted to establish themselves as proper religious leaders.[12]

These debates show very clearly the differences between the Protestant and the Catholic missions. The Catholic missions were influenced by a century-long debate on the precise definition of civilization, and specifically on the fine distinctions between morality and religion, philosophy and virtue. It was a discussion which saw no difficulties in enfolding non-Christian philosophies and moralities in a wider Christian framework, as the aim of any encounter with the 'other' was always to establish a universality, a totality in which the non-Christians may have been subordinated to the Christians, but in which none the less every human phenomenon belonged in the same category.[13]

In the Protestant missions, on the other hand, a totally different understanding of the 'other' is apparent.[14] By now the emphasis is on the diversity of civilisations, and the ranking of non-Christian and non-European civilisations in a hierarchical framework, where to be different was both to be of inferior status, and definitely outside the sphere of Christianity, civilisation and progress.[15] This view, which was to be confirmed later in the century by the theory of evolution, gave the Protestant missionaries ample scope for regarding Indian social phenomena, in this case the caste system, as something that should be eradicated in order to bring about Christianity and civilisation – which were intimately linked and almost identical.

THE AREA OF THE MEP MASS MOVEMENTS

Not only were the Roman Catholic and the Protestant missions different in their views on Indian society. The area where the MEP mass movement occurred was also different from the Krishna-Godavery and Kaveri river deltas, where a number of the most significant Protestant mass movements took place. To ascertain whether Duncan Forrester's view that the mass movements were preceded by significant social changes also holds true for the French mission area, it is necessary to discuss the social and economic conditions in some detail.

In the diocese of Pondicherry the mass movements were not evenly spread. They were concentrated in the areas around the mission stations in the northern part of South Arcot and the southern part of North Arcot, i.e. in the area lying between the two lines of the railway which came together in Villapuram and from there ran north to Madras through Tindivanam and Chinglepet, and north-west to Vellore through Tiruvannamalai and Polur.

It was an area which suffered from low rainfall and frequent droughts. There were no rivers from which water could be obtained for irrigation, which meant that cultivation depended on private wells or on the storing of rainwater in public tanks. Dry crops (i.e. crops that did not depend on irrigation) were predominant, especially the sturdy types of millet such as *ragi*, *kambu* and *varagu*.[16] In 1891 about 48% of the *ragi* in the entire South Arcot district was grown in the *taluqs* of Tiruvannamalai, Tindivanam and Villapuram.[17] The distribution of castes was different from what was found in wet areas. There were not many Brahmins, and those who lived in the area were not the wealthy landowning Brahmins of the wet areas, but rather poor, landless Brahmins, working as temple-priests or domestic priests, whose only income was the salaries paid by the families who had the various rites performed.[18] There was a larger percentage of trading castes such as Chetties and Kaikalars. There was also a larger percentage of Idaiyars, the chief shepherding caste, a fact which was related to the importance of cattle in the rural economy. Livestock was important both as providers of power for ploughing and working the water-wheels, as providers of cow-dung for fuel and fertilizer, and as providers of saleable items such as milk and curds. Cattle-markets were common in the neighbouring towns of Polur, Vellore and Tiruvannamalai.

The ratio of landless labourers to landowners was small. Furthermore, the bargaining position of the labourer was stronger than in the wet areas, because agricultural production on the one hand was dependent on the control of labour, and on the other hand it was easier for the labourer or small-holder to set up as independent cultivator. The millets and other tough food grains grown on the small plots left the cultivator with enough spare time to earn an additional income as a wage-labourer, but the additional work was not necessary for survival, as the small plots gave just enough for subsistence.

CHANGES IN THE MEP AREA

The last half of the nineteenth century was a period of change in the dry regions where the MEP mass conversions occurred. The first to be noticed was the improved lines of communication, especially the two lines of railway, which were completed between 1875 and 1895. Hereby the relatively isolated dry areas were put in direct contact with markets and commercial centres which traded not only with the major cities of India but also with overseas markets.

The triangular area between the railway lines was the area which in the last half of the century developed into the centre of ground-nut production in South India.[19] It was a crop which grew equally well on wet and on dry lands, and which did not require the heavy capital outlay of other commercial crops. It took only a short time to grow, freeing the land for a second crop. It was a crop which favoured small holdings. In the years from 1870 to 1914 the area under ground-nut in South Arcot grew from 10,000 acres to more than 300,000 acres, which was more than a third of the total area under ground-nut in the entire Tamil area.[20]

The pattern of landholding in the dry areas has been debated fiercely. It seems however that there was a general tendency towards greater equality of landholding in the dry districts of the Madras Presidency than in the wet districts.[21] Furthermore, we know that the cultivated area in South Arcot and North Arcot expanded significantly in the last decades of the nineteenth century. This expansion probably, as Bruce Robert has argued for other dry districts, came about through the introduction of a large number of small and marginal landholdings established on the previously more or less communally held wastelands.[22] Most of these wastelands had been used as grazing grounds for the cattle, which was so important in the economy of the dry zones. By putting this land under plough the basis of the agricultural economy changed from a pastoral economy to a crop-oriented economy. Furthermore, a gradual settlement took place, whereby farmers and peasants replaced the nomadic, shepherding groups, showed a high percentage of landholders and only a small percentage of labourers. All this points to a situation where the number of landowners actually grew in the late nineteenth and early twentieth centuries.

This settlement however, did not mean that the mobility of the population was curbed. On the contrary, we find in this area a far higher level of mobility than in the wet zones. Whereas the population generally grew only little and the density of population remained on the same low level from 1871 to 1901, the urban centres in the ground-nut area (Tindivanam, Tiruvannamalai, Polur, and Vellore) increased at a much higher rate than the other urban centres in southern India.[23]

In the last decades of the nineteenth century we thus find a movement towards integration with a wider economic network. Expansion of the cultivated area, change from a pastoral nomadic economy to a settled agricultural economy, migration and urbanisation, improved lines of communication, economic integration – everything points to a type of development which in later years was to be described as 'modernisation'. Here economic development and social development did not necessarily take place within the framework of an established social order. Instead, the framework itself was undergoing subtle changes. In most of the areas where the Protestant mass movements took place, we find social and economic change resulting in marginalization of the poorest sections of society. We find village communities being dissolved, with the traditional ties of dependency between labourer and landlord being eroded.[24] In this case it was not surprising that the poor should look elsewhere – i.e. to the Christian missions – for social and religious security. This was not the case in the MEP area. Here the poor sections of society were offered new opportunities. And they took these opportunities to establish new cropping patterns of landholding, new commercial networks – and to establish new religious identities for themselves.

THE FRENCH MISSION AND THE MASS MOVEMENTS

The reaction of the French mission to the mass movements took on a form which clearly signalled the willingness of the MEP to act as both spiritual and worldly leaders for their congregations. Contrary to most Protestant missions, the French mission saw nothing wrong in extending temporal help to catechumens and converts. As early as 1872 Mgr. Laouënan had decided to pay a fixed sum of money to the catechumens to recompensate them for the loss of daily wages suffered during the time they were under instruction to become Christians.[25] Some of the French missionaries were not very happy with this arrangement, which they considered smacked of paying people to get baptized – in other words, the French mission would hereby do exactly what the Protestants accused them of doing: attracting converts who were nothing but 'rice-Christians'. However, the arrangement continued, even during the famine of 1876–1878.[26] During the famine, when the French mission established a wide network of relief camps, large numbers of people demanded to be baptized. Afterwards, a number of missionaries deplored the conversions which had taken place during the famine, judging these conversions to be too hasty and the converts to be unworthy of baptism. As proof of this Father Fourcade held that a number of 'new Christians' in his district had participated in the village festivals which were held as thanks-offering to the village goddess who was supposed to have ensured the long-awaited rain and plentiful harvest of 1879.[27] However these objections were considered to be the enthusiastic and somewhat uninformed views held by a young missionary recently arrived from France, and were brushed aside. Mgr. Laouënan argued that the number of apostates was relatively small and certainly not a sufficient reason to discontinue the practice of supporting the catechumens while under instruction.

During the first wave of mass conversions in 1874–1875, i.e. before the famine, the French missionaries did not stop at this kind of help. They also actively took part in a court case concerning a group of agricultural labourers in Alladhy who had been repeatedly beaten up by their landlords. The case was first heard at the local court, where the judge demanded a bribe of 60 Rupees to let the case fall out in favour of the Christians. Rather than complying with this, the missionaries then took the case to the sub-collector in Tindivanam.[28] How it ended, the sources do not tell us, but the important thing was the action taken by the missionaries, and the implicit promises of support they hereby gave the Christians.

Another action taken by the French mission which was of great symbolic significance, was the visitation of Mgr. Laouënan in the mass conversion villages during the month of March 1875. He was received everywhere with enthusiasm and joy, and every village did its best to venerate the first Bishop in fullest pontifical costume they had ever seen. Mgr. Laouënan was received with fireworks, music, drums and torches, and – even more important – with offerings of bananas, coconuts, flowers etc., signifying his importance as a spiritual and worldly leader, a person of almost kingly status.[29] By this action the mission had demonstrated to the new Christians that they did indeed belong in a new, larger network of spiritual authority.

During the famine several groups turned to the mission both to be baptized and to receive help. The French mission entered into a cooperation with the Protestant missions in the area to establish private relief camps, as well as with the British government. This was not done without some misgivings, and with several declarations of how difficult it was to work with Protestants.[30] The French mission was able to hand out seeds and food even during the second year of the famine, when the lack of rain threatened to make all but the most prosperous members of the society destitute. Handing out grains and seeds to the poor Christians had two effects, apart from the primary effect of holding off immediate starvation. The French mission acquired, or maybe rather stabilized, the position as a just ruler, one who fulfilled the expectations laid down in *raja-dharma*, the position of a ruler who took care of the spiritual needs of his people and at the same time secured peace and prosperity. Significantly, this position was acquired not by upsetting the moral and social framework of society, but by accommodation to the existing rules and expectations.

During the famine the French mission extended yet another kind of help to their congregations in which the Protestant missionaries would never have dreamed of partaking. In 1876 Father Darras was asked by a few members of his congregation in Melkallur to let them have the statues of St. Anthony and the Holy Virgin, and that these could be carried around in the village to ward off the cholera epidemic. The non-Christian village leaders were against it, but the Christians did as they had planned, and the Christian families were not touched by the epidemic. This is an example of the attempts to ward off epidemics and disaster by making not only the entire village but also the leaders of the supra-locality (in this case, the leader of the mission) participate in rites to propitiate the gods and to make them put an end to the disaster.[31] Once again, the French mission by their accommodating practices had succeeded in bringing about change, because the entire village hereafter decided that the Christian saints must be more powerful than the village gods and goddesses, and all demanded to be baptized.

Thus we see that the French mission made extensive use of precisely the 'tools' which were most despised by the Protestant missions – the practice of accommodation and the handing out of money and food to people who considered becoming Christians. They did this deliberately, and with great success. The French mission was not bothered by thoughts of rice-Christians, as were the Protestant missions. Instead they succeeded in providing adequate answers to the demands of the converts, and managed to secure a position as secular and religious leaders, indispensable to their converts in the changing times of the late nineteenth century.

NOTES

1 The first major study of the mass movements was J.W. Pickett, *Christian Mass Movements: A Study with Recommendations*, (New York, 1933). For specific studies on South India, see P.Y. Luke and J.B. Carman, *Village Christians and Hindu Culture: Study of a Rural Church in Andhra Pradesh*, (London, 1968). The most influential research however remains the studies by G.A. Oddie, 'Protestant missions, caste and social change in India, 1850–1914', *Indian Economic and Social History Review*, vol. 6 (1969); 'Christian conversions in the Telugu country, 1860–1900: A case study of one Protestant movement in the Godavery–Krishna delta', *Indian Economic and Social History Review*, vol. 12 (1975), and the most recent, *Hindu and Christian in South-East India*, (London, 1991).

2 J. Richter, *Indische Missionsgeschichte*, (Gütersloh, 1906), pp. 213–214. See also the statistical tables in *The Missionary Conference of South India and Ceylon, vol. II*, 1879, pp. 481–488 ('Comparative Statistics of Missions in South India, 1857–78') and the discussion of missionary statistics vs. Census statistics in G.A. Oddie, 'Christians in the Census: Tanjore and Trichinopoly Districts, 1871–1901', in N. Gerald Barrier, ed., *The Census in British India: New Perspectives*, (Delhi, 1981), esp. pp. 127–135.

3 See for instance Duncan B. Forrester, *Caste and Christianity: Attitudes and Policies on Caste of Anglo-Saxon Protestant Missions*, (London, 1980), pp. 72–73.

4 *Die katholischen Missionen* (188), p. 9 and *Die katholischen Missionen* (1900–1901) p. 186.

5 Forrester, *Caste and Christianity*, pp. 75–80.

6 In this view they were supported by Anglo-Saxon and German administrators, historians and anthropologists. See E. Valentine Daniel, *Fluid Signs: Being a Person the Tamil Way*, (Berkeley/London, 1984), pp. 1–12; Nicholas B. Dirks, *The Hollow Crown: Ethnohistory of an Indian Kingdom*, (Cambridge, 1987), pp. 3–16, 256–261; and Clive Dewey, 'Images of the Village Community: A Study in Anglo-Saxon Ideology', *Modern Asian Studies*, vol. 6 no. 3 (1972) pp. 314–328.

7 Rosalind O'Hanlon, *Caste, Conflict and Ideology: Mahatma Jotirao Phule and low caste protest in nineteenth-century western India*, (Cambridge, 1985), pp. 50–87, 156–163, 193–213.

8 See Kenneth W. Jones, *Socio-Religious Reform Movements in British India (The New Cambridge History of India, vol. III no. 1)*, (Cambridge, 1989), pp. 1–14, 164–209, who stresses the socio-political and anti-colonial character of many of the movements of the late 19th century. See also Robert Eric Frykenberg, 'On roads and riots in Tinnevelly: Radical change and ideology in Madras Presidency during the 19th century', *South Asia*, vol. V no. 1 (1982), pp. 34–52.

9 Paul Hazard, *Die Krise des europäischen Geistes 1680–1715*, (transl. from French, *La crise de conscience européenne*), (Hamburg, 1939), pp. 47–51; Roland Mousnier, *Les XVIe et XVIIe siècles*, (Paris, 1954), pp. 203–2024,

338–340; for a bibliography see Donald A. Lach and Edwin J. Van Kley, *Asia in the Making of Europe*, (Chicago, 1993), vol. III, book 2, pp. 222–269, and vol. III, book 4, pp. 1731–1753.

10 Confucius was seen as a philosopher not a priest, and was therefore acceptable.

11 See my *Mission and Tamil Society: Social and Religious Change in South India, 1840–1900* (forthcoming) pp. 44, 48–50.

12 J.A. Dubois, *Letters on the state of Christianity in India; in which the Conversion of the Hindoos is considered as impracticable*, (London, 1823), pp. 28–47.

13 This shift has mainly been discussed for the New World, but not properly for the European encounter with Asian civilisations. See Anthony Pagden's important works, *The Fall of Natural Man: The American Indian and the Origins of Comparative Ethnology*, (Cambridge, 1982), and *European Encounters with the New World*, (Cambridge, 1993).

14 I am here talking of the Protestant missions of the 19th century, as the Halle missionaries of the late 18th century belonged in a different category.

15 See Johannes Fabian, *Time and the Other: How Anthropology makes its Object*, (New York, 1983), pp. 2–21; Margaret T. Hodgen, *Early Anthropology in the Sixteenth and Seventeenth Centuries*, (Philadelphia, 1964), pp. 213–223, 254–269, 389–408; Jörg Fisch, 'Zivilisation/Kultur', *Geschichtliche Grundbegriffe*, vol. VII, (Stuttgart, 1992), pp. 696–704.

16 Christopher John Baker, *An Indian Rural Economy 1880–1955; The Tamilnad Countryside*, (Oxford, 1984), pp. 34–56, 138–155.

17 *Statistical Atlas of the Madras Presidency* (1895) pp. 236–237.

18 The Danish missionary Herman Jensen estimated in 1900 the monthly salary for a temple Brahmin in Tiruvannamalai to vary between 6 and 12 Rupees. Herman Jensen to the Board, *Archive of the Danish Missionary Society* vol. 256, 21 February 1900. This should be compared to the salary for an agricultural labourer, estimated by Dharma Kumar to vary between 2 and 3 annas per day, i.e. 4 and 5 Rupees per month. Dharma Kumar, 'Agrarian Relations: South India' in Dharma Kumar and Meghnad Desai, eds., *Cambridge Economic History of India, vol. 2: 1757–1907*, (Cambridge, 1983), pp. 206.

19 See map 7.B. in Baker, *Rural Economy*, p. 386.

20 *ibid.*, pp. 145–147.

21 Dharma Kumar, 'Landownership and inequality in Madras Presidency: 1853–54 to 1946–47', *Indian Social and Economic History Review*, vol. 12 no. 3 (1975), pp. 242–254. For other views, see David Washbrook, 'Country politics: Madras 1880–1930', *Modern Asian Studies*, vol. 7 no. 3 (1973), pp. 476–499; David Washbrook, 'Economic development and social stratification in rural Madras: The "dry" region 1878–1929', in Clive Dewey and A.D. Hopkins, eds., *The Imperial Impact: Studies in the Economic History of Africa and India*, (London, 1978), pp. 68–82, and as a critique of Washbrook, Bruce Robert, 'Economic change and agrarian organization in "dry" South India 1890–1940: A reinterpretation', *Modern Asian Studies*, vol. 17 no. 1 (1983) pp. 59–78.

22 Robert, 'Economic change', pp. 64–67.

23 Baker, *Rural Economy*, pp. 385–388. See also R. Lardinois, 'Une conjoncture de crise démographique en Inde du Sud au XIXe siècle', *Population*, vol. 37 (1982), pp. 385–387.

24 See my *Mission and Tamil Society*, pp. 146–167.

25 'Mandements de Mgr. Laouënan' (15 March 1872), quoted in A. Launay, *Histoire des Missions de l'Inde: Pondichéry, Maïssour, Coïmbatour*, (Paris, 1898), vol. 4, p. 7.

26 Launay, *L'histoire*, vol. 4 pp. 20–21, See also the letter from Father Fourcade to Father Ligeon, 10 October 1874, *Archive des Missions Étrangères de Paris*, vol. 1004, pièce D.1.

27 Launay, *L'histoire*, vol. 4, pp. 58–60.

28 *Die katholischen Missionen* (1875), pp. 39–40, 171–174.

29 *Compte rendu des Traveaux de la Société des Missions Étrangères* (1875) pp. 45–46.

30 J.F.M. Darras, *Cinquante ans d'apostolat dans les Indes sous les auspices de Notre-Dame de Lourdes*. (Pondicherry, 1907), pp. 155–161, 168–172.

31 Darras, *Cinquante ans*, pp. 81–83. *Die katholischen Missionen* (1878) pp. 108–110. David Arnold, 'Famine in peasant consciousness and peasant action: Madras 1876–78', in Ranajit Guha, ed., *Subaltern Studies*, vol. 3 (1984) pp. 71–74.

Chapter 5

The Beginnings of the Theosophical Movement in India, 1879–1885

Conversion and Non-Conversion Experiences*

Edward C. Moulton

This paper originated from a conference panel on religious conversion in India and focuses on that issue as it pertained to the operations of the Theosophical Society from the time of the arrival of the founders, Helena P. Blavatsky and Henry S. Olcott, in 1879 until the enforced departure of the former in 1885. Theosophy sought the fundamental truths which it believed to underlie all religions and in theory did not require conversion of its ordinary members. The case was different in principle, however, for those who wished to give themselves completely to the work of Theosophy as *chelas* or dedicated pupils. But in practice, as we shall argue, Theosophy in its subcontinental setting articulated such strong support for ancient Indian religions and cultures that some Indian elites were able to become part of the inner circle without modifying their religious beliefs or practices. The exception to this appeared to be young Indian adherents who became a part of Blavatsky's headquarters inner circle, and for whom she became a powerful female guru. The one prime instance in this period on which we have considerable data is Damodar K. Mavalankar, whose case will be examined in the paper.

The second thesis is that the Indianizing of Theosophy meant that it was impossible for Europeans, who belonged to a Christian

* Research for this paper was made possible by grants from the Social Sciences and Humanities Research Council of Canada and the Shastri Indo-Canadian Institute. I wish to thank my colleague, K. Klostermaier, an expert on Hinduism, and the editor, Geoffrey A. Oddie, for helpful comments on an earlier draft of the paper. Alice Moulton provided valuable research and proofing assistance.

and western cultural tradition, to become *chelas* or even *lay chelas* (devotees who were married) without undergoing a conversion process. By that is meant a basic change in beliefs or practices which could happen quickly or be a long drawn out process. The most important cases in point in this period are those of Alfred P. Sinnett, editor of the influential newspaper, *The Pioneer*, and Allan O. Hume, a prominent Indian Civil Service officer. In these years they were the most prominent Europeans in India to become deeply involved in the Society and play formative roles in its development. Sinnett converted quickly and completely but for Hume the process was long-drawn out and he was never free of doubts about the founders and their teachings. Extensive data exists on their contrasting Theosophical experiences and the paper gives much attention to this subject. Hume's case is of particular interest not merely for our understanding of Theosophy and conversion but because his experiences impinged upon his subsequent involvement in the organization of the Indian National Congress.

THEOSOPHICAL ORIGINS, TRANSPLANT TO INDIA AND INDIANIZATION

The word theosophy derives from classical Greek, connotes wisdom concerning things divine and has close affinities with mysticism. Beginning with an acceptance of the idea of God, it claimed that insights into the nature of both the universe and the divine could be achieved through direct knowledge, philosophical inquiry or physical processes. In the Western tradition Neoplatonists and Gnostics were often considered theosophists, as were Protestant thinkers such as the German religious mystic, Jakob Boehme (1575–1624) and the prominent Swedish scientist and mystic, Emanuel Swedenborg (1688–1772).

In its modern nineteenth century avatar, theosophy refers to the ideas and beliefs of the Theosophical Society as formed and developed by Blavatsky and Olcott. Blavatsky was born in southern Russia in 1831. She came from a privileged family of German-Russian origins and was reputed by her family to have been psychic, rebellious and strong-willed from childhood.[1] Pressured in her late teens into a marriage with 40 year old N. V. Blavatsky, a vice-governor in Armenia, she promptly ran away to Constantinople and became something of a world traveller until 1873 when she settled in the United States and became a citizen. By then she was heavily into spiritualism and the performance of occult phenomena, then much in vogue among religious liberals on the eastern seaboard where she lived.[2] This was the link which brought her into contact with Olcott, a lawyer and journalist who had earned the rank of colonel in Lincoln's army and subsequently developed an interest in spiritualism. They first met in the autumn of 1874. Olcott, who was a year younger than Blavatsky, was fascinated by her power as a medium. She saw him as a potentially loyal and trustworthy associate and they became close friends. In her New York flat, popularly known as 'the lamasery,' Blavatsky presided over many discussions on the occult and eastern spiritualism. At one such meeting in September 1875, she and Olcott took the initiative in founding the Theosophical Society.

The Society failed to flourish in its American setting,[3] and by the latter part of 1878, Blavatsky and Olcott, who were respectively the life-time corresponding secretary and president, left for India in the hope of finding a more favourable spiritual and cultural environment for the growth of the movement.

A year earlier Blavatsky had produced the first major literary underpinnings for Theosophy, namely *Isis Unveiled: A Master Key to the Mysteries of Ancient and Modern Science and Theology*, a massive two volume publication. Bruce F. Campbell, in his recent critical but sympathetic history of Theosophy, has succinctly summarized the strong scholarly evidence subsequently presented by the American orientalist and spiritualist, W. E. Coleman, that extensive portions of these volumes were plagiarized by Blavatsky.[4] While that assessment is sound and undermines the book's philosophic originality, it is still important for our purposes to understand its essential views. Blavatsky's purpose was to rediscover the authentic roots of 'the spiritual aspirations of mankind,' in an effort to counter the 'materialism' which was threatening to engulf all humanity.[5] These roots she believed to exist in the writings of the 'ancient philosophers and religious teachers,' who had resided in the East but whose doctrines had not reached the West because of the 'prejudice and bigotry' of Christianity.[6] The West had lost not merely a knowledge of true theology but also of science. Psychology, for example, was 'alone . . . understood' in the East, and '*pretended*' Western authorities on 'modern psychological phenomena,' needed to '*go to the Brahmans and*

Lamaists of the far Orient, and respectfully ask them to impart the alphabet of true science.'[7] The most saintly among these religious leaders constituted a continuing brotherhood of morally and intellectually perfected beings known as *adepts,* masters or *mahatmas.* Indeed, Blavatsky presented *Isis Unveiled* to the world as 'the fruit of a somewhat intimate acquaintance with Eastern adepts and study of their science.'[8] Her book constituted a statement on behalf of 'divine religion' and 'spiritual freedom' and a 'plea . . . for enfranchisement from all tyranny, whether of Science or Theology.'[9]

Two themes in *Isis* explain why Theosophy was to prove broadly attractive to many of India's new intellectual classes. One was the focus on ancient Indian religion and culture. In a chapter entitled 'India the Cradle of the Race,' she contended that as a result of advances made in the study of Sanskrit, it had been 'discovered' that the 'very same ideas' of the ancient Egyptian philosophers were earlier expressed in 'almost identical language . . . in the Buddhist and Brahmanical literature.'[10] The other was a vehement attack on organized Christianity. The Church was symbolized by the inquisition, which had shed 'torrents of human blood . . . unparalleled in the annals of Paganism,' and by Catholic clergy, who 'surpassed . . . the "heathen"' in *sorcery*'.[11] Moreover, Jesus was only a pale, later image of the Buddha, who had developed the religion to perfection. Buddhism, unlike modern Christianity, did not 'curse the "heathen"' or condemn 'him and his religion to "eternal damnation".'[12] Instead, the Buddhist doctrine was 'entirely based on practical works' and had as 'its nucleus' a 'general love of all beings, human and animal'. Later in the volume Blavatsky referred to the '*Vedas*' and 'Brahmanical literature' as the source of 'identical cosmical myths, symbols and allegories,' which underlay Judaism, Christianity and Gnosticism.[13] An understanding of these myths and allegories was 'possible only to those who have inherited the key from their inventor.' This was where the *adepts* came in, for they alone knew true 'Magic' or 'spiritual wisdom' and its 'material ally,' nature.[14] Blavatsky's special gift was to be able to communicate transcendentally with these masters.

It is clear from the above that prior to their arrival in Bombay in February 1879 the Theosophical founders had a rudimentary familiarity with Indian religious literature as translated by Western orientalists. Moreover, during their last months in America they had also become aware of the reformist Arya Samaj and had established written contact with its leader, Dayananda Sarasvati.[15] One of their initial objectives in India was to use that relationship as a springboard to enlist support among Indian reformist elites. Their strategies for this latter purpose included making India the international headquarters of the movement, recruiting a small core of personal devotees to assist in the work of the Society, extensive travel and use of the public platform and press to spread the message. In this latter connection, in October 1879 the Society established its own monthly journal, *The Theosophist*, with Blavatsky as editor. The Society also developed an explicit statement of purpose which was well attuned to the Hindu cultural-intellectual ethos. While the main focus was on winning support among Indian elites, the founders understood the realities of political power relations in British India and were anxious to gain adherents among influential members of the European community.

The Society's first formal statement of principles in its new Indian context was worked out at a meeting which the founders held with Dayananda in Banares in December 1879.[16] The first principle stated: 'The Theosophical Society is formed upon the basis of a Universal Brotherhood of Humanity.' In all, seven specific purposes were identified – namely, to 'keep alive' man's 'spiritual intuitions;' to 'counteract' all forms of 'bigotry . . ., whether as an intolerant religious sectarianism or belief in miracles or anything supernatural;' to 'promote . . . brotherhood among nations' and 'assist . . . international exchange of useful arts and products;' to seek and diffuse 'knowledge of all the laws of Nature, . . . especially . . . the Occult Sciences;' to disseminate 'correct information' about 'ancient philosophies, traditions and legends;' to foster 'the spread of non-sectarian education;' and finally to 'encourage and assist individual Fellows in self-improvement, intellectual, moral and spiritual.' These objectives fitted closely with the values of many thinking Indian leaders.

In 1881 the Society refined its goals into a more succinct version incorporating much of the above but also providing an explicit commitment to the study of Indian philosophy and culture. The revised statement of principle was as follows:

First. To form the nucleus of a Universal Brotherhood of Humanity, without distinction of race, creed or colour.

Second. To promote the study of Aryan and other Eastern
literature, religions and science and vindicate its importance.
Third. To investigate the hidden mysteries of Nature and the
Psychical powers latent in man.[17]

Gone were explicit commitments to assisting improvements in
livelihood and to the promotion of education, though such
reforms remained of interest to the movement. What remained
was in accord with the general ethos of Hinduism and Buddhism
and clause two was obviously appealing to Indian cultural
nationalists.

The process of Indianizing the Society can be further
illustrated by a brief examination of Olcott's inaugural address
in Bombay and of the first issue of *The Theosophist.* Olcott was
neither an original nor profound thinker, but he enjoyed public
speaking and his first Indian speech was a masterly production.
Entitled 'The Theosophical Society and its Aims,' the address was
cast in the form of answers to numerous questions about
Theosophy raised by interested Indian friends during their first
month in Bombay. Olcott emphasized that the Society, founded
by more than coincidence in the same year as the 'Arya Samaj of
Aryavarta,' had begun its life in 'the enemy's country, with foes
all about, public sentiment hostile, the press scornful and
relentless' and 'traitors' working to undermine the organization.[18] In addition, Christian clergy had 'denounced' the
Theosophists as 'the children of Satan, doomed to eternal
damnation along with the wretched "Heathen."' In his introduction to the published text he stated that the founders had chosen
to 'settle' in India, because they were thoroughly 'Hindoocized'.
They were 'enraptured with the ancient learning and philosophy
of India' and for India had 'left their homes and sacrificed all
worldly considerations.'

After assuring the audience that the Society was non-political
and would not interfere in social institutions such as marriage or
'filial or parental relations,' he spelled out its essential philosophy.
Theosophy believed that there was 'one Absolute Truth' underlying all established religions and accepted the 'immortality of the
human soul'. It supported the systematic study of 'occult science,'
first, because it taught that there was 'a world of Force within this
visible world of Phenomena,' and second, because it stimulated

the 'student to acquire, by self-discipline and education, a knowledge of his soul-powers and the ability to employ them.' This 'occult science,' not that of the modern West, was the key to the 'sacred science' which was the core of all truth and explained the very nature of life. This core truth had been discovered by the ancient sages of 'Tibet, India, Persia, Chaldea, Egypt and Greece,' and still survived and was 'practised by men who carefully guard their knowledge from profane hands.' Then, sounding like a Vedantist, he spoke of the contrast between 'our narrow physical life and the *Bhāvitātman*, or soul universalized – the soul having sympathies with the Universal Good, True, Just, and being absorbed in Universal Love!'

Olcott identified the Society with indigenous religious and cultural reform organizations rather than with traditional and orthodox Hindu leaders. He particularly welcomed adherents of the 'Arya, Brahmo, Prarthana, and all other minor Samajes which represent the progressive mind of Young India.' Olcott concluded with various moral injunctions, generally in accord with the ideas of these Societies. He appealed to Hindus to 'rise above their castes and every reactionary influence' in order to 'regenerate' their country. He also made a pitch for 'non-sectarian education for native girls and married women,' which Theosophists regarded as 'the corner-stone of national greatness'. He promised that the Society would aid in promoting such education, as well as the introduction of 'cheap and simple machines,' which could be used to ease manual labour and promote India's 'prosperity'. His only explicit criticism of modern India was that it 'completely' ignored the 'achievement of ancient Aryavarta.' He added, presumptuously, that he and Blavatsky knew 'more of the essence of Vedic philosophy than the direct descendants of the Rishis themselves.' On this point, as they were later to discover, Dayananda was to disagree profoundly.

The first issue of *The Theosophist* repeated many of the general themes which Olcott had identified in his inaugural address. Even its sub-title, *A Monthly Journal Devoted to Oriental Philosophy, Art, Literature and Occultism: Embracing Mesmerism, Spiritualism and other Secret Sciences*, emphasized its identification with the East. Educated Indians, used to the berating of their culture by Western officials and missionaries, must have been flattered by the Journal's first titled article, 'Namaste!', which gave the rationale for its establishment. The prime purposes were twofold.

The first was to provide an 'organ through which the native scholars of the East could communicate their learning to the Western world' by expounding the 'sublimity of Aryan, Buddhistic, Parsi and other religions'.[19] The second function was that of a 'repository' especially for 'facts' about occultism. Members might adhere to any religion but they could not use the Journal to exclusively promote their own sect. It promised not to suppress facts and asked for 'courtesy of language' to be used against opponents, something which Blavatsky herself was to find difficult to observe. In a later issue, noting the numerous contributors, who varied so greatly in 'literary merit' as well as in 'race and creed', Blavatsky proudly described *The Theosophist* as 'the Asiatic People's Magazine.'[20]

The extent of the Society's Indianization can also be seen in its articulation of guidelines for members. From its early months in India the Society's expectations regarding its members envisaged two different levels of commitment, depending upon whether one was interested in 'exoteric' or 'esoteric' Theosophy. The first involved support for the general philosophic principles of the Society. In his 1879 Bombay address, Olcott emphasized that it was not necessary for general members of the Society to forego marriage and that even as president he had merely given up his former moderate wine drinking and other worldly pleasures such as frequenting clubs, theatres and race courses. Only the *adepts* were obliged to forsake obligations to 'country, society and family,' and follow a 'life of strict chastity.'[21] Later Hume, writing on behalf of the Society, detailed the behaviour code for *chelas*, by which he meant followers of 'esoteric' Theosophy who were involved in sustained endeavours to understand the divine wisdom of the *mahatmas*. To become such an adherent required a 'complete change of life, mind and heart,' and 'most strict and long-continued preparation'.[22] This involved abstaining from 'all spirituous liquors;' living a 'perfectly pure and chaste life;' being 'perfectly truthful, just and honest, in all . . . words and deeds;' maintaining a state of mental 'serenity' and banishing 'all passion, pride, hate, malice, envy, anger, greed and craving for worldly advantages;' subordinating 'self to others,' filling one's heart with 'loving kindness towards all living beings;' watching for 'opportunities of doing secret kindness to all within reach;' and, finally, accepting 'the empty and transitory character of all earthly things,' and centring one's 'desires . . . on the unseen and imperishable, and on the attainment of that higher knowledge which leads to these'. This code was well attuned to the ideas of Indian religious reformers, while the Society accepted as ordinary fellows all who sympathized with its general objectives.

Many devout Hindus and religious reformers already lived according to the principles required of *chelas*, which meant that they could even become a part of the Theosophical inner circle without having to undergo changes of belief or lifestyle. By the same token few Westerners in India were likely to be in that category. Indeed, the more the Society became Indianized, the greater was the change required in belief and lifestyle for Europeans who wished to become *chelas*. The case was probably similar for a small number of young Indians who were entrusted by Blavatsky to work at headquarters. But the great majority of Indian supporters were interested only in 'exoteric' Theosophy and that required no changes in belief or behaviour. It will be useful first to examine some specific cases of Indian non-conversion and conversion.

CONVERSION AND NON-CONVERSION AMONG INDIANS OF THE THEOSOPHICAL INNER CIRCLE

While Theosophy had obvious appeal for Hindu religious or social reformers, as well as more secular nationalists, the position was more difficult for orthodox Muslims and Indian Christians. Muslims regarded the *Koran* as 'revealed' truth, and for devout Christians the same was true of the *Bible*. Christians had another problem, for even though Theosophy claimed not to have preferences among the established religions, it was clear from Blavatsky's writings that she had intense contempt for institutional Christianity. Moreover, Christian missionaries in India tended to be overtly hostile to Theosophy. It is not surprising, therefore, that Indian Christians did not become involved in the Society in this period. The absence of Muslim involvement was more marked given the overall size of that community. The only Muslim name prominently associated with the movement in this early period was Mirza Murad Ali Beg, a council member for several years and an occasional writer for *The Theosophist*. However, his real name was Godolphin Mitford, a Madras-born Englishman, who, at the time when he came into contact with Blavatsky and Olcott in early 1881, claimed to be a follower of Islam. According to Blavatsky, he subsequently went through brief successive phases as an atheist, mystic, Roman Catholic and atheist again by the time of his death from insanity in the mid-1880s.[23]

Among the leading Indian religious reformers, the person most systematically cultivated by Blavatsky and Olcott was Dayananda, the dedicated founder of the Arya Samaj. Obviously he required no change in lifestyle to qualify for a close association with the Society. In the spring of 1879 Blavatsky and Olcott travelled to Saharanpur in north India to meet him and then accompanied him to Meerut.[24] That meeting was evidently cordial and in December they met again, this time at Banares, where Dayananda participated in a small council meeting of the Society which spelled out its objectives in the manner noted above. For a time relations between the Theosophical founders and Dayananda were amicable and the Society proudly designated him as 'Supreme Chief of the Theosophists of the Arya Samaj.'[25] There were, however, inherent differences in the beliefs of the Samaj and the Society which soon became apparent to both sides. The main ideological problem was that the Theosophists did not believe in revealed literature, whereas a belief in the infallibility of the *Vedas* was a fundamental creed of the Arya leader. It may well have been that Dayananda also became wary of Blavatsky's spiritual credentials as he got to know her. In any case, in the spring of 1882 after various efforts by Dayananda to discuss their differences were evidently ignored, he vehemently condemned the Theosophical founders in a public lecture.[26] According to extensive and partly verbatim reports in *The Theosophist*, Dayananda accused them of such radical changes in their basic beliefs as to constitute '*fraud* and *treachery.*'[27] Whereas the Theosophical founders had initially said they were coming to India to study 'Vedic Religion' and were neither 'Buddhists, Christians nor . . . believed in the Puranas', they had subsequently claimed to have been Buddhists for many years. He further contended that the founders did not believe in the '*Ishwar*' or personal god preached by him. Indeed, they 'believed in no religion'. He also complained of broken promises of financial and library assistance to the Samaj and failure to live up to understandings on relations between the two organizations.

Responding for the Theosophists, Blavatsky threw the blame back on Dayananda, and accused him of bad faith. '[W]hile telling us privately,' she wrote, 'that *Yoga-Vidya must not* be taught promiscuously as it was a sacred mystery, he laughed at the Spiritualists, denounced every spiritual and occult phenomenon as a *tamasha*, a juggling trick, and pooh-poohed publicly at that which *we all know to be* undoubted and genuine facts, capable of demonstration and verification.'[28] She concluded that he must have decided to keep his knowledge of 'practical *Yoga* . . . secret from the present generation.' Henceforth, therefore, Theosophists would be 'content' with their 'Buddhist esotericism.' In any case, the Theosophists had 'never agreed' with Dayananda's teachings though they had respected him as a 'great Sanskrit scholar' and a 'useful Reformer'. Now however, she declared, the alliance between the Society and the Samaj was 'broken.' Olcott was more generous. While regretting Dayananda's 'wild misconceptions' about Theosophy, he commended him as 'a loyal champion of Aryan culture' and an Indian patriot, and suggested these virtues were more important than his continued alliance.[29] What is obvious is that Dayananda's beliefs and practices were not altered by his relations with Theosophy. Rather, he found that the founders did not live up to his initial hopes and no longer merited his continued support.

There is every reason to assume as well that the leading Hindu spokesman for Theosophy following the break with Dayananda, the Madras Telugu Brahmin, T. Subba Rao (1856–90), did not have to undergo any form of conversion in order to assume his new role. Rao was western-educated, obtaining B.A. and B.L. degrees at Madras, where he built up a successful legal practice.[30] Although according to his family he showed no early evidence of interest in metaphysics, he established contacts with the Theosophists by late 1881 when he wrote Blavatsky a detailed letter of exposition on 'Aryan-Ahrat Esoteric Tenets'.[31] In January 1882, when Blavatsky quoted excerpts from that letter in *The Theosophist*, she referred to Rao as a 'layman' who was 'perhaps better versed in the Brahmanical Occult Sciences' than anyone else in India who was 'outside the inner conclave of adepts'.[32] This suggests that at the outset he more than met the Society's standards for *chelaship* and in April 1882, during a visit to Madras, Blavatsky and Olcott, 'privately' inducted him into the Society ,[33] the privacy perhaps accounted for by a desire on his part not to offend orthodox members of his community. He also became corresponding secretary of the Madras branch of the Society which was established during that same visit by the founders.

Rao's initiation followed closely on Dayananda's break with the Society and he quickly became the leading authority for *The Theosophist* on Hindu philosophical themes. In February 1883, when Blavatsky got him to comment upon some fine points in *advaita* philosophy raised by Swami Paramahamsa of Almora, she characterized Rao as a top authority in India 'concerning the esotericism of the Adwaita philosophy.'[34] According to Olcott, Rao was instrumental in the decision of the Society in 1882 to transfer its headquarters from Bombay to Madras and thereafter he sometimes acted as editor of *The Theosophist* during Blavatsky's absence. Following Rao's premature death in 1890, Olcott claimed that on his initiation into the Society there had 'suddenly opened to him' a 'storehouse of forgotten experience'.[35] He remembered his 'preceding birth,' 'recognised his Guru,' the *adept* Morya, who was also Blavatsky's teacher, and 'thenceforth held intercourse with him and other Mahatmas, . . . personally . . . and by correspondence.' Rao proved to be a loyal supporter of Blavatsky through the Adyar shrine exposure crisis of 1885, but subsequently disengaged himself from her and the Society.

In contrast to Dayananda and Rao, already mature, educated and experienced by the time they encountered Theosophy, some younger and more impressionable Indians who came under Blavatsky's sway as members of her headquarters entourage were transformed by the experience. The first case in point was that of Babula, a Bombay lad of fifteen when in early 1879 he became Blavatsky's personal servant, a position in which he was to demonstrate exemplary devotion.[36] It was subsequently claimed that he spoke six languages and he developed an impressive bearing. When he accompanied Blavatsky on her extended visit to Europe in 1884 she reported that he was a 'sensation' at Marseilles where he had an 'admiring audience of 500 men strong, running after him to admire his gold earrings and theosophical livery.'[37] His life was dramatically altered by his involvement with Blavatsky and Theosophy, though we do not know the extent of change in his belief system.

Another far more important Indian member of her staff, and a convert in the fullest sense of the word, was Damodar K. Mavalankar (1857–1885). He came from a wealthy Maharashtrian Brahmin family of Ahmedabad, and by his own testimony was educated by his father in the tenets of orthodox Hinduism and also given 'every facility for acquiring an English education.'[38] The principal Theosophical work on his life asserts that he had two critical illnesses in his youth during which he had visions of a man who saved his life.[39] Through circumstances which are unclear he turned up at the Theosophical headquarters in Bombay around mid-July 1879 and in early August was initiated into the Society by Olcott. According to Olcott's diary entry, 'the dear boy' was 'as thin as Sarah Bernhardt, with lantern jaws and legs . . . like two lead pencils,' and appeared an unlikely candidate for *chelaship*.[40] However, according to his own testimony, Damodar then had 'the inestimable good fortune to read' *Isis Unveiled*, which dramatically changed his life, creating an 'unfathomable abyss' between his former and new existence.[41] Until then he had been 'ardently ritualistic,' simply practising his religion 'without understanding it' and 'not really enjoying happiness and peace of mind,' his aspirations being only for 'more Zamindáries, social position and the gratification of whims and appetites.' *Isis* opened his eyes to the 'nature and powers' of man and the 'possibilities, duties and joys' of life and convinced him that his former aspirations were mere 'vapours'. Now 'the perfection of his spiritual self' became the 'grand object of his efforts.' Indeed, so determined was he to follow his new convictions and to maintain his 'freedom of action' that in the spring of 1880 he formally renounced his caste affiliation, even though this was not a requirement for *chelaship*. His justification was that the broader principles of Theosophy enjoined one to regard 'all men as equally my brothers, irrespective of caste, colour, race or creed.' He adhered to this resolve despite intense pressure from his family, all of whom severed their Society membership. According to his biographer, Damodar's action also involved breaking off relations with the bride to whom he had been betrothed since childhood and to whom he now generously made over his ancestral lands worth some Rs.50,000.[42]

From the outset Damodar assisted Blavatsky in her role as editor of *The Theosophist* and quickly became an important member at headquarters. In 1880 he was designated formally as assistant to the corresponding secretary for Marathi and English. From the following year he assumed the more responsible position of joint recording secretary for the Society. He was the closest of Blavatsky's Indian associates and usually went with her when she travelled in the subcontinent. Indeed, he confessed to a prominent American founding member of the Society, lawyer

William Q. Judge, that he regarded Blavatsky as his 'benefactor,' 'revered' her as his 'Guru' and 'loved her more than a mother.'[43]

From his early days at headquarters it was clear that Damodar had psychic inclinations. According to Eek, his first encounter at headquarters with a picture of the *mahatma*, Koot Hoomi, led him to the realization that this was the very man who had appeared to him in visions during his life-threatening childhood illnesses.[44] Soon he was claiming that the *adepts* were appearing directly to him and discussing philosophical teachings, the first such visit occurring during his trip to Ceylon with the founders and other leaders of the movement between early May and mid-July 1880. These incidents Damodar described a year later in letters to Judge.[45] He also assured Judge that he had received numerous written communications from the *adepts* and on one occasion they had appeared to him at night in his headquarters bungalow and transported him in his 'astral body to the real place of Initiation' in the Himalayas of Kashmir.[46] Damodar claimed to have been assured that if he proved 'deserving' of the 'blessings' of the *adepts* he would be taken back there in his body for 'the Ceremony' of initiation. This seemingly came true in the autumn of 1883 when Damodar, while visiting Jammu with Olcott, was reported by the latter to have disappeared for two days from the house at which he had been staying. Olcott telegraphed Blavatsky that Damodar had been 'called' by his 'blessed masters'.[47] When Damodar returned after two days Olcott noted in his diary that he was greatly 'changed!' 'He left,' Olcott wrote, 'a delicate-framed, pale student-like young man, frail, timid, deferential; he returned with his olive face bronzed several shades darker, seemingly robust, tough and wiry, bold and energetic in manner'. The secret to the change, Olcott reported, was that 'he had been at the Master's retreat (*ashram*), undergoing certain training.'

In some respects Damodar was outdoing Blavatsky, if not in his relations with the *mahatmas* then in the facility with which he appeared to change from his physical to his astral body and travel great distances in the latter state. If Blavatsky had concerns on this latter score she did not reveal them publicly. In an editorial note in *The Theosophist* in December 1883, Blavatsky announced, in obvious reference to Damodar's astral experiences in Kashmir, that although he had been a *chela* only for four years, he had 'lately' demonstrated 'remarkable psychic powers.'[48] The note added that 'whenever the phenomenon of the separation of the astral from the physical body takes place, . . . he falls invariably asleep or into a trance a few minutes before.' Damodar became increasingly influential in the running of *The Theosophist* and at headquarters and was a key member of the board left in control at Adyar during the extended visit of the founders to Europe from February to November 1884.

There were also two Europeans associated with headquarters from the outset. These were Rosa Bates, a former English school teacher, and Edward Wimbridge, an architect from New York and early member of the Society, both of whom had accompanied the founders to Bombay. Bates appears to have become household manager at the new headquarters and Wimbridge designed the attractive cover of the first issue of *The Theosophist,* a design which was used for a considerable period.[49] In late March 1880 they were joined by Emma Coulomb, née Cutting, and her French husband, Alexis.[50] Blavatsky had evidently met Emma in Cairo in 1871, but she had later married and moved to Ceylon. In mid-1879, when they were reputedly in some financial difficulty, Emma wrote to Blavatsky, the upshot of which was that some months later the Coulombs arrived at the Bombay headquarters. At the annual meeting in April 1880, and presumably on Blavatsky's doing, Emma was named assistant to the corresponding secretary, sharing with Damodar responsibility for European languages – in her case French and Italian. Evidence suggests that for the next few years she was a trusted confidant of Blavatsky. Indeed, in August 1880 following the return from their highly successful mission to Ceylon, Blavatsky and Olcott sided with Emma Coulomb in an acrimonious dispute which had developed between her and Rosa Bates. Olcott described the incident as the 'hell of an explosion between Rosa and us,' the result of which was that she immediately left the headquarters, accompanied by Wimbridge, and resigned from the Society.[51] As a consequence Emma Coulomb became an important part of the inner circle at headquarters. Her husband shared that influence, for although he was basically a draughtsman and carpenter, in 1882 he was formally designated as the Society's librarian.[52] The Coulombs were later to be designated as part of the board of control at headquarters during the prolonged absence of Blavatsky and Olcott in Europe in 1884. While we do not know whether the belief systems of the Coulombs were altered by their connection with Theosophy, it is clear that for a number of years their lives were dominated by the Society.

No reliable published data appears to be available on the actual number of members the Society had in India in these early years. Published data is available, however, on the number of branches, which grew from 10 in 1881, to 39 in 1882, to 77 by 1883 (85 including Ceylon), and to 85 by the end of 1884, but we know little about the size of membership in the branches. At its 8th anniversary convention, held at Madras in December 1883, the Society claimed an attendance of 'nearly 500 members and delegates,'[53] and later clarified that 58 of these were delegates.[54] At the subsequent convention a year later there were 99 delegates, 6 of whom were from Europe and America and the rest from 39 Indian branches. One letter in *The Theosophist* of November 1883, protesting recent extreme criticism of the *mahatmas* by Dr. George Wyld, former head of the London branch, claimed signatures from 'over 400 Hindu Theosophists' belonging to 30 of the country's branches.[55] That works out to an average of 13 members per branch, but we do not know what proportion signed. Even if we estimate an average branch membership of 50, which is probably high, the total Indian membership in early 1885 would have been just over 4,000. They were overwhelmingly from the new educated classes, for the movement offered little for the masses. There is no reason to think that Theosophy transformed the personal lives of many of these members, but collectively its positive attitude to ancient Indian culture was psychologically reinforcing. Moreover, the influence of the movement extended far beyond the number of formal adherents.

EFFORTS TO RECRUIT INFLUENTIAL EUROPEANS: BEGINNING AND CONSOLIDATION OF THE A.P. SINNETT – A.O. HUME CONNECTION

From the outset the founders were also anxious to recruit influential members of the British community. This was a slow process, partly because the increased Indianization of Theosophy meant that European members normally had to undergo a greater change in values than was necessary for Hindus. Furthermore, European adherents in India had to put up with a considerable degree of ostracism because of the extensive deprecation of the credentials of Blavatsky and Olcott by the

British press and the general hostility to mysticism and occult phenomena. Nonetheless, a few resident Europeans became members of the Theosophical Society.

The first such formally initiated recruits appear to have been Lieutenant Colonel William Gordon of the Bengal Army Staff Corps and his wife, Alice, who were based in Calcutta. They came to Theosophy via spiritualism and were formally initiated as fellows in August 1879.[56] They were both active in the Society for several years but do not appear to have aspired to *chelaship*. Another early European recruit was Ross Scott, a young Irish member of the Indian Civil Service in the North-Western Provinces who had returned to India on the same ship as Blavatsky and Olcott.[57] Blavatsky tried to interest Scott in Theosophy and he undoubtedly had a part in bringing the Hume family into contact with the movement. While we do not know the background circumstances, in February 1880 Ross Scott and Maria Jane or Minnie Hume, the daughter and only child of Allan O. Hume and his wife Mary, along with three Indian members, were initiated into the Society by Blavatsky at her bungalow in Bombay.[58] According to Blavatsky, 'Miss Hume,' who was her house guest for three days, had already been associated with the Society for ten months. While we have no corroborating evidence on this latter point, the first list of paid up subscriptions to *The Theosophist*, printed in the December 1879 issue, contained Minnie's name, as well as that of Scott. Blavatsky described Scott as a 'Christian' and Minnie as a 'Christian follower of Swedenborg,' the Swedish mystic. She further alleged that though Minnie had lived in India for ten years she had 'never touched the hand of any *native*' until the evening of her membership initiation. Blavatsky confessed that she was utterly 'bored' with Minnie before the visit ended, but she had much greater interest in Scott and later, as we shall see, attempted to draw him into the inner circle.

Far more significant for the Society was the contact which started in February 1879 with Alfred P. Sinnett (1840–1921), editor from late 1872 of the influential Allahabad newspaper, *The Pioneer*. Sinnett had begun his journalistic career in Hong Kong in the late 1860s, after which he returned to London in 1870 and became an editorial writer for *The Evening Standard*.[59] That same year he married Patience Edensor, who went with him two years later to his prestigious new position in Allahabad. During a three months' London furlough in 1875 Sinnett became heavily influenced by spiritualism. He heard about *Isis Unveiled* shortly after its publication and when he saw a note in a Bombay newspaper about the arrival there of Blavatsky and Olcott, he published an item about them in *The Pioneer*. Olcott wrote to him on the basis of that news item and Sinnett, in turn, invited the founders to visit Allahabad. The visit materialized in early December 1879, when Blavatsky and Olcott, accompanied by Babula and Damodar, arrived in Allahabad as the guests of the Sinnetts. According to Damodar, the Sinnetts wanted Blavatsky to demonstrate her occult powers but she declined until she consulted Dayananda, who was then in Banares.[60] In mid-December, the Sinnetts, along with Mrs. Alice Gordon, went with the founders to Banares, where they witnessed what Damodar described as flowers dropped 'by invisible hands' on a table around which the group were sitting. Evidently satisfied, the Sinnetts returned to Allahabad where the founders soon rejoined them for a further week. During that stay Sinnett and his wife were formally admitted as fellows of the Society.[61] This was a major coup, Sinnett being one of the most influential, non-governmental Englishmen in India. It was equally significant for the Sinnetts, transforming their lives and constituting a conversion experience.

The Allahabad visit also captured the first sparks of interest in another prominent Briton, Allan O. Hume (1829–1912), who had just taken up residence in that city. He too had a certain prominence, or more accurately notoriety, among the British community in India, but was in the opposite camp from the conservative Sinnett on political, social and intellectual issues. Hume was the product of a liberal utilitarian family background, and like his Radical M.P. father, Joseph Hume, had little evident interest in institutional Christianity. He was essentially a rational empiricist, deeply interested in natural science and by that time recognized as the leading Indian ornithologist.[62] While ornithology was his passion, his professional career since 1849 had been that of an Indian Civil Service officer. Until 1867 he had been involved in district administration in the North-Western Provinces, after which he spent four highly successful years as commissioner of inland customs and from 1871 to 1879 was secretary to the Indian government's newly created department of revenue, agriculture and commerce.

Given this background, how and why did Hume become interested in Theosophy? The circumstances of his first contact are clear enough. Hume had been a zealous secretary of his department but as a critic of government policies and reform activist he became a thorn in the side of his superiors. The result was that in June 1879 the government took advantage of an ostensibly cost-cutting restructuring of central administration to abolish Hume's department and demote him to junior member-ship of the revenue board in the North-Western Provinces.[63] This explains his presence in Allahabad when the Theosophical leaders visited. Hume was invited to introduce Olcott at their public meeting on 13 December. While he had undoubtedly heard about Theosophy through his daughter, at the meeting Hume stated that he knew little about the Society except for what he had 'gleaned from the first three numbers of *The Theosophist*' and from 'a few all too brief conversations' with Olcott and Blavatsky.[64]

In his introductory remarks Hume emphasized the humanitarian message of Theosophy. Its 'fundamental' objective, he informed the audience, was the 'institution of a sort of brotherhood in which, sinking all distinctions of race and nationality, caste and creed, all good and earnest men, all who love science, all who love truth, all who love their fellow-men, may meet as brethren, and labour hand in hand in the cause of enlightenment and progress.' This was a 'noble idea' and, while only the future would prove whether it would be translated into 'reality,' he believed that 'no honest efforts for the good' of humanity were 'ever wholly fruitless'. For these reasons, one 'must necessarily sympathize with the Theosophists'. In an oblique reference to the occult, Hume referred to 'other aims' with which he declined to 'entirely identify' himself. However, he whole-heartedly supported the Theosophists in their 'desire to break down all artificial barriers between the various sections of mankind and unite all good and true men and women in one band, labouring for the good of their fellows'. Hume's interest was genuine though tinged with liberal scepticism.

Sinnett, by contrast, was deeply interested in spiritualism and was primarily attracted to Blavatsky by her commitment to the occult. Being more socially conventional than Hume, Sinnett found Blavatsky's personality difficult to accept. He later acknowl-edged having found her 'rugged manners and disregard of all conventionalities,' including her ready use of 'expletives' and 'vehement tirades' against the good-natured Olcott, rather off-putting.[65] Even though she was 'too violent a departure from accepted standards' to be well received in general Anglo-Indian circles, Sinnett characterized her first visit 'an unqualified success'. As it turned out, he and his wife were on the road to being lifetime believers. For more than six months following the December visit nothing further occurred to involve Sinnett or Hume actively in the Society. But the Sinnetts were already fellows and anxious to pursue occult inquiries. Consequently, they invited Blavatsky and Olcott to spend the autumn season of 1880 at their home in Shimla. This visit, which lasted from early September to late October, was very important for the development of the movement for it turned Sinnett into a true *chela*. At the same time, the visit deepened the interest of Hume, who was then living in Shimla and got to know Blavatsky better.

Sinnett was already convinced that Blavatsky was 'in possession of some faculties of an abnormal character.'[66] Nevertheless, he still wanted 'absolute certitude' as to the existence of the *adepts* and their 'wonderful powers,' including the ability to teach human beings 'positive knowledge concerning . . . their own spiritual nature.' Hume's interest was more humanitarian. It was psycho-logical as well for he was facing a traumatic mid-life crisis. Being a very energetic and goal-oriented person, he felt the need for a new mission in life. In 1879 he was 50 years old, had spent 30 years in the I.C.S., and considered his provincial revenue position boring and demeaning. Accordingly, in May 1880 he arranged an eighteen month leave as a forerunner to his planned early retirement at the end of 1881. The object of his leave was to undertake a pioneering ornithological expedition to Manipur and to complete a 3 volume publication *The Game Birds of India, Burmah, and Ceylon*, which he was producing in conjunction with C.H.T. Marshall. By the autumn of 1880 when Blavatsky and Olcott came to Shimla that project was nearing completion. Given his scientific orientation, it seems likely that Hume also had a theoretical interest in the claims of Theosophy as a higher science for the exploration of human consciousness and the natural universe.

Hume also had a lively intellect, an enquiring mind and a wide range of interests in social and political issues. At the same time his family life was not very stimulating; indeed his wife Mary Anne (née Grindall), who was five years older than her husband, appeared by then to have a serious alcohol problem. It was hardly surprising, therefore, that Hume found Blavatsky personally and intellectually fascinating as he got to know her better that autumn in Shimla. Blavatsky had a very fertile imagination and her striking individuality and feisty temperament resembled Hume's. While these common traits helped to bring them into close association, they were to prove significant factors in explaining why the intellectual relationship between them was to prove both stormy and relatively short-lived.

Meanwhile, Blavatsky's 1880 season in Shimla was marked by her precipitation of a rash of phenomena. These began with a 'happening' during a late September picnic on Prospect Hill, involving Mary Hume, Patience Sinnett and Blavatsky, in which their on-the-spot request to receive a communication from the *adepts* was answered with a note on a nearby bush.[67] Next, on 3 October at a breakfast picnic, at which Hume and Sinnett were both present, a seventh person had unexpectedly joined the group at the time of their starting out. As they prepared to eat somebody asked Blavatsky to produce a needed extra cup and saucer, whereupon she directed them to dig in the ground nearby and to their amazement a cup and saucer matching the other six was located.[68] That same evening at the Humes' luxurious bungalow, Rothney Castle, located on Jakko Hill overlooking the Shimla Mall, the most sensational phenomena of the series occurred. Including Blavatsky and Olcott, there were eleven people present, among them the Sinnetts and Alice Gordon. During post-dinner conversation Blavatsky asked Mary Hume if there was anything that she especially wished for, whereupon she mentioned a brooch which she had given away, possibly to her daughter, who had allowed it to pass from her possession. After a period of concentration, Blavatsky had a premonition that the brooch had just fallen into a certain flower bed in the garden. Sure enough, a search there quickly located the missing brooch. What was special about this incident was that all nine witnesses signed a written account of what had transpired, including an expression of their belief that it represented 'unimpeachable . . . evidence of the truth of the possibility of occult phenomena.' The statement was promptly released to the press and quickly gained country-wide publicity.

While press reports coming out of Bombay and elsewhere soon cast doubts on the authenticity of the 'brooch incident',[69] another development of more significance was the beginning, via

Blavatsky, of transcendental correspondence from *mahatma* Koot Hoomi to Sinnett and Hume. This new development began with the more captivated Sinnett. Since Blavatsky produced phenomena only through the agency of the *adepts*, Sinnett wished to consult them about the crucial importance of providing 'perfect and unassailable' demonstrations of their occult powers.[70] Blavatsky agreed to attempt to transmit such a letter to the brothers. Anxious to prove beyond doubt 'the possibility of obtaining by occult agency physical results which were beyond the control of ordinary science,' Sinnett presented a brilliant test, one in which Hume evidently had input – namely, 'the production in our presence in India of a copy of the London *Times* of that day's date.'[71] After a few days Blavatsky learned via 'her psychological telegraph,' that a 'Brother' had agreed to receive and answer the letter. Sinnett was so excited that he immediately dashed off another letter and on the evening of 15 October found on his desk a lengthy letter from 'Koot Hoomi Lal Singh' responding to both his communications. Even though the letter categorically rejected the London newspaper test, Sinnett was deeply moved by the contact with the *mahatmas*, who kept up a sustained correspondence with him until November 1884.[72] The explanation for not precipitating a copy of *The Times* was that humanity was still totally 'unprepared' for such a phenomenon and would either regard it as a 'miracle' or attribute it to 'dark agencies'.[73] Indeed, Sinnett was not as yet worthy of 'such phenomena,' which had 'ever been reserved as a reward for those who have devoted their lives to serve the goddess Saraswati – our Aryan *Isis*.' The letter reminded Sinnett that he had already witnessed 'a greater variety of phenomena' than 'many a regular neophyte' and that his duty, as the 'trustworth[y]' editor of an influential newspaper, was to publicize news of the recent phenomena effected by Madame Blavatsky. If Sinnett complied, Koot Hoomi promised 'further evidence.' While he may not have been altogether satisfied with this response, Sinnett was predisposed to believe and was on the way to becoming a faithful *chela*.

HUME'S SEARCH FOR THEOSOPHICAL CERTAINTY, (OCT. 1880–OCT. 1881)

Sinnett's profound elation over the establishment of written contact with a *mahatma* rubbed off on Hume, who determined to write to Koot Hoomi. Unfortunately, no copy of Hume's letter, dated 17 October, is known to have survived. However, we know much about its contents from a summary by Sinnett and from the reply of Koot Hoomi to Hume. Sinnett's synopsis was as follows:

> More favourably circumstanced than I for such an enterprise, he [Hume] had even proposed to make a complete sacrifice of his other pursuits, to pass away into any distant seclusion which might be appointed for the purpose, where he might, if accepted as a pupil . . ., learn enough to return to the world armed with powers which would enable him to demonstrate the realities of spiritual development and the errors of modern materialism, and then devote his life to the task of combating modern incredulity and leading men to a practical comprehension of a better life.[74]

In short, Hume offered himself as a *chela*, who would henceforth devote his whole life to the Theosophical cause.

Koot Hoomi replied to Hume in a letter postmarked Amritsar, where Blavatsky, the exchange medium for these transcendental communications, had gone after leaving Shimla. The letter expressed the appreciation of the *mahatma* 'fraternity,' who were particularly interested in India's welfare, 'for an offer of help whose importance and sincerity no one can doubt.'[75] However, instead of focusing on that offer, which was what really mattered to Hume, it then proceeded to the issue of establishing a separate 'Anglo-Indian Branch' of the Theosophical Society, an idea mooted by Blavatsky but in which Hume had little interest. To Hume this was off-putting, as was the response to his thoughtful queries as to why the *mahatmas* had failed to 'leave any mark upon the history of the world,' and what 'good' was to be attained for humanity through 'occult sciences.' The answer to the first was to question Hume's capability of knowing their impact on the world and to confess that they were not 'demi-gods' but only wise men who could 'divert' some of the world's 'energy into useful channels.' As for occult sciences, interest in it by 'high officials,' would encourage 'the natives' to 'openly . . . study' their 'ancestral sciences and philosophies'. The letter concluded with the snide comment that if Hume would only devote to his fellow men 'half the attention' that he bestowed on his 'little birds,' he would 'round off a useful life with a grand and noble work.'

To Hume, who had offered to redirect his whole life to the Theosophical movement, this reply was decidedly unsatisfactory. Unlike Sinnett, who asked many questions of the *mahatmas* but did not tend to challenge their responses, Hume's reply was characteristically argumentative. He criticized Koot Hoomi for only partly understanding his position and failing 'to touch the more important points' on which he desired 'enlightenment.'[76] He insisted that 'one good' direct 'conference' would be infinitely preferable to 'any amount of correspondence.' '[I]s it not possible,' Hume queried, 'for you to arrange to deal with me *conversationally,* in or out of the body, under your own condition of time, place, secrecy and the like?' He believed that his personal 'weaknesses' and 'follies' were 'eradicable,' and that he already had 'so much in common' with the *mahatmas.* 'We might become friends and fellow workers in earnest,' Hume continued, 'if you . . . are what I would fain believe, men purified from ordinary human errors, devoid of all selfish views, inspired by one sole desire of doing good'. To work with them in such a cause 'would be the dearest desire of my heart,' Hume added, 'to attain which, nothing on my part would seem an unreasonable effort.'

Hume emphasized both his yearning to believe in the *mahatmas* and his need for proof. He already accepted the 'possibility' of their existence and '*almost*' believed in them as a reality. As a near-convert, he was fully conscious of how such belief would be regarded by 'most Western minds' – namely as 'pure idiotcy.' They would question whether 'the wild talk of a clever but most erratic minded, and in many ways inaccurate woman' such as Blavatsky and 'a few strange phenomena that *might* be . . . mere tricks,' were 'reasonable' grounds for 'even entertaining the notion of such a brotherhood, possessed of such knowledge and powers' as the Theosophical leaders claimed. However, since Hume was already ostracized by his fellow administrators, the attitude of the British Indian community to his adhesion Theosophical involvement was inconsequential. Moreover, he was 'essentially a believer in the unseen universe'. Indeed, he had 'always admitted . . . the possibility' of special 'psychical training and development' and even had 'at odd times' in his life 'glimpses of something like' the 'philosophy' of the *mahatmas.* 'It would be such a boon to me to find my dreams true,' Hume added, 'that I am anxious to grasp any chance of proving them so.'

Hume went on to deconstruct Koot Hoomi's reply and to criticize the Theosophical founders. He considered the notion of imparting their 'higher knowledge' as a reward for deserving work immoral. With their superior insight the brothers should know whether sharing their knowledge with him would make him 'more useful' to humanity, and in which case they were 'bound by all eternal laws of right and wrong so to enlighten'. Hume did not care 'a fig for the knowledge and the philosophy' unless it enabled him 'to work in earnest instead of wasting' his life on 'comparatively trivial matters' because he could not see his 'way to meddle safely with more serious concerns of human life'.

As for an Anglo-Indian Theosophical branch, Hume contended that it could only amount to 'blind leaders of the blind,' as long as the *mahatmas* declined to provide special guides to Sinnett and himself. As a result Hume regarded Koot Hoomi's further suggestion that he and Sinnett provide 'ideas of the plan on which the branch should be organized' as patently stupid. Hume bridled at the accusation that he was refusing 'to give a helping hand to humanity,' by insisting upon special *adept* guidance. This was 'an utterly distorted and misleading resumé' of his case – so much so, that he speculated that in a former existence Koot Hoomi must have been 'a lawyer trained "to make the bad appear the better cause".' Having been given no meaningful knowledge of the wisdom that the brotherhood were supposed to possess, Hume was worried that the outcome might be the overwhelming of 'peace and good government' instead of the 'crushing [of] our common enemies, ignorance and vice'. How can I yet be sure,' Hume candidly asked, 'that this is not all moonshine?' 'I have seen many shams,' he continued, 'many windbags, many star-crowned, flower decked lies and before I move I require to be thoroughly satisfied as to course and consequences.' Not a person who was modest about his own moral commitment and intellectual acuteness, Hume added:

> If you want men to rush on blindfold, headless of ulterior results – stick to your Olcotts – if you want men of a higher class, whose brains are to work effectually in your cause, remember that such men are as fully impressed with their responsibility for their acts as you can ever be, and that you must convince them and take them into your confidence before you can expect them to do your work.

Hume bitterly resented Koot Hoomi's slighting of his ornithological work and general hostility to modern science. The *mahatma* had 'too narrow' a conception of science and failed to see its connection with 'moral nature' and 'Philanthropy.' Science, Hume insisted, taught 'a love of truth for its own sake' and led to 'a purely disinterested exercise of intellectual facilities'. It was the 'next best thing to spiritual culture,' and closely related thereto. Only when science copied the stance of its defeated foe, theology, and became dogmatic did it warrant denunciation. Hume admonished Koot Hoomi to realize that 'laws are the backbone of all science' and that science ministered 'in ten thousand thousand ways' to the 'comfort' and alleviation of the 'sufferings' of 'humanity'. As for his own work in Indian ornithology, it was undertaken 'for wide reaching moral effects that follow the implanting of scientific tasks.'

In a similar vein, Hume frankly questioned the *adepts*' veneration of eastern philosophy over what he regarded as the central truth of 'all western religions – Thou shalt love thy highest conception of goodness, knowledge and love with all thy heart and thy neighbour as thy self.' That precept, he believed, was superior to 'all the theologies Eastern and Western.' Moreover, he questioned the wisdom of the *mahatmas* in wishing to revive 'ancient Indian civilization,' which, like all civilizations, was the product of a particular environment and time. That civilization was 'dead' and the *adepts* were wasting their 'talent' and 'energies' in seeking to revive it. Similarly, instead of trying to revive 'another Golden Age of Sanscrit literature' the *mahatmas* should 'call from its tomb all the flowers of thought that survive it and plant them in the garden of the present'.

Hume contended that in the present age intellectual culture could best be 'acquired thro[ugh] the study of Western literature' and 'the handmaid of the soul,' science. Acknowledging that the East had much to offer in spiritual culture, Hume challenged the *mahatmas* to give that 'culture . . . with open hand, and leave to cosmic energies the fashioning of that age-harmonized form of civilization which must necessarily follow the preserve of combined mental and spiritual culture.' Instead, Koot Hoomi and his 'fraternity' were 'smothering' this spiritual culture with their 'traditional laws' and 'rules of practice,' which were the fossilized relics' of earlier ages. Indeed, he feared that the *mahatmas* were 'a perishing organization, no longer possessing the vital capacity for the readjustment of internal organization in correspondence with the changes in external conditions.' Their 'glorious association,' Hume warned, would be 'doomed' unless they could reform 'its conditions to meet the altered circumstances of modern life.' In fact, Hume was not even sure whether they existed or were merely the 'creation of M[adame] B[lavatsky]'s prolific imagination'.

In addition to criticizing the *adepts*, Hume expressed his misgivings about Blavatsky and Olcott. He knew '*nothing*' about their '*antecedents*,' but they seemed 'to be earnest and well intentioned' and had communicated to him 'matters . . . quite incredible.' However, Hume continued, neither of them possessed 'intellectual capacities, sufficiently great to enable me to feel certain that they are not themselves in error.' Blavatsky was 'decidedly clever' but she was 'clearly neither stable in mind, nor accurate in statement.' On the other hand, she had exhibited 'certain phenomena' for which Hume could not account by 'natural laws'. These 'may have been mere clever tricks' but he was not yet prepared to rule out that they were 'bona fide results of a knowledge of natural laws exceeding' his own. Because he believed in 'the unseen universe,' he had not 'pooh pooh[ed] the whole matter,' as had the 'majority' of his fellow Westerners. Indeed, if this 'new gospel' were 'true,' it could infinitely benefit 'humanity' and at the same time enable Hume personally 'to regain that faith in the potency of human effort, the fading of which has so embittered my life and paralysed my energies'. What he found inexplicable was the unresponsiveness of the *mahatmas*. As he bluntly phrased it, he had asked Koot Hoomi 'for bread' but received only 'a stone.'

Not surprisingly, a long silence followed Hume's critical letter. Assuming, as any secular rationalist must, that Blavatsky and her *mahatmas* were one and the same entity, this was not an easy letter to deal with. On the one hand, Hume clearly suspected that the *adepts* were the creation of Blavatsky's imagination, but this was accompanied by a passionate desire to believe in them, intertwined with a questioning of their wisdom and morality. An answer that would draw Hume into the Society required careful thought. Before any response was forthcoming, Sinnett sent Hume a copy of his latest letter from Koot Hoomi. In it he had informed Sinnett that Russia was 'massing her forces' for a 'future invasion' of Tibet and that the *adepts* were trying to stop it.[77] This was intended to demonstrate how they were working for good in the world. Koot Hoomi had also spoken approvingly of Olcott, who 'never questions, but obeys,' and had 'pledged' his 'faithful service' to them 'come well, come ill.'

This letter only reinforced Hume's concerns about the *adepts*. On 20 November he wrote to Koot Hoomi regarding the letter to Sinnett. 'I cannot bear the idea,' Hume emphasized, 'of your throwing me over under any misconception of my views.'[78] But instead of displaying the kind of submissiveness that Koot Hoomi desired Hume gave a candid critique of the letter. He was unimpressed about claims of restraining Russia, observing that if he thought Russia would govern Tibet or India in a way which made the 'inhabitants . . . happier than they are under the existing governments,' he himself would 'welcome and work for her advent.' However, since he judged the Russian government to be a 'corrupt despotism, hostile to individual liberty of action and therefore to real progress,' surely it was axiomatic for the *adepts* to oppose her expansion. As for praising Olcott's unquestioning obedience, it was reprehensible. 'This,' Hume declared, 'is the Jesuit organization over again'. '[T]his renunciation of private judgement, this abnegation of one's own personal responsibility, this accepting the dictates of outside voices as a substitute for one's own conscience,' he expostulated, 'is to my mind a *sin* of no ordinary magnitude.' If 'this doctrine of blind obedience' was 'essential' to the 'system' of the *adepts*, Hume doubted whether 'any spiritual light' it might confer could 'compensate mankind for the loss of that private freedom of action, that sense of personal, individual responsibility of which it would deprive them.' He himself would never accept instructions from the *adepts* 'without understanding the why or the wherefore, without scrutinizing consequences' and would never act in a 'blind and heedless' manner. As an 'avowed enemy of . . . military organiza- tion' and an 'advocate of the industrial or co-operative system,' Hume warned that he would never join any Society which 'purports to limit or control my right of private judgement.' He feared that he was 'too essentially a radical at heart, to be accepted' into the 'naturally conservative order' of the *adepts*.

Hume's criticisms angered Koot Hoomi, who, as soon became evident, was anxious to project himself as a traditional Indian guru who did not take kindly to being challenged by his followers, much less a mere aspiring *chela* such as Hume. In a lengthy response to Hume himself and in other comments to Sinnett, Koot Hoomi was scathing. He attributed Hume's reactions to his nationality, asserting that it was easier for oil and water to mix than for even the most 'intelligent, noble-minded and sincere' Englishman to 'assimilate . . . exoteric Hindu thought, let alone its esoteric spirit.'[79] By contrast, the 'Hindu mind' was 'pre-eminently open to . . . the perception of the most transcendental . . . abstruse metaphysical truths,' and hence oriental adepts would always be 'Masters' of Europeans in 'spiritual sciences'. He deplored Hume's criticisms of Olcott and infinitely preferred his loyalty to Hume's 'fierce combativeness'. He also drew unfavourable contrasts with Sinnett, who 'believes and will never repent,' whereas Hume had allowed his 'mind to become gradually filled with odious doubts and most insulting suspicions.' Hume was so filled with 'that haughty and imperative spirit which lurks at the bottom of every Englishman's heart' that he would be uncomfortable with an oriental guru. On the other hand, Koot Hoomi assured Sinnett that he was the exception to the haughtiness which was a 'national feature' of the English and thus 'would ever consent to have a "nigger" for a guide or leader'.[80] While Sinnett was also egotistical he did not mount 'philanthropical stilts' like Hume and therefore had much greater likelihood of learning 'a good bit of occultism.' Hume, however, was the very embodiment of the 'egotism of this age' and hence the prospect of the *adepts* developing an '*entente cordiale*' with him was remote.[81] Koot Hoomi ominously warned that Hume's 'suspicion' threatened to become a 'hideous monster' which would likely prevent him from realizing his 'highest ideals' and leave him in 'worse darkness than before'.

Koot Hoomi's response to Hume's letter of 20 November was to suspend correspondence with him while venting his outrage to Sinnett. He accused Hume of wanting to disturb the 'moral, pure hearted, simple people' of Tibet by imposing on them his own 'ideal of civilization and Govt.'[82] He added with withering satire that Hume 'ought to be sent by an international Committee of Philanthropists . . . to teach our Dalai Lamas – *wisdom*.' Men like Hume, he acknowledged, might make 'able statesmen, orators, anything you like but – never Adepts.' Later, when rejecting Sinnett's plea that he was being 'too hard' on Hume, Koot Hoomi speculated that Hume found 'in his quiet daily life too meagre a field' with his wife 'Moggy' and and his taxidermist, Davidson.[83]

Consequently, his mind 'bursts the dam and pounces upon every imagined event,' and being a 'skilled workman in intellectual mosaic' he delighted in picking out 'ingredients' of the *adepts'* teachings to 'daub' their 'faces with.' Koot Hoomi was pleased that the 'spiritual light' was burning within Sinnett and urged him to publicize the Theosophical movement and the revelations from the *mahatmas*.

SINNETT'S FIRST PROSELYTIZING ENTERPRISE: THE OCCULT WORLD

While Hume went on with his ornithological work and continued to brood over Theosophy, Sinnett, with all the conviction of a true believer, responded to the promptings from Blavatsky and Koot Hoomi and decided to inform the wider world about the 'truth' of the movement. He must have realized that in so doing there was some risk to his career as editor of the *Pioneer*, for a letter of Koot Hoomi's of December 1880 noted ominously that the editors of the paper even objected to any 'mention of occultism' in its columns.[84] Nonetheless, Sinnett took advantage of a furlough in England in early 1881 to publish *The Occult World*. The book, whose chapters focused on 'Occultism and its Adepts,' 'The Theosophical Society,' Recent Occult Phenomena,' and 'Teaching of Occult Philosophy,' represented a vigorous defence of Blavatsky and her movement. It gave extensive information on the phenomena which Blavatsky had precipitated, particularly at Shimla, and contained excerpts from some of the early Koot Hoomi letters to himself and Hume. Sinnett was a respected journalist and his book brought Blavatsky and her movement unmistakably onto the world stage.[85]

Home News of 29 July 1881 gave it a sympathetic review and acknowledged the strength of occultism in 'India and adjacent countries'.[86] It rightly noted that Sinnett had failed to give a satisfactory explanation of why occultism had remained 'secret property' through the ages. While not convinced by his arguments, the reviewer acknowledged that Sinnett's book raised 'a host of vague speculations in the mind of the reader, and startles and fascinates him'. The book was just what Blavatsky and Koot Hoomi had wanted Sinnett to produce and the latter, in a communication to the author on his arrival back in India in July 1881, greeted him as 'good friend and brilliant author'.[87] The first edition sold out quickly and the following year Sinnett published a new edition with further updates on ensuing developments. Although it soon became evident that the book included a letter of Koot Hoomi's containing plagiarized material from a prominent American spiritualist, Henry Kiddle, that did not jeopardize its popularity or propaganda value for the movement.[88]

HUME'S ONE YEAR COMMITMENT TO THEOSOPHY: NEAR-BELIEF, PRIVATE QUESTIONING AND PUBLIC CRITICISM, 1881–1882

Although Koot Hoomi had suspended correspondence with him, Hume's interest in the humanistic ideals of Theosophy remained. Moreover, his daughter was still involved in the movement, as was the man soon to become her husband, Ross Scott. As late as July 1881, Koot Hoomi complained to Sinnett that Hume, the 'once promised . . . champion fighter in the Battle of Light against Darkness,' was displaying 'an attitude of armed neutrality wondrous to behold.'[89] Significantly however, Koot Hoomi added, that he still respected Hume. Nor had Hume abandoned hope that Theosophy might yet fulfil his need for a new mission in life. Perhaps encouraged by Minnie and Ross Scott, the Humes received Blavatsky as their house guest in Shimla in late July 1881. Sinnett later joined them and Blavatsky remained with the Humes until late October. This period was to mark the beginning of a new level of public commitment by Hume to full-time work for Theosophy. On this occasion there was no emphasis on occult phenomena, but on more substantive organizational issues. The result was the creation that August of Blavatsky's long desired Anglo-Indian branch, formally named the Simla Eclectic Theosophical Society. Rather surprisingly, Hume and not the committed believer, Sinnett, became president. Perhaps this was because Hume was a freer agent than Sinnett, being already in the process of arranging his early retirement from the I.C.S. at the end of the year. Ross Scott was chosen as secretary and Sinnett became the vice-president. The prime objective of the Society was to demonstrate to the 'Native community that many Europeans respect, sympathise in and are desirous of promoting' the Theosophical movement.[90] We have no contemporary record of Hume's sentiments at the time of the formation of the Eclectic branch, but some months later he recapitulated the circumstances to Blavatsky.[91] Hume indicated that he had 'engaged' to devote himself to the work of Theosophy 'for one year' and during that time would do all he could 'honestly and fairly'. '[B]ut if within that period,' Hume continued, 'I can acquire no certainty, I shall retire from the Society feeling that true or false, it is not true for me.' He would not 'give up the life' in as far as he had 'succeeded in living it'. The latter reference was vegetarianism and temperance, which he had evidently practised from October 1880 when he first offered to become a *chela*. In short, he would continue to support exoteric Theosophy but abandon the pursuit of the esoteric work on which he embarked in earnest when he became president of the Eclectic branch.

The period from the autumn of 1881 until the latter part of 1882 marked the high point in Hume's involvement in Theosophy. His formal commitment expressed itself in the form of concerted study of the writings of Blavatsky, the *adepts* and authorities on Hinduism, Buddhism and mysticism and in extensive writing on behalf of the Society. Most of this writing was published in *The Theosophist* from the autumn of 1881 until the spring of 1883, some of it under his own name and other items under two pseudonyms which he regularly employed, namely 'Aletheia' (truth) and 'H. X.' At other times his writings appeared in the form of pamphlets or booklets sponsored by the Theosophical Society. Here we shall refer only to his writings which relate to his struggle to believe and to be accepted as a *chela*.

One recurring theme of Hume's was the lack of charity on the part of the founders in response to criticisms by Christian missionaries. While he held no brief for the missionaries or other Christian clerics, Hume thought that it was incumbent on the leaders of Theosophy to respond to attacks with Buddha-like charity. This was one of the points he made in his first article reviewing Olcott's *A Buddhist Catechism*, prepared for Theosophical mission work in Ceylon. Hume had high praise for Buddhism, a religion 'inculcating as pure a code of morality as it is possible for the human intellect to conceive' and 'in no way *practically* antagonistic' to Christianity. [92] He strongly chided Olcott for being at times 'distinctly aggressive' towards Christian missionaries in Ceylon. This, he thought, was not in keeping with the 'pure spirit' of either Buddhism or Christianity. Hume returned to this same general theme later in a letter under the pseudonym,

Aletheia. The case concerned articles in *The Theosophist* 'redolent with hatred and malice' against Rev. Joseph Cook, a Boston preacher who had been travelling around India criticizing Theosophy and Spiritualism.[93] 'Is it for us, who enjoy the blessed light,' the letter queried, 'to imitate a poor unenlightened creature (whom we should pity and pray for) in the use of violent language?' No great religious reformers had ever won adherents without consistently observing their own teachings. 'Think now,' the letter continued,

> if the Blessed Buddha, assailed, as he passed, with a handful
> of dirt by some naughty little urchin wallowing in a gutter,
> had turned and cursed, or kicked the miserable little imp,
> where would have been the religion of Love and Peace?
> With such a demonstration of his precepts before them,
> Buddha might have preached . . . through seventy times
> seven lives, and the world would have remained unmoved.

Instead of 'returning good for evil, 'the founders of the Society, 'straightway . . . fume and rage, and hurl back imprecations and anathemas, which even the majority of educated gentlemen . . . would shrink from employing.' Such behaviour could only lead the world to ignore the divine message of Theosophy.

Hume's first major publication was a series of three essays, 'Fragments of Occult Truth,' published in *The Theosophist* from October 1881 to September 1882 and subsequently issued in pamphlet form.[94] These essays show him trying to comprehend Theosophical teaching as it was being revealed piece-meal by Blavatsky and the *adepts* and also to spread the message. The essays were in response to criticisms of an Australian spiritualist, W. H. Terry, who argued that occultists did not understand the phenomena of spiritualism.[95] In the first essay, Hume explained the Theosophical notion that human beings consisted of seven components (physical body; vital principal or *jiva-atma*; astral body; astral shape or body of desire; physical ego; spiritual ego; and spirit or emanation of the Absolute) not three (the body; the animal soul; and spiritual soul), as the spiritualists believed.[96] According to Theosophy the first three components dissipated at death. Then, according to the 'Universal Law of Affinity,' either of two things happened. If during life the 'spiritual Ego' had been 'material in its tendencies,' it continued to 'cling blindly' to the physical bodily elements, in which case the 'true spirit severs itself from these and passes away elsewhere . . . still guided . . . by the irresistible cyclic impulse which first projected it through the veil of primitive cosmic matter.' If, however, 'the tendencies of the Ego' had been 'towards things spiritual,' then at death the ego would 'cling to the spirit' and pass with it into a new state of being where it would be 'reborn' into a world 'higher in the spiritual scale'. By deductive logic it followed that 'no Spirits of the departed can appear . . . in the phenomena of Seance-rooms' but merely the 'animal souls' or 'shells of the deceased'. In his third article, he dogmatically contended that the knowledge of the spiritualist medium was 'unreal' and 'untrustworthy,' in contrast to that of the *adepts,* who 'alone possess the real knowledge, their minds alone *being en rapport* with the universal mind.'[97]

Hume appeared to write with the assurance of a believer, but privately he worried about the weakness of some of his arguments. The main problem related to *adept* teachings about the fate of the spirits of those who died premature deaths from suicide, violence or epidemics. Theosophy taught that only a minority of phenomena in seance rooms derived from these spirits, but statistics showed that in Britain, for example, some 85% of the people died before 'their normal death period'.[98] Another problem was that Theosophy maintained that 'the spirits of . . . good people dying *natural* deaths remain[ed] some time in the earth's atmosphere,' but failed to explain why they could not communicate through seances. Thirdly, Hume was convinced Theosophy grossly underestimated the 'number of pure high spirits,' thousands of which he was convinced 'appear in pure circles and teach the highest morality'. In support of that view he cited the books of the French spiritualist, Alan Kardec, noting at the same time that 'pages and pages' of his books were 'identical' with what the *adepts* taught. If he suspected plagiarism, he did not level that charge against Koot Hoomi. What he did warn was that 'unless the whole theory' was 'properly set forth,' Theosophy would 'never win over the spiritualists.' 'Better tell the *outside* world *nothing,*' Hume argued, 'than to tell them half truths, the incompleteness of which they detect at once, the result being a contemptuous rejection of what *is* truth'.

The publication of *Fragments of Occult Truth* overlapped with Hume's most substantial discourse on Theosophy, *Hints on Esoteric Theosophy,* issued under the pseudonym 'H.X.' and published in book form by the Theosophical Society in the first part of 1882. It was written in response to two letters addressed to Hume by thoughtful questioners of Theosophy. The proposition of the first of these, as paraphrased by Hume, was that the Theosophical Society was a 'delusion' and that there was not 'a shadow of evidence of the existence of Brothers,' the phenomena and correspondence being 'the result of Madame Blavatsky's mesmeric, clairvoyant and mediumistic powers.'[99] The letters also criticized the founders and their management of the Society. Hume attempted to address these issues, but in so doing he candidly acknowledged certain problems regarding Theosophical beliefs and practices.

Hume agreed that the Society had as yet achieved much less than it 'might and ought to have . . . done,' but argued that it was already having some success in bringing together India's 'myriad classes, castes, sects and races'.[100] On the Society's second objective, that of promoting 'ancient languages, science and religion,' Hume conceded that little had '*apparently*' been accomplished, but contended that 'some of the most learned Pundits, Sanscritists and Pali Scholars of India' had joined the movement.[101]

On the issue of whether the *adepts* were real, Hume admitted in the original edition that he had 'no absolutely conclusive proof' of their existence.[102] He contended, however, that 'the existence of a Lodge of persons, such as the Brothers . . . is a hypothesis (monstrous as it must seem to all outsiders) less difficult to accept . . . than any other . . . suggested'.[103] One of the problems, Hume admitted, was that until one became a *chela* and submitted 'absolutely' to the brothers' guidance they would provide none of their secret knowledge out of fear that otherwise it might be misused.[104] But Hume maintained that even among those who were aspiring or recognized *chelas* 'none of us feel disposed to subordinate our wills entirely to those of other people, Adepts or non-Adepts.' The result was that, except for Olcott, no European in India had yet become a regular *chela*. But even he could still 'perform no phenomenon' and in Hume's opinion was 'nearly as far from the great secret as any of us.' Blavatsky alone was on a 'different footing,' being not only a *chela* but having 'passed through several of the stages which precede the lowest stage of adeptship.' As such, she possessed 'powers' and could 'communicate at will with the Brothers'. Only Blavatsky, Olcott and one other 'cultivated European,' whom Hume did not name, had ever 'seen and conversed' with one of the Brothers.[105] However, Damodar and other 'natives' had 'publicly testified to seeing one or other of the Brothers.' Indeed, there were 'a large number of natives who have received absolute proof and possess an absolute certainty of the existence of the Brothers, under whom many of them are working, and in whose steps they are treading.' The other factors which supported the hypothesis of the reality of the *adepts* were, Hume argued, 'a long series of phenomena, several of which are outside all authenticated spiritualistic experiences,' and written 'communications supposed to have come from them,' which in some cases Blavatsky could not 'possibly have had access to, or even knowledge of'.

Hume also dealt with the secretiveness of the *mahatmas* and their refusal to deal directly even with a 'selected number of Theosophists, and thus pave the way for the gradual infusion of the truths about them amongst mankind,' but instead leaving them all 'in the pitiable state of uncertainty'.[106] The answer, Hume reasoned, was that mankind, being most deeply stirred by 'mysteries of death and the possible world beyond the grave,' was not yet ready to absorb peacefully the news of the existence of *adepts* 'who not only knew all about death, but . . . watch[ed] the progress of the immortal portion of man after death, witnessed what befell it, and knew why and how in each case this occurred'.[107] Given the existing state of mankind, Hume argued that 'the public appearance and ministry of the Brothers' would 'give birth to a new crop of bainful superstitions, . . . disorganise society, disturb the whole course of public affairs, and not improbably extinguish finally that small Brotherhood, in whose sole custody remains the secret knowledge of the universe.' Even the frustratingly slow revelation of the fragments of the truth being doled out to Theosophical devotees was preferable in Hume's mind to such social upheaval.

Another issue was that of the obvious preference of the *mahatmas* for orientals instead, as Hume's questioner put it, of 'more enlightened and better educated Europeans.'[108] In particular, Hume's questioner had queried why the brothers had bothered to 'waste time with a half-educated slip of a boy' like Damodar. Even though Hume was no fan of Damodar, he challenged the questioner's dismissal of him as a 'monomaniac' who saw 'anything and everything!' Instead, he noted that Damodar had 'deliberately given up high caste, family, friends and an ample fortune, all in the pursuit of truth'. Hume thought that the *adepts'* 'love [for] the natives' occurred because India was the 'earliest traceable home of Occultism,' and 'adeptship' had been known there for 'at least 4,000 years'. Moreover, he believed that the physical character of 'Easterns,' due partly to climate and 'vegetarian diet,' was more 'favorable to the development of psychical powers than the more robust animal-food-fed organisations of the Westerners.' All this explained why the 'large proportion' of *adepts* appeared to have been 'natives of India.' This posed no problem for Hume, who was not tainted by racism and had already decided to stay on in his adopted home of India rather than return to Britain.

Hume also dealt with the sensitive topic of aspersions on the characters of Blavatsky and Olcott and their management of the Society. After having closely observed Olcott for months, Hume was convinced no 'mere man' could have led 'a purer, better life' than he had following his arrival in India.[109] As for Blavatsky, Hume had to contend with severe strictures from his questioner, who had remarked on 'her restlessness of mind, loose and inaccurate habits of speech, . . . her irascible temper, her want of charity to all who oppose or doubt her, her dogmatic and imperious spirit and vehemence of speech'.[110] Hume admitted 'a substratum of truth' in these comments but argued that they were seriously exaggerated.[111] With an air of male superiority, he considered that 'like most other women' she was at times 'irritable and fractious,' but he had never been able to detect 'any malicious or revengeful spirit in her.' He further acknowledged that when faced with 'some new and outrageous calumny' she sometimes became 'very angry' and showed 'a great disposition to abuse her assailants roundly' or to fire off a sharply worded letter. But afterwards she was always sorry for her behaviour. Hume also emphasized that she had incredible aggravations to contend with. 'When you . . . have sacrificed everything in life . . . to spread truth and do good to your fellows,' he wrote, ' it *is* . . . aggravating to see yourself continually denounced, in the public prints, by anonymous writers, as a swindler, impostor, liar and what not.' A true philosopher might merely smile and disregard such abuse, but Blavatsky 'had not one grain of this philosophic temperament'. Hume further admitted that she was 'by no means in all respects' what the *adepts* 'should have desired'.[112] Evidently accepting much of the existing myth about Blavatsky's past, Hume noted that she had inherited a 'special capacity . . . for . . . occult studies' from 'an Adept ancestor,' possessed an 'innate yearning' to 'penetrate' the 'secrets' of ancient wisdom which had 'led' her to Tibet, and there had become 'thoroughly grounded in the science'. This special background, coupled with total rejection of 'all worldly objects' and 'absolute singleness of heart' in her devotion to the *mahatmas*, led them to accept her as 'on the whole the fittest instrument available.'

Notwithstanding this defence of Blavatsky, Hume concluded with two severe criticisms. The first was her inaccuracy. Again showing his own male chauvinism, he contended that 'most women' were inaccurate, but Blavatsky was 'more than normally so'.[113] This he attributed to her long and difficult life and her health, which had been 'failing for years'. She suffered 'morbidly from the vulgar slander' with which she was 'assailed;' her memory was 'undoubtedly impaired' and she frequently made 'incorrect, if not absolutely false, statements.' Her second disconcerting tendency was her 'humorous combativeness,' which at times when she was in 'high spirits' led her 'to propound absolute fictions of malice prepense.' On such occasions even her closest friends could not be certain whether she was acting in 'fun or in earnest,' whether she was 'telling a truth or simply bamboozling an adversary'. Hume deeply regretted such a 'habit' in a leader of her position and considered it the source of much 'enemy' criticism.

In addition, Hume insisted that even the *adepts* were not without serious faults. On the basis of Koot Hoomi's letters, Hume considered him to be 'quite as dogmatic and imperious, and far less polite, than his poor *chela* Madame Blavatsky ever has been or could be.'[114] He could 'seldom avoid some fling at the stupidity of . . . "*Pelings*"' (foreigners) when it came to grasping 'abstruse metaphysical idea[s]'. These faults Hume attributed to Koot Hoomi's not having completely shed the residue of his 'haughty' Rajput heritage, which made him 'intolerant of all opposition and thoroughly hating and despising of Europeans.' Most disconcerting of all to those of the inner circle, Hume confessed, was the 'fact that the Brothers themselves' had at times 'formed very erroneous conceptions of the state of mind of some of those with whom they were dealing.'[115] Hume's explanation was that their 'psychic force' sometimes became exhausted, but he did not himself appear to find it very convincing. In his view the shortcomings of the *adepts* and Blavatsky were 'grievous stumbling blocks' to the development of the movement.[116]

The second part of Hume's *Hints* was subtitled *Swedenborg and Theosophy* and was a response to criticisms by a follower of that mystic. Here Hume portrayed himself as a Theosophical believer and sought by essentially dogmatic assertions to convince his critic of the inadequacy of Swedenborg's spiritualism and his belief in the personal God of Christian teaching. Hume accepted Swedenborg as one of the 'greatest natural mystics' and 'witnesses to the truth' during an age of 'dark . . . materialism'.[117] He was an 'untrained seer' whom the *adepts* had tried to lead to 'absolute truth,' but had failed because Swedenborg had the 'erroneous . . . western notion of an *omnipotent* Personal God,' which 'absolutely barred his ever rising to the perfect light'. Hume contended that the Theosophical 7th principle (the Spirit) was 'Christ, . . . God, or what you like,' but it was 'impersonal, and a scintilla only of the Universal Divine, which is *in* and *is* everything.'[118] The object of modern Theosophy was 'to bring men back to the basic and eternal truths from which Christ and Buddha alike drew their inspiration.' In the case of Christianity this could never be done by the institutional church, for its preachings bore 'no resemblance' to those of Jesus.[119] Moreover, the teachings of Jesus existed only in a 'most imperfect form,' and were 'nothing more than a repetition of a portion of the teachings of Buddha, and other ancient eastern religious teachers'.

Hume also discoursed at some length on how Theosophy alone, by its return to the eternal verities from which all religions sprang, could ensure human salvation and social order in a world threatened by materialism. The gravity of the latter threat explained why after 'thousands of years of secrecy' the *adepts* had now decided to 'share some portion of their knowledge with mankind.'[120] The established religions were 'perishing' from 'spiritual dry rot' and the 'most cultivated and intellectual men,' influenced partly by developments in physical sciences, were doubting 'a continued existence after the death of the body'. Consequently, 'divine laws' were losing their hold on 'the minds of mankind,' with resulting decreased 'respect for human laws'. The world was becoming 'rapidly demoralised,' not merely by 'reckless, murderous Nihilism, Communism, [and] Fenianism,' but by the 'general weakening of the moral sense amongst all bodies, political, commercial, professional' and not merely in the public but also the private lives of their members. The real threat to social order would appear when the 'ignorant masses,' already lacking 'self-respect and self-control,' adopted the 'non-beliefs' of the intellectuals. Only the truth offered by Theosophy could avert 'the coming terrors of a godless, soulless, materialistic age'. It alone could 'show experimentally' that there was 'something in man independent of his physical and death-doomed body'. Esoteric Theosophy taught all 'willing and worthy to learn how to obtain for *themselves* . . . proof positive of their distinctness from and capacity for existence apart from, their physical bodies.' At the same time, Theosophy was to 'rehabilitate the divine law of retributive justice, . . . a justice that exactly requites every human being for every deed, good or bad.' This was the Hindu concept of karma on which Theosophy put much stress. Finally, Theosophy would restore 'the old divine idea of Universal Brotherhood,' and, either in its own name or through the total transformation of one of the world's existing religions, become the 'religion of the future'.

In reality, Hume was far less confident of the truth of Theosophy than his published discourse suggested. This he candidly admitted to Blavatsky in early January 1882, just after he had finished writing the first part of *Hints*. His opening sentence, in which he confessed that at times he was 'desperately inclined' to believe that she was an 'imposter,' but that he 'love[d]' her nonetheless, gave a foretaste of what was to follow.[121] Hume pleaded that he could not be more conclusive about the brothers unless he had more convincing proof. '[T]hough I may convince others,' he confided, 'I have almost unconvinced myself.' 'Never till I came to defend it,' he added, ' did I realise the extreme weakness of our position.' He then proceeded to chide Blavatsky severely:

> *You*, you dear old sinner (and wouldn't you have been a reprobate under normal conditions?) are the worst breach of all – your entire want of control of temper – your utterly un-Buddha and un-Christlike manner of speaking of all who offend you – your reckless statements form together an indictment that it is hard to meet . . . .

Hume hoped that his candour regarding her deficiencies would 'stop others' mouths' but 'I personally am not satisfied,' he added. The *adepts'* 'supposed explanation' that Blavatsky was a 'psychological cripple ' because one of her 'seven principles' was 'in pawn in Tibet,' Hume found unconvincing. He deplored the 'fatuity of superior beings' who sent Blavatsky 'to fight the world armed with only a part' of her faculties and surrounded by a 'network of such contradictory and compromising facts' as to make it 'impossible' for even 'loving' friends not to doubt the existence of the *adepts* and her 'good faith.' The situation, Hume thought, threw suspicion on the whole notion of a sagely brotherhood.

Hume added perceptively that in many other areas the 'more one looks into things, the less they seem to hold water.' Instead, they looked like 'contrivances thrown out on the spur of the moment to meet an immediate difficulty.' He failed to understand why the *adepts* could not explain their philosophy in its entirety. Assuming that the brothers existed, Hume's most fervent prayer was that they would make Blavatsky 'more what a great moral reformer should be' and thus strengthen the hands of people like himself and Sinnett to 'defend . . . and advance' the cause.

Elaborating on his own position, Hume warned that the brothers were making a 'mistake in crippling' his 'energies' by leaving him 'without any certainty of their existence'. As a result he was harassed with 'doubts' whether he might 'not be preaching doctrines' which were 'founded on a fraud'. He worried that he might be 'wickedly wasting' his 'time and brains over a chimera, time and energies' that he might devote to a 'truer' and better cause. The thought that the *adepts* might be an illusion brought forth Hume's most acerbic comment:

> If they *don't* exist what a novel writer you would make! You certainly make your characters very consistent. When is our dear old Christ – I mean K. H., again to appear on the scene – he is quite our favourite actor . . . .

On a more sober note, Hume concluded that 'if put into the witness-box,' he '*could* swear' that he believed Blavatsky to be 'a perfectly true woman,' but 'could not swear that the whole story about the Brothers was not a fiction'. All he could say was that 'on the whole' he '*believed* it to be more likely to be true than false.'

In this continued questioning Hume contrasted himself to Sinnett, a 'lucky fellow' who 'has no shade of doubt'. He was confident that Sinnett, with 'his *conviction* – position and abilities,' would be a 'tower of strength' both to Blavatsky and to Theosophy. One result, Hume added, was that he himself would 'have less compunction' in washing his hands of the 'business' knowing that she would not be 'left without a champion in the hands of the Philistines.'

Hume sent the proofs of *Hints* to Blavatsky, with a warning not to 'weaken' the criticisms, arguing astutely that 'the strongest position is always gained, by putting out *yourself* all that can possibly be said against you.' Much as Blavatsky disliked Hume's criticisms, she did not revise the manuscript. Had she attempted to do so she would have had a nasty fight on her hands and that she obviously had the foresight to realize. The first edition of part 1 of *Hints* sold well and by June 1882 Hume had completed a second edition, with some additional material about the recent activities of the *mahatmas*. It also contained the following revealing footnote by H.X.: '*now* I can say that I am *quite* certain of the existence of the Brothers'.[122] While there is no reason to doubt this profession of belief, it does not mean that Hume was satisfied with the piece-meal way in which they revealed their teachings or with Blavatsky and her inner circle. These factors were to lead in the autumn of 1882 to Hume's termination of his one year commitment to the Society. The circumstances surrounding his disengagement merit examination.

THE PARTING OF THE WAYS BETWEEN HUME AND BLAVATSKY AND HER MAHATMAS

As 1882 opened the brothers still had not resumed correspondence with Hume but continued to criticize him in their communications with Blavatsky and Sinnett. The *adept* Morya, active from September 1881 when Koot Hoomi went on retreat,[123] disapproved of part one of the *Hints* pamphlet, characterized Hume's reference to K.H. as an 'actor' as 'blasphem[ous],' and insisted that the brothers would '*never*' appear to Hume.[124] Morya cautioned Sinnett that while Hume might 'shine in a Durbar or as the leader of a scientific society' that was no assurance of 'his fitness for occult research' or his 'trustworthiness' with their 'secrets'.[125] The *adepts* did not need to 'dribble facts thro' him, to be dressed for the public meal with a currie of nauseous doubts and biting sarcasm fit to throw the public stomach into confusion'. To Hume nothing was 'sacred;' his was a 'bird-killing and a faith-killing temperament;' and he would callously 'desiccate' Sinnett, 'K. H. and the "dear Old Lady"' and make them all 'bleed to death under his scalpel . . . with as much ease as he would an owl'. He even warned that Hume's 'bad karma' was reacting on Sinnett to his 'detriment'. Above all, Sinnett was to stop sharing with Hume confidential matters that Blavatsky had intended for him alone.

For his part, Hume acknowledged in a private letter to an Indian fellow Theosophist, probably written around the end of 1881, his profound misgivings about the movement. 'I am entirely in the professions of the Theosophical Society,' he wrote, 'but I can not approve the practice in a dozen different ways of most of the leaders and *chelas*.'[126] He added: 'theirs is the *upasana* of *sakti*, not of *anand*.' He complained that Damodar was so 'sore' at his 'plain speaking about their Mahatmas' that he would not even answer correspondence, while Blavatsky was 'overbearing and intolerant'. Moreover, he found the organizational 'system of the society . . . most distasteful,' and believed it was 'fraught with danger for all those who meddle with it.' However, he was not prepared at that time to make a public issue of these matters.

Frustrated by his lack of accord with the *adepts*, in the spring of 1882 Hume evidently proposed what Koot Hoomi described as the 'insane idea of going to Tibet' to try to contact them first hand.[127] Koot Hoomi assured Sinnett that neither Hume, nor even 'an army of Pelings' who had upset the 'the Chohans' the way he had, would ever find anything out about the brotherhood, even if they went all the way to Lhasa. By contrast, those whom the *adepts* desired 'to know' would find them at 'the very frontiers' of Tibet. Koot Hoomi, therefore, warned Sinnett to persuade Hume to abandon his 'insane plan,' or face the prospect of an 'absolute separation between your world and ours.' Sinnett acted accordingly and Hume did not persist, though the incident undoubtedly increased his doubts about the *mahatmas*.

Another negative influence on Hume's relations with the Society in the spring of 1882 was family related. In December 1881 his daughter Minnie had married Ross Scott, in a civil ceremony held in the Hume home before the marriage registrar, an event publicized in the Society's journal as 'A Marriage of Theosophists.'[128] Scott had earlier become secretary of the Shimla Eclectic branch and Blavatsky was intent upon bringing him more closely into her inner circle. After leaving Shimla in October 1881

Blavatsky had spent some time with Scott at his official post in Dehra Dun. Later that autumn Scott was invited to chair the sixth anniversary Theosophical convention in Bombay but he declined because of 'official duties'.[129] By May 1882, however, the relationship between Scott and Blavatsky had soured and she learned that he had become suspicious of her. She was unsure of 'how much or in what' Scott suspected her, but threw some interesting light on her previous relations with him.[130] She indicated that Scott had had a medical problem with his leg and that she had 'repeatedly' requested the *adepts* to 'cure' it, but was advised instead to 'provide him with a wife'. Koot Hoomi had suggested that 'Miss Hume would do first rate for him,' and that if he proved 'faithful and true' they would 'attend to his leg'. Accordingly, the *adepts* allowed him '*six months probation*' but he failed the trial. Blavatsky attributed the failure to the 'petty jealousy' of his wife Minnie, who was afraid that she or the *adepts* would retain their 'hold upon her husband'. There is no corroborating evidence on this point, but in any case Scott and Minnie severed their ties with the Society. Undoubtedly, this episode had a negative influence on Hume.

Later that spring some comments by Olcott on organizational developments prompted a strong public protest from Hume. Olcott had announced that Theosophy desired 'the formation throughout India of affiliated societies, *the members of which should recognise the necessity for the strictest discipline and the most perfect subordination to their leaders*'.[131] Hume was sure that Olcott's comments would refuel earlier troublesome speculation that the Society was 'only a thinly-veiled disguise for a political purpose.'. He was even more worried that such an organisation '*might* lend itself to political purposes utterly foreign to the objects of Theosophy'. He was equally concerned that it would lead 'to the creation of a new spiritual despotism,' to him a total anathema. Hume suggested that the above statement must have 'fallen' from Olcott in an 'unguarded moment,' and he was confident that the *adepts* would never allow anyone to 'pollute' Theosophy with 'any worldly or political purpose'.

Despite Hume's troublesomeness, Blavatsky's *adepts* remained anxious not to lose him. Indeed, by summer 1882 Koot Hoomi not only resumed correspondence with Hume but acknowledged his 'sincere desire' to serve the Society and humanity and assured him that there was nobody else in India better able to 'disperse the mists of superstition and popular error by throwing light on the darkest problems.'[132] He even suggested that Hume, having become a thorough vegetarian, now had 'more chances' of being given further wisdom than Sinnett, who evidently had not yet abandoned 'feeding on animals'. However, on Hume's primary desire of obtaining 'a clearer comprehension of the extremely abstruse . . . theories of our occult doctrine,' Koot Hoomi's only assurance was that Hume would not die before completing his 'mission'. While his own 'Master,' the 'hitherto implacable Chohan,' had permitted him to 'devote . . . a portion' of his time to the 'progress' of the Shimla Eclectic, he could not reveal further information about the nature of their organization or 'impart' to Hume 'the secrets concerning . . . the seventh round' of existence. Indeed, understanding of 'the higher phases of man's being on this planet' could not be attained by 'mere . . . knowledge'. As for Hume's request to 'converse' with him 'through astral light,' Koot Hoomi did not think Hume's 'psychical powers of hearing' could develop sufficiently to make that possible.

This letter plunged Hume into agonizing soul-searching as his self-imposed, one year deadline to achieve certainty regarding the *adepts* and their teachings approached. He expressed his spiritual turmoil in two private letters to Blavatsky in July 1882. Commenting on the recent refusal of the *adepts* to permit Blavatsky to re-visit their Tibet headquarters, Hume confessed that only the 'hope of doing good' prevented him from 'taking warning' from their disregard for her and cutting his 'connection' with the Society.[133] '[E]quilibrium is their God,' Hume complained, 'and the more . . . any of us push – the more they will push in the opposite direction.' Unless wiser counsels prevailed among the 'conservative element' of the senior *adepts*, the Society was almost certain to 'break down.' 'It is grievous,' Hume added, 'but we are helpless.' All roads forward seemed to be blocked by the un-cooperativeness of the *adepts*. Hume believed there were only 'two ways of carrying convictions to the world's leaders,' who needed to be won over in order to influence the 'millions'. One way was 'by *phenomena*,' but the *adepts* evidently wanted to restrict it 'to *clinch[ing]* a nearly formed conviction' in the cases of 'picked men' – a position with which Hume had no philosophic disagreement. The second way was 'by giving a complete philosophy, which by its completeness should carry indirect intellectual conviction.' Unfortunately, Hume complained, the *adepts* would only 'allow' that 'to be taught in a *mutilated* form'. Consequently, Hume added, 'my hopes of getting a complete system which . . . would in itself have carried conviction have vanished.' He observed despondently that if nothing came of Theosophy his life would be 'ruined and wasted'.

The tone of his second letter a week later was even more dejected. Hume revealed that he had initially hoped to win 'others to the truth' through 'preaching by phenomena' but by July 1881 'found that could not be permitted.'[134] He had then attempted to 'get out a complete system of philosophy, that would really stand fire,' but now that also had been disallowed. Moreover, the 'Fragments' they were 'allowed' to propagate could 'be knocked into a cocked hat by any clear thinker.' 'I could smash them up amongst the unextinguishable laughter of the world,' Hume added, 'and that's what someone will do sooner or later and throw us back fifty years.' If Theosophy continued to 'push these scraps sufficiently' some of 'the leading thinkers' would eventually 'tackle' them and make the Society 'the laughing stock of the western world at any rate.' '[S]eeing how very thin the ice is, I *am* despondent,' he added. He had, after all, given up ornithology, in which he had been 'doing some little good,' to take up Theosophy only to find that 'circumstances and the peculiar organization and traditions' of the *adepts* precluded his doing 'any good'. He had 'given up every thing' for the Theosophical cause and now his life was threatened with ruin. He concluded, plaintively:

> Time after time have I prayed and prayed–let me be sacrificed–and happen what may to me–but let me help others–let me do good . . . .
> I would give my life with pleasure–but I want some good to others in exchange for it–and this it seems to me I shall not get–and I cannot see my way to be a bit nearer being useful in a future rebirth.

Given the unhappy fate of his government service career, one can understand Hume's anguish over the dashing of his cherished hopes for a worthwhile mission in Theosophy.

During August and September 1882 the mounting difficulties between Hume and Theosophy came to a head over doctrinal contradictions raised by C. C. Massey, the first President of the

Theosophical Society in England, who published an article in *Light*, exposing discrepancies between *Isis Unveiled* and recent issues of *The Theosophist.* Blavatsky's attempts to explain the differences in the August 1882 issue of *The Theosophist* did not convince Hume and he insisted on having his say in a letter in the ensuing issue. Hume's letter, written under the familiar initials, 'H.X.', proved to be dynamite. Asserting that the reply given to Massey was neither 'satisfactory or sufficient,' Hume launched into his own assault on *Isis Unveiled.*[135] 'I think it a pity,' he wrote, 'that it is not plainly said that 'Isis Unveiled' . . . *teems* with . . . errors.' 'Passages on passages' conveyed 'to every ordinary reader, wholly erroneous conceptions.' Isis had not been 'unveiled' and instead, only 'a few rents were torn in the veil, through which *those knowing how to look* can obtain glimpses of the Goddess.' The book was 'essentially destructive' and 'never seriously aimed at reconstruction'. Another difficulty was that the text, much of which was written by 'different adepts imperfectly acquainted with English,' had to be 'put into shape' by Blavatsky, who was 'no great English scholar' and by Olcott, who was then 'quite ignorant . . . of occult philosophy.' This, Hume advised, should be 'plainly' admitted, thus avoiding the 'perpetually recurrent demand for the reconciliation of apparent discrepancies between passages in 'Isis' and passages in articles in the Theosophist.'

Hume then launched into a critical assault on the *adepts.* Their insistence on giving only 'stray glimpses' of their truth to 'lay disciples' like himself was nothing short of 'a *sin*'. 'I hold,' Hume contended, 'that be a man an adept or what not, all the knowledge he possesses, he holds, simply, in trust for his fellow-men.' An *adept* might be justified in reserving 'for specially tried disciples, such knowledge as would invest men with abnormal powers over their fellows, but the rest' he was '*bound* to give.' Instead, the *adepts* held that the knowledge they possessed was 'their own especial property, to communicate . . . as they please'. Furthermore, there were problems in their manner of teaching, which differed in '*toto*' from Western notions. 'If we wanted to teach any thing,' Hume explained, ' we should teach it piece by piece, and each branch with perfect accuracy.' The *adepts*, however, appeared 'to care nothing about complete accuracy.' They also seemed content to convey merely a 'general conception of the outline.' Worst still from Hume's liberal perspective, they appeared unwilling to impart their 'philosophy' to anyone 'not bound to them by obligations rendering them practically their slaves'. Hume boasted that 'in one week' he himself 'could teach any ordinarily intelligent man, all, that in eighteen months, we . . . have succeeded in extracting' from the *mahatmas.*

Hume contended that from an 'educated European' viewpoint the behaviour of the *adepts* was completely 'unreasonable and unsatisfactory,' but acknowledged that from an 'Oriental point of view' it posed little difficulty. '[M]any of my native friends,' he conceded, 'seem to look upon it as not only natural and what was to be expected, but as actually reasonable and right.' Hume was anxious that 'European Theosophists' should understand this situation. They needed to know too that 'one might as well try to argue with a brick wall as with the fraternity, since when unable to answer your arguments they calmly reply that their rules do not admit of this or that.' Hence, dealing with the brothers was 'very far from a hopeful business'. Their 'system and their traditions' were 'opposed' to European 'ideas of right and wrong,' and they themselves were neither 'altogether just, nor generous'. '[I]n a dozen different ways,' Hume continued, 'they fall short of the European ideal of what men so elevated in learning and so pure in personal life should be'. Hume acknowledged that the brothers 'honestly believe themselves to be entirely right in all their ways' and that 'Asiatics see it as the Brothers do'. In summation, he added:

> We have to deal with a set of men almost exclusively Orientals; . . . learned beyond the conception of most Westerns, very pure in life, very jealous of their treasured knowledge, brought up and petrified in a system that can only recommend itself to Eastern minds, and saturated with a stream of thought flowing directly at right angles to that in which runs all the highest and brightest modern Western Thought.

Looking at the issue from what Hume characterized as 'Mr. Gladstone's now traditional formula' there were three possible courses. These were to 'accept the Brothers as they are' and 'accept gratefully such small crumbs as fall from our Masters' tables;' secondly, 'to give up the Brothers and their painfully doled out glimpses of the hidden higher knowledge altogether, but to work . . . to unite all we can in bonds of brotherly love;' and thirdly 'to cut the concern altogether'. At the time he wrote his letter Hume stated that his own preference was still for the first 'alternative'.

Blavatsky, who received Hume's H. X. letter in her capacity as editor of *The Theosophist*, was livid. She confided to Sinnett that Hume, after depicting her as '*a consummate liar, a chronic humbug*' in his *Hints* was now '*absolutely*' insisting on denouncing *Isis* and labelling 'the Brothers . . . selfish Asiatics.'[136] 'Why . . . *should he* come in like an African *Simoon*,' she railed, 'blasting and destroying all on his passage, impeding my work, showing my *mediocrity* in a blaze of light, criticising all and everything, finding fault with everybody and forcing the whole of India to point a finger of scorn at me'. Since Hume had begun writing for the 'alleged good of the Society,' she had received more 'insults' and 'kicks' from him than anybody she knew. Her instinct was to throw the letter 'into the fire,' but Koot Hoomi directed her to publish it. The upshot was that *The Theosophist* published the letter though Blavatsky included with it a long editorial clarifying that she did so 'under a strong personal protest.'[137] Predictably she condemned the author for daring, as a European, to 'judge' by his standards the *adepts*, who were 'exempted from judgment even by their own people – the teeming millions of Asia'. She emphasized the cruelty of depicting the brothers in a totally 'false light' and having them 'cut up piece-meal by one dissatisfied student for the benefit of a few who are not even lay-chelas!'

Hume's claimed purpose had been to answer the charges of critics in Britain,[138] but he had left himself open to Indian counterattack by his strong indictment of the Asiatic *adepts*. Blavatsky's closest Indian devotees were quick to pick up on that point. In the same issue of *The Theosophist*, and directly following the H.X. letter, was one protesting against it signed by Damodar and ten other 'Hindu *Chelas* of the Himalayan Brothers'. Nine were listed as fellows of the Society, and the other two, identified as Deva Muni and Paramahamsa Shub-Tung, reportedly belonged 'to the confidential chelas of the Chohan himself.'[139] The most prominent of the fellows was T. Subba Rao, the Society's leading expert on Hindu theological issues. All were undoubtedly close to Blavatsky or Damodar. They latched strongly on to the racial issue, satirically describing themselves as 'inferior' Asiatics. No full *chela*, they asserted, much less a lay one like H.X., had a 'right to openly criticize and blame' the masters on the basis of his own 'unverified hypotheses'. They made no apologies for their '*slavish*' devotion, for it was precisely because *chelas* had 'always blindly followed the dictates of their Masters' that some of them, after years of self-sacrifice, had become *adepts*. H.X. should have been grateful for any 'crumbs of knowledge' the *adepts* deigned to give him. Though his letter was 'indisputably clever . . . from a literary and Intellectual stand-point,' as 'natives' they perceived its essence to be 'an imperious spirit of domineering' that was 'utterly foreign' to Indian character.

Hume was neither impressed nor repentant. Informed by telegram from Blavatsky that the Chohans and Subba Rao had protested against his letter, Hume responded that if the *adepts* could so totally 'misconceive' the purpose, 'spirit and practical bearing' of an intervention for which they 'ought to give thanks' then the situation was 'hopeless'.[140] Theosophy was like a ship with a captain who did not know navigation. 'I give it up,' Hume categorically stated. To Sinnett, he complained that the Chohan superiors expected 'obedience'.[141] 'Well they won't get it from me,' Hume asserted.

His exasperation was expressed most graphically in a long letter to Blavatsky. Referring to an *adept* who had precipitated some pictures of the *mahatmas*, Hume directed Blavatsky to inform 'Gjuakual, or whatever his blessed name may be, not to make a goose with his sham occult pictures'. 'Tell him,' Hume continued, 'I can make quite as good pictures as he can.[142] At the same time he accused Damodar of taking the letter of an aspiring *chela*, Edmund Fern, producing a 'facsimile' of his 'handwriting' and then telling Fern that it was 'done by occult means!' Damodar should stop such 'infernal nonsense' and remember that he had a 'big microscope' and could himself 'reproduce by similar occult means every single handwriting' he chose. 'I don't go in for this,' Hume added, 'because we call it forgery – but I can do it a great deal better than D. M. to judge by the sample.' He warned Blavatsky that if she did not 'keep these boys in hand' they would 'play the duce' with the Society.

Hume then vented his wrath against the *adepts*, terming Koot Hoomi's response to his recent letters as 'fatuous'. 'Ask him to be reasonable in the matter of occultism and occult philosophy,' Hume added. It was one thing to accept Koot Hoomi as his master, but 'when he says a thing is black one day and white another – I ask him to "exercise his ingenuity."' Koot Hoomi 'ought to be grateful' to him since his criticisms had as their 'only object . . . the more satisfactory turning out of *his* work.' Hume still claimed 'sincere affection' for Koot Hoomi personally, but 'wholly' disapproved of 'much of . . . the organization and system of the Brotherhood'. He was profoundly sad to see all around him 'Brothers and non-Brothers, persuade themselves that good can come out of evil – and that crooked paths can prove short cuts'. Theosophy's promise of 'good and blessedness' was being undermined by the 'perverse' and 'fossilized' system of the *adepts*, which was 'no longer in harmony with the age and therefore an abiding source of discord.' In short, Hume placed the blame for what had occurred on Blavatsky and the brothers.

Hume's public and private letters created a storm in the higher echelons of the movement. Blavatsky wanted no more letters from Hume. She informed Sinnett that the 'Boss,' Olcott, was 'fearfully mad with Hume,' fearing the latter had 'spoilt all his work'.[143] In another letter she confided to Sinnett that she thought Hume was 'beginning to be *off his head.*'[144] 'He bamboozles himself,' she wrote, 'into the insane belief that he is fast becoming an adept and he *sees sights* and believes in them as revelations.' She feared that he wanted to 'sink' the existing Society and create a '*new one*' with the 'help of a few insane mystics–spiritualists, whom he *will go on bossing.*' Hume was '*doomed,*' Sinnett was her 'only true and faithful' English friend in India and she could now see the 'difference between a *Conservative* [Sinnett] and a *Liberal* [Hume]!! Oh Jesus.'

The *adepts* too, mainly in correspondence with Sinnett, voiced their displeasure against Hume. Morya insisted that he would not resume correspondence with Hume. After 'centuries of independent existence,' they would never become the 'puppets of a Simla Nawab . . . [or] submit to the rod of a Peling schoolmaster.'[145] He also indicated that Blavatsky was again seriously ill and in danger of 'falling to pieces' because of 'constant anxiety for the Society' produced by Hume's behaviour. Koot Hoomi, for his part, accused Hume of writing 'words so filthy as to pollute the very air that touched them.'[146] While he thought Asiatics were unlikely to be affected by Hume's 'egotistical thrusts,' he feared a very harmful effect on 'European readers'. He thought that after Hume's outrageous H.X. letter 'people' would 'regard him more than ever a lunatic,' while 'Hindu members' would 'blame him for years, and our chelas can never be made to look upon him but in the light of an iconoclast, a haughty intruder, incapable of any gratitude, hence – unfit to be one of them.'[147] He had no recourse but to 'denounce' Hume and would never again mention his name to the Chohan. Surprisingly, however, Koot Hoomi then affirmed that he had been 'ordered not to break with him until the day of the crisis comes.' This implied that the *adepts* wanted Hume himself to initiate any formal break with the Society.

By that time Hume had had his fill of Blavatsky, Olcott, the Theosophical Society and the organizational system of the brotherhood. He felt a duty to complete some further publications, mostly of a general intellectual or cultural nature, but in early October 1882 he resigned the presidency of the Shimla Eclectic and thereby, except for his intervention in the crisis of 1885, severed his active association with the Society and its founders.

Blavatsky and the adepts claimed a certain amount of satisfaction over Hume's defection but this was mostly false bravado. In reality there was much concern over Hume's potential for damage. For example, in early January 1883, Koot Hoomi appealed to Sinnett to visit Britain in order to counteract the 'harm' caused by Hume's letters before it was too late to 'undo the mischief.'[148] Hume was a 'prolific letter writer' and, now that he was free of 'all restraints,' could become a real loose cannon. He compared his defection to that of Dayanand. Hume was the victim of the same 'demon – Vanity' which had 'ruined Dayanand,' though he feared that the 'Avatar' of 'Jakko' was preparing an 'assault upon us and the T.S. far more savage than the Swami's.' Obviously, Koot Hoomi felt that he was damning Hume by putting him in the same camp as Dayananda. In fact, given the Arya leader's deserved reputation as a true swami, he was paying Hume a high compliment. On another occasion Koot Hoomi accused Hume of 'diabolical malice' in fomenting the opposition of Anna Kingford and her Christian mystic allies in the London branch and of 'plotting and scheming to make us all into a holocaust'.[149] Finally, Blavatsky herself in one of her last major jibes against Hume at this time informed Sinnett that she would rather 'emigrate to Ceylon or Burma' than remain in India with Hume, 'our Jhut-sing of Simla'.[150] At the same time she criticized Hume for associating himself with Lord Ripon's liberal reforms, to which she was adamantly opposed. Obviously the leadership took Hume's loss seriously and continued to fear his influence.

POSTSCRIPT: HUME, SINNETT, INDIAN CHELAS AND THE THEOSOPHICAL SOCIETY CRISIS OF 1885

While Hume gave up on Theosophy as a lost cause under the existing leadership and brotherhood, he did not abandon his pursuit of Indian religion and culture. On the contrary a careful reading of the Mahatma Papers indicates that beginning in early 1882 Hume established contacts with a Hindu *advaitist* guru, Swami Paramahamsa of Almora. As early as February 1882 Koot Hoomi had warned Sinnett that Hume was 'under the baneful influence' of 'a weaker but more cunning' mind, boding 'ill to him, to you and to the Society.'[151] Little is known about the Swami except that he was an authority on Hindu, non-dualistic *advaitism* and contributed five articles to *The Theosophist* between August 1882 and July 1883.[152]

The first direct reference to the Swami by Hume was in correspondence with Sinnett in September 1882, when he indicated that he had 'received a communication from a representative of another School.'[153] 'I have replied,' Hume added, 'and am awaiting an answer – if favourable, while still aiding the Theosophical Society to the utmost, I shall take a great deal of my teaching from elsewhere.' Hume continued:

> All are equally awaitees – all equally desire the good of mankind – all say that the time has come for new (tho[ugh] old) truths to dawn on the world – but the other school is more Xn [Christian] – it lays more stress on love – and is less cold and selfish than ours. Moreover the very words of my letter to the O[ld] L[ady] . . . in which I say that I have intuitively unified the negative and the positive are quoted with approval as being the real highest knowledge. . . .

This turn to *advaitism* was resented by Koot Hoomi, who complained that Hume 'impresses himself with the illusion that he is 'far more of an *Adwaitee*' than either M[orya] or myself'.[154] This, however, only showed Hume's lack of understanding because the *adepts* 'never were Adwaitees'.[155] He even suggested that Hume had become an *advaitist* partly to spite him and to prove him at 'fault'.

Hume's best explanation of his position was in a letter to Blavatsky in which he asserted that he had been a 'staunch . . . adwaitee' all his life.[156] 'I claim,' he continued, 'a higher intuitional generalization which cannot properly be expressed by any words, whereby I know that the impersonal, the unconscious, the unintelligent is also the positive of all these negatives.' That knowledge, he maintained, had come to him '*three* . . . times in everlasting glory'. Consequently, it was 'nonsense' for Koot Hoomi to regard him as a 'personal god worshipper and creator of the *ordinary* low *dualistic* type.' Hume elaborated:

> I am a pukha *adwaitee* of the most unswerving character – but admitting that . . . the human mind cannot see beyond this, I hold . . . that the *soul* may and can, and that my soul has so gone and possesses a conception that language, fettered by laws of contradictions does not permit me to formulate, exploring the behind the veil and unifying the negative and the positive.
>
> When I say C'être est l'être with E. Levi – I mean that I, you, God, the universe are all one and the same – that all distinctions are matter-created delusions – that my own existence proves . . . God, man and the universe.

Clearly, Hume was fully in tune with Swami Paramahamsa and his philosophy and seems to have maintained the relationship until his *advaitist* guru died in December 1883.

Outwardly, Hume's split with Theosophy had little immediate negative effect. That was because he still supported the humanitarian goals of the movement and did not publicize his break. In fact, he appears to have explained what had occurred only to a few close associates. We have records of only two such instances. The first of these was a letter which he wrote to a leading Madras Theosophist, Judge P. Sreenivas Rao, on 22 November 1882.[157] It is also the most outspoken statement we have by Hume on his complete disillusionment with Blavatsky's *adepts*. Hume confided to Rao that he found 'the Brotherhood a set of *wicked selfish men*' who cared for 'nothing but their own spiritual development'. Moreover, their 'system' was one of 'deception and *tainted largely with sorcery* in that they employ spooks' or 'elementals to perform their phenomena.' The deception occurred because once a person became a *chela* and 'bound himself' by the vows which the *adepts* exacted, '*you cannot believe a word he says*'. 'Every chela,' Hume insisted, was 'a slave of the most abject description – a slave in thought as well as in word and deed'. The result was that the Society was a noble 'edifice' only in 'outside show,' and in reality was built 'on the shifting sands of atheism' and 'full of deceit and the dead bones of a *pernicious, jesuitical system*'. Significantly, Hume informed Rao he was free to make use of his letter 'inside the Society,' thus implying that he did not want it publicized.

The second instance of Hume's private disparagement was in a letter to Lord Ripon, the Gladstonian Liberal viceroy with whom he had developed close bonds because of their common interest in political reform in India. In January 1884 Hume informed Ripon of his Indian transcendental contacts. He explained that initially Blavatsky and Olcott had been partially 'aided' by them, but the Theosophical founders had not proved to be 'quite honest,' but had 'drifted away into a maze of falsehood, or at any rate exaggerations and deceptions, and have been gradually left almost wholly to their own devices'.[158] Hume claimed that though Blavatsky and Olcott had proved untrustworthy they had helped in the first instance to reunite him with a network of mystics with whom he had had brief contact in Paris in 1848, just prior to his coming to India. Hume was undoubtedly referring to the famous French mystic, Eliphas Levi, whom he obviously now linked to his Indian transcendental community. Hume maintained that the Theosophical founders were 'working with a lower Association' which the 'friends' with whom he was now associated 'did not acknowledge or approve because its principles' were not 'at all as rigidly pure, nor its objects as elevated.' 'Peace, order, brotherly love, freedom and progress,' he assured Ripon were 'the key-notes of our people.' Hume appeared in a happier frame of mind with *advaitist* philosophy and the resulting but ill-defined transcendental associates than he had ever been with Theosophy.

Meanwhile, Sinnett remained active in the inner circle of Theosophy. At the height of their collaboration he and Hume had spent 'long hours together, day after day, in trying to develop the unmanageable hints . . . obtained in the form of written answers to questions' to the *mahatmas*.[159] Sinnett respected Hume's intellectual acumen and expressed his 'lasting regret' that he became 'alienated from the undertaking.'[160] By the autumn of 1882, Sinnett's involvement in Theosophy got him in trouble with the owners of *The Pioneer,* who gave him notice of his termination as editor.[161] This did not, however, shake his commitment to the movement. After the failure of an attempt by the founders to launch a new newspaper with Sinnett as its editor, he and his wife returned permanently to England in April 1883. Later that year he published his second book, *Esoteric Buddhism*, designed to further the Theosophical message. This book, which expanded upon many of the themes developed in his earlier *Occult World*, went through three English editions within about a year and in 1884 had its first American edition. These two books and the publicity which they gave to the letters from the *mahatmas*, as Campbell has observed, 'gave Theosophy wide publicity both in India and the West, and were important to the development of the movement.'[162]

The kind of troubles for which Hume had long feared the Theosophical Society was headed erupted in 1884. In May of that year, while Blavatsky and Olcott were visiting Europe, Emma and Alexis Coulomb, assistants and confidants of Blavatsky, were expelled from the Adyar headquarters. They revealed what they claimed were authentic letters of Blavatsky showing that they had been her accomplices in facilitating various occult phenomena in the shrine room at Adyar and elsewhere. Then in September and October, while the founders were still in Europe, the *Madras Christian College Magazine* created a sensation by publishing an exposé of the Adyar occult phenomena, based on the Coulomb letters.[163] While Hume had long before become distrustful of Blavatsky and her devotees at headquarters, his initial reaction to the news was that Blavatsky was too clever to have allowed herself to fall into the hands of ordinary assistants such as the Coulombs. Notwithstanding his break with Blavatsky, he went to the trouble of publishing a letter expressing this opinion.[164] However, as Hume acquired more information about the Coulomb affair, he obviously changed his mind. When in December 1884 the newly established Society for Psychical Research, based at Cambridge University, sent G. Hodgson, a capable young scholar, to India to investigate Blavatsky's occult phenomena at the Adyar headquarters, Hume became a prime cooperator in the inquiry.

Hume spent much of February and March 1885 in Madras working with Hodgson. He and Hume, with several others, were informed by Dr. Franz Hartmann, one of the prominent Theosophists at Adyar who had been present when the shrine was examined prior to being destroyed, that it had had a false back – a sliding panel that could be accessed from the adjoining room.[165] Hodgson concluded that the Adyar phenomena were fraudulent and that Blavatsky was the creator of the correspondence from the *adepts.* Hume did not go nearly so far. His position, as he explained it to Hodgson, was that

> despite all the frauds perpetrated, there have been genuine phenomena, and that, though of a low order, Madame [Blavatsky] really had and has Occultists of considerably though limited powers behind her; that K.H. is a real entity, but by no means the powerful and godlike being he has been painted, and that he has had some share, directly or indirectly . . . in the production of the K.H. letters.[166]

In short, Hume still believed Blavatsky had occult contacts and that Koot Hoomi was a *mahatma* of a lower order.

Hume's final action in connection with the Society during the crisis of March 1885 was to attempt to reshape the organization by ousting the founders, Damodar and 13 other members of headquarters and introducing major reforms, but he could not persuade Subba Rao and other Brahmin leaders of the Society in Madras to go along.[167] This ended Hume's involvement. Instead of the radical reforms he advocated more modest changes were effected, the main action being to oblige Blavatsky to resign as corresponding secretary of the Society and leave India at once. In poor health and even poorer spirits, and furious with Hume and Hodgson, Blavatsky left India for the last time at the end of March 1885. Olcott managed to stay on as president and introduced organizational reforms, including the down-playing of the occult.

While the events of 1885 marked the definitive end of Hume's relations with the Theosophical Society, Sinnett stuck with Madame Blavatsky and in 1886 published a highly sympathetic account of her life, entitled *Incidents in the Life of Madame Blavatsky.* He remained a convinced and active Theosophist until his death in 1921. As for Blavatsky's closest Indian confidant, Damodar, he became a martyr to the cause. Accused of being a confederate of Blavatsky in the phenomena at Adyar, Damodar left Madras in February 1885 to join his master in Tibet. He died in the Himalayas, while still en route, though Olcott and Theosophical believers were convinced that he actually reached his guru.[168] Subba Rao first supported Blavatsky in the 1885 crisis but subsequently changed his position and left the Society the following year.[169]

Hume, for his part, gave every evidence that following the split with the Theosophical Society in late 1882 he established an ongoing relationship with more noble transcendental contacts, achieved through his Hindu *advaitist* association. In November 1886, Hume confided to the new viceroy, Lord Dufferin, that he was 'working under the advice and guidance of advanced initiates'.[170] Some months earlier he had informed Dufferin that, thanks to this transcendental brotherhood, he sometimes received 'precipitated facsimiles' of official state papers.[171] He made the same point to another prominent official, A. P. Macdonnell, hoping that some day even cynics might realize that 'there are things in heaven and earth outside the every-day world philosophy.'[172] These are the last known references by Hume to this brotherhood connection but he remained a devout vegetarian until his death in 1912. While he found his new and most satisfying life mission in the promotion of Indian national politics from 1883 onward, one can assume that he continued to approve Theosophical efforts for India's educational and cultural revitalization and for improved human understanding.

CONCLUSION

In these early years Theosophy moved so extensively to identify itself with broad principles of early Hindu and Buddhist thought that it appears to have done little to transform the personal lives of its general Indian supporters. However, Blavatsky's devotees at headquarters undoubtedly had their lives reshaped by the experience, much as religious cult followers might today. This transformation was most evident in the case of Damodar, who gave up family ties and caste to work for the movement and ultimately died in his attempt to join the *adepts* in Tibet. While Theosophy may have transformed the lives of few Indians, the movement by its promotion of ancient Indian culture did much to advance the country's national regeneration. Among the British in India, Sinnett is the principal example during this early period of an influential adherent whose life was transformed by Theosophy. Hume provides an excellent case study of a European who fervently wanted to believe, but whose intellectual questioning of the fragmentary teachings of the *adepts* and philosophic disagreements over the organization and leadership of the movement precluded his total belief or being accepted as a *chela*. Surprisingly, given his intellectual acumen, he allowed Blavatsky to define Indian *chelas* as people who obediently accepted her teachings. The refusal of Dayananda ultimately to buy into Blavatsky's schema should have alerted him to the realization that some Indian searchers for higher truth insisted upon the right to query. Hence it was that Hume's journey from near-belief to his break with Blavatsky was a highly personal journey of the mind. While his disillusionment with Theosophy from the latter part of 1882 cleared the way for him to find a new and more satisfying mission in the promotion of Indian political reform and national regeneration, his commitment to vegetarianism and temperance and, as far as one can tell, his belief in *advaitism* continued to influence his remaining years. Theosophy brought Hume closer to Indian culture and enhanced his ability to relate to India's new intelligentsia. Theosophy too remained a part of India's cultural mosaic and under Blavatsky's successor, Annie Besant, was to become intimately involved with the Congress organization that Hume did so much to create.

Notes

1 A. P. Sinnett, *Incidents in the Life of Madame Blavatsky Compiled from Information Supplied by her Relatives and Friends* (London, 1886), 14–74. There is extensive writing on Blavatsky, generally either by Theosophical enthusiasts or hostile opponents. Sinnett's is the earliest of the former category.

2 Bruce F. Campbell, *Ancient Wisdom Revived: A History of the Theosophical Movement* (Berkeley, 1980), 13–20.

3 Blavatsky complained around November 1878 that 'very few' even of the 'Fellows' of the Society attended meetings in New York. (C. Jinarajadasa, ed., *H. P. B. Speaks.* vol. 1. Adyar: Theosophical Publishing House, 1950, 106).

4 Campbell, *op. cit.*, 32–35.

5 Blavatsky, *Isis Unveiled*, vols. I & II (The Theosophical Company, 1975), xlv. This is a photographic reproduction of the original, New York 1877, publication.

6 *Ibid.*, xliv-xlv.

7 *Ibid.*, xlv.

8 *Ibid.*, v. Blavatsky claimed to have first visited India in 1852, a second time around 1856 to early 1857 and again around 1868, when she spent considerable time in Tibet and first met one of her principal *adepts*, Koot Hoomi (*H. P. Blavatsky Collected Writings, 1874–1878* [hereafter *B.C.W.*] I, 2nd. ed. Wheaton, Illinois: Theosophical Publishing House, 1977, xl–xlviii). The compiler of the *Collected Writings* acknowledges that Blavatsky's Tibetan stay 'is wrapped . . . in considerable mystery,' but for an account which assumes the certainty of the Indian and Tibetan visits, see Jean O. Fuller,

Blavatsky and her Teachers: An Investigative Biography (London: East-West Publications, 1988), 13–15 & 24–27. Campbell is a better guide when he concludes that there is no 'reliable account' of Blavatsky's life during the 25 years following her escape to Constantinople (op. cit., 4).

9 *Ibid.*, xlv.

10 *Ibid.*, I, 626.

11 *Ibid.*, II, 5–6.

12 *Ibid.*, 288.

13 *Ibid.*, 405.

14 *Ibid.*, 590.

15 Campbell, *op. cit.*, 77.

16 *B. C. W.,1879–80* II, xxix; and *The Theosophist* I (Apr. 1880), 179.

17 *A Report of the Proceedings of a Public Meeting . . . Bombay, on the 12th of January 1882, to Celebrate the Sixth Anniversary of the Theosophical Society* (Bombay, 1882), 5.

18 *Address Delivered by Col. H. S. Olcott . . . at . . . Bombay on March 23rd, 1879* (Bombay, 1879), 1–2. Where, as in the ensuing passages, there is a sequence of quotations from the same speech, article or letter only an initial citation is provided.

19 *The Theosophist* I (Oct. 1879), 1.

20 *Ibid.*, (June 1880), 229.

21 *Address . . . by . . . Olcott . . ., 1879, op. cit.*, 13–15.

22 *Hints on Esoteric Theosophy.* 2nd. ed. (Calcutta, 1882), 20–25. 'H. X.', a pseudonym used by Hume in much of his extensive Theosophical writings from 1881 to 1883, appears frequently in the text but not on the title page. *The Indian Mirror* publicly identified 'H. X.' as Hume (*The Theosophist, Supplement* IV (June 1883), 9.

23 *B.C.W., 1883–85* VI, fn., 241–44.

24 K.W. Jones, *The New Cambridge History of India III.1 Socio-religious reform movements in British India* (Cambridge, 1989), 169.

25 *The Theosophist* I (May 1880), 214.

26 For a cogent, analytical account of Dayananda's break with Theosophy see J. T. F. Jordens, *Dayananda Sarasvati: His Life and Times* (Delhi, 1978), 211–13.

27 *The Theosophist, Extra Supplement* III (July 1882), 1–10.

28 *Ibid.*, *Supplement,* III (Apr. 1882), 8.

29 *Ibid.*, (May 1882), 7.

30 *B. C. W., 1883* V, 267–72.

31 *B. C. W., 1881–82* III, 400–18.

32 *The Theosophist* III (Jan. 1882), 92–93.

33 G.E. Linton and V. Hanson, *Readers' Guide to the Mahatma Letters to A. P. Sinnett.* 2nd. ed. (Adyar, 1988), 343.

34 *The Theosophist* IV (Feb. 1883), 118.

35 *B.S.W. 1883* V, 268–69.

36 Fuller, op. cit., 65.

37 Mahatma Papers, (British Library) Add. Mss. 45,287, f. 116–17 (hereafter M.P. and mss. number). Reprinted in A.T. Barker, ed., *The Letters of H.P. Blavatsky to A.P. Sinnett and Other Miscellaneous Letters*

(hereafter *B. L.*), Reprint of 1925 ed., (Pasadena: Theosophical University Press, 1973), 83–84.

38 D.K. Mavalankar, 'Castes in India.' *The Theosophist* I (May 1880), 196–97.

39 Sven Eek, *Dâmodar and the Pioneers of the Theosophical Movement* (Adyar, 1978) 4–5.

40 Quoted in *ibid.*, 3.

41 *The Theosophist* I (May 1880), 196–97.

42 Eek, *op. cit.*, 6.

43 *Ibid.*, 40.

44 *Ibid.*, 5.

45 *Ibid.*, 55–58.

46 *Ibid.*, 58–62.

47 *Ibid.*, 350.

48 *B.C.W., 1883–85* VI, 71.

49 Linton and Hanson, *op. cit.*, 317 & 346.

50 *Ibid.*, 323.

51 *B.C.W., 1879–80* II, xxxii.

52 *The Theosophist, Supplement* III (Mar. 1882), 8.

53 *A Full Report . . . of the General Convention of the Theosophical Society and Celebration of its Eighth Anniversary* (Madras, 1884), 1.

54 *The Theosophical Society: Official Report of the Ninth Session of the General Convention . . . at Madras* (Madras, 1885), 1.

55 The actual number specified in the letters was 282. The Editor, taking account of the category 'others', estimated 400 (*The Theosophist, Supplement* V (Nov. 1883), 20–21).

56 *B.C.W. (1879–80)* II, xxviii, and Linton and Hanson, *op. cit.*, 331.

57 Linton and Hanson, *op. cit.*, 344.

58 C. Jinarajadasa, ed., *op. cit.*, 226.

59 Linton and Hanson, *op. cit.*, 349–56.

60 Eek, *op. cit.*, 36–37.

61 *B.C.W., 1879–80* II, xxix–xxx.

62 For Hume's involvement in ornithology see, Moulton, 'The Contributions of Allan O. Hume to the Scientific Advancement of Indian Ornithology,' *The Indian Archives* XLI (Jan.–June 1992), 1–19.

63 Moulton, 'Allan O. Hume and the Indian National Congress: A Reassessment,' *South Asia* VIII (June–Dec. 1985), 7.

64 [Hume's speech], printed in *The Pioneer,* 16 Dec. 1879.

65 Sinnett, *op. cit.*, 223–24.

66 Sinnett, *The Occult World* 9th ed. (London, Theosophical Publishing House, 1969), 42–43. The original edition was 1881.

67 Hume to the Editor, *The Pioneer,* 23 Oct. 1880. Hume, who first published the account, has his wife finding the note whereas Sinnett described his wife as central (*Occult World*, 54–55).

68 Hume to the Editor, *ibid.*, and Sinnett, 58–60. Olcott's account did not include Hume among those present (Eek, *op. cit.*, 156–58).

69 J.N. Farquhar, *Modern Religious Movements in India* (New York, 1919), 229–31.

70 Sinnett, *Occult World*, 82.

71 *Ibid.*, 82–83.

72 A valuable research guide to these letters, the originals of which are in the British Library, is Linton and Hanson, *op. cit.*, according to whom (pp. 307–09) the last two *mahatma* letters to Sinnett were dated September or October 1885.

73 M. P., 45,284, f.1–9. Printed in *M.L.*, 1–6.

74 Sinnett, *Occult World*, 90–91.

75 Printed in Margaret Conger, *Combined Chronology for Use with The Mahatma Letters to A.P. Sinnett and The Letters of H.P. Blavatsky to A.P. Sinnett* (Pasadena: Theosophical University Press, 1973), 29–38.

76 M.P., 45,289B, f. 39–60.

77 M.P., 45,284, f.24–32. Printed in *M.L.*, 11–17.

78 *Ibid.*, 45,288, f. 151–71. A short excerpt of this letter is printed in *M.L.*, 428–31.

79 *Ibid.*, 45,285, f.56–66. This letter is undated but the context indicates it is a direct reply to Hume's letter of 7 November. Printed in *M.L.*, 205–15.

80 *Ibid.*, 45,284, f.33–37. Printed in *M.L.*, 17–21.

81 *Ibid.*, 45,285, f.56–66.

82 M. P., 45,286, f. 148–49. Printed in *M.L.*, 427–28.

83 *Ibid.*, 45,284, f.39–42. Printed in *M.L.*, 22–24.

84 *Ibid.*

85 Campbell, *op. cit.*, 57 and 81.

86 Printed in *The Theosophist* III (Oct. 1881), 3–4.

87 M. P. 45,284, f. 62. Printed in *M.L.*, 38.

88 Campbell, *op. cit.*, 58–59, gives a succinct and insightful account of this case of plagiarism.

89 M. P., 45,284, f.62–74. Printed in *M.L.*, 38–41.

90 *The Theosophist, Supplement* III (Oct. 1881), 1.

91 M.P., 45,288, f. 166–69. Printed in *B.L.*, 305–10. The letter is dated 4 Jan. 1881 but the context indicates that the year was 1882.

92 *The Theosophist*, II (Sept.1881), 270–71.

93 *Ibid.*, III (June 1882), 223. The issue of Apr. 1882 (183–84) had contained an editorial on Cook entitled 'A Theological Snob.'

94 Hume's name did not appear on the articles but contemporary Theosophical correspondence indicates that he wrote the first three essays in this series.

95 For brief information on Terry, see Jill Roe, *Beyond Belief: Theosophy in Australia, 1879–1939* (New South Wales University Press, 1986), 2–3, 12–13 and 38.

96 *The Theosophist* III (Oct. 1881), 17–21.

97 *Ibid.*, (Mar. 1882), 158.

98 M. P., 45,284, f.166–69.

99 *Hints on Esoteric Theosophy. No. 1. Is Theosophy a Delusion? Do the Brothers exist?* 2nd. ed. (Calcutta, 1882), 17.

100 *Ibid.*, 18.

101 *Ibid.*, 19.

102 *Ibid.*, 41.

103 *Ibid.*, 71.
104 *Ibid.*, 30.
105 *Ibid.*, 41–42.
106 *Ibid.*, 39–40.
107 *Ibid.*, 38.
108 *Ibid.*, 42–45.
109 *Ibid.*, 52.
110 *Ibid.*, 15.
111 *Ibid.*, 64–65.
112 *Ibid.*, 53–54 .
113 *Ibid.*, 68–70.
114 *Ibid.*, 63–64.
115 *Ibid.*, 70.
116 *Ibid.*, 65.
117 *Hints on Esoteric Theosophy. No. 2 Swedenborg and Theosophy, 1882* (Calcutta, 1883), 12–13.
118 *Ibid.*, 28–29.
119 *Ibid.*, 42.
120 *Ibid.*, 21–24.
121 M. P., 45,288, f. 166–69. Printed in *B. L.*, pp. 305–10. Hume mistakenly dated this letter 1881 instead of 1882.
122 *Hints on Esoteric Theosophy. No. 1*, op. cit., 71.
123 Linton and Hanson, *op. cit.*, 8–10.
124 M.P., 45,288, f.170–75. Printed in *B.L.*, 310–11.
125 *Ibid.*, 45,285, f.122–27. Printed in *M.L.*, 255–59.
126 *The Mahratta*, 27 Oct. 1912, 343. This letter was published following Hume's death earlier that year.
127 M.P., 45,287, f.3. Printed in *B.L.*, 4.
128 *Supplement* III (Feb. 1882), 16.
129 *Ibid.*, 3.
130 M.P., 45,287, f.28–33. Printed in *B.L.*, 15–17.
131 Hume to the Editor, *The Indian Daily News*, 23 June 1882.
132 M.P., 45,289A, f.33–46. Printed in *M.L.*, 59–66.
133 *Ibid.*, 45,289B, f.150–51.
134 *Ibid.*, f. 152–57.
135 *The Theosophist* III (Sept. 1882), 324–26.
136 M.P., f. 55–59. Printed in *B.L.*, 29–34.
137 *The Theosophist* III (Sept. 1882), 324.
138 M.P., 45,285, f.210–26. Printed in *M.L.*, 322–31.
139 *Ibid.*, f. 165–70. Printed in *M.L.*, 284–90.
140 *Ibid.*, 45,288, f.176b. Printed in *B.L.*, 311.
141 *Ibid.*, 45,289B, f.165–66.
142 *Ibid.*, f.182–93.
143 *Ibid.*, 45,287, f.64–65. Printed in *B.L.*, 37–38.
144 *Ibid.*, f. 60–63. Printed in *B.L.*, 34–36.
145 *Ibid.*, 45,285 f. 138–40. Printed in *M.L.*, 264–66.
146 *Ibid.*, f. 93–96. Printed in *M.L.*, 239–41.
147 *Ibid.*, f.165–70. Printed in *M.L.*, 284–90.
148 *Ibid.*, f.210–26. Printed in *M.L.*, 322–31.

149 *Ibid.*, f.36–37. Printed in *M.L.*, 364–66.
150 *Ibid.*, f.45,287. Printed in *B.L.*, 43–44.
151 *Ibid.*, f.132–37. Printed in *M.L.*, 260–64.
152 *The Theosophist*, III (Aug. 1882), 273–74; (Sept. 1882), 297–98; IV (Feb. 1883), 118; (Mar.1883), 128; and (July 1883), 246–48.
153 M.P., 45,289B, f.169–70.
154 *Ibid.*, 45,284, f. 165–70. Printed in *M.L.*, 284–87.
155 Hume probably assumed otherwise because the leading Hindu *chela*, Subba Rao, was an advaitist, though he and the Swami of Almora disagreed on interpretations of the philosophy (*The Theosophist*, IV (July 1883), 248–51).
156 M.P., 45,289B, f.182–93.
157 This letter is quoted at length by Koot Hoomi in writing to Sinnett (*Ibid.*, 45,285 f. 210–26. Printed in *M.L.*, 322–31).
158 Hume to Lord Ripon, 11 Jan. 1884, Ripon Papers. Add. Mss. 43,616.
159 Sinnett, *Incidents in the Life of Madame Blavatsky, op. cit.*, 244.
160 *Ibid.*, 245.
161 *B.C.W., 1882–1883*, IV, xxvi.
162 Campbell, *op. cit.*, 57.
163 See *ibid.*, 88–91, for a succinct account of this important episode.
164 *The Statesman*, 20 Sept. 1884.
165 *Proceedings of the Society Psychical Research* 3, IX (1883), 224.
166 Quoted in *ibid.*, 275.
167 M.P., 45,286, f. 242–51. Printed in *M.L.*, 461–62.
168 Campbell, *op. cit.*, 91–92.
169 *B.C.W. 1883* V, 270.
170 Hume to Dufferin, 27 Nov. 1886, Dufferin Papers, F142\42g.
171 Hume to Dufferin, 31 July 1886, *ibid.*, F130/42C.
172 Hume to Macdonnell, 1887, *ibid.*, Microfilm 534, vol. 2, 369–70.

Chapter 6

George Uglow Pope contra Vedanayagam Sastriar

A case-study in the clash of 'new' and 'old' mission

Antony Copley

Conversion is a process. Be it Pauline or long drawn-out, the moment of conversion is not the end of the story: beyond conversion lies a long process of adjustment between the demands of the new faith and former loyalties. Nineteenth century Protestant Mission invariably made the mistake of concentrating its energies on winning new converts and failing to meet the needs of its new Christian communities. So called 'new' mission had quite unreasonable expectations that their convert communities would shake off all previous loyalties, above all to caste, and come into line with the narrow, sectarian demands of Evangelical Christianity. Mission had not always been so. The Lutheran mission to Tranquebar, above all associated with the name of Christian Schwartz, had trod far more gently. So likewise had Catholic mission. Both continued to do so on into the nineteenth century. Here was a situation ripe for conflict between 'new' and 'old' mission. One classic example of this was to occur in mid-nineteenth century Tanjore (Thanjavur).

Tanjore itself was seen as a great prize for mission: as one account has it, 'the district abounds in places connected with Hindu mythology and legend and is par excellence sacred country for Hindus. It is still the home of orthodox Brahminism and year after year replenishes the strength of the Hindu intelligentsia all over India. The Tamil Brahmin has now the largest share in the intellectual, economic and administrative life of the country'. Next to Tinevelly (Tirunelveli), it has been the field of longest Christian evangelist effort in the country.[1] The neighbouring town of Trichinopoly (Tiruchirupalli), as distinct from the district, is also here under review.

Initially we have to set the scene, to portray the religious and cultural life of Tanjore on the eve of this assault by nineteenth century Protestant new mission. We have also to describe its Lutheran and Catholic antecedents or old mission. This will better show why both Christian converts and Hindus were so often alienated and hurt by new missionaries.

One highly indicative conflict was to be between The Society for the Propagation of the Gospel (SPG) missionary, George Uglow Pope and Vedanayagam Sastriar (or the Tanjore poet, as he was always named). Pope's career well exemplifies both the tensions and the strengths and weaknesses of Protestant mission in mid-century. It is a story that only emerged from the records.[2] H. P. Thompson has a brief account on his setting up the Seminary at Sawyerpuram and his Tinevelly years; 'in teaching and discipline he was relentless and he did wonders with poor material'.[3] If Stephen Neill acknowledged his prowess as a Tamil scholar, somewhat elliptically he continued: 'he was his own worst enemy. Again and again irascibility betrayed him into unwisdom and in the end it led to his withdrawal from India'.[4] This is quite untrue; it only led to his resignation as a missionary. He continued to enjoy a highly distinguished career as an educationist in India. This is in large part an attempt to explore Pope's controversial Tanjore years.

THE SOCIETY AND CULTURE OF TANJORE

Missionaries like moths to the flame were attracted to the great centres of Hinduism. How promising a field was the Kaveri delta for their endeavour?[5] The river dominated. It took its name from Kaveri, the daughter of Brahma: to honour her father she became this sacred river. Indicative of just how sacred is the fact that in the 1860s eight out of the twenty largest festivals in the Presidency of Madras took place on its banks. Here was a major pilgrimage centre, supported by its monasteries, to be strengthened by an expanding railway system from mid-century. This was temple territory. According to the findings of the Collector of Tanjore in 1841, 2784: the Collector of Trichinopoly counted 4,701 in his district in 1828. Pride of place in Tanjore went to the great Brihadeshwara temple, built by Rajaraja the Great, (985–1014), most outstanding of the Chola dynasty, an architectural master-piece – 'amplifying the standard components of the Chola complex to stupefying proportions'[6] – though, surprisingly, not one of its most sacred temples. According to legend, Apper, the Saivite saint, was refused entry and hence he and his fellow Saivite saints did not celebrate the temple. More sacred were the temples of Tiruvedi, some six miles north of Tanjore city, seen as a miniature Benares. There was also a major temple complex, with its great Chola Darasuram temple, at Kambaconam, one of South India's most sacred towns. Here, every twelfth year, took place the Mahamagham festival: Ganga, according to belief, polluted by all the myriad bathers in the river Ganges, comes to purify herself in the Mahamagham tank. North of Trichinopoly, on an island where the Kaveri divides, with the Coleroon running to the north, stands South India's largest temple, Srirangam.

Many temples were managed by maths or monasteries. This monastic tradition goes back to the ninth century and Shankara. His followers, the Smarta Brahmins, look in part to the Sringeri math in Karnataka, Shankara's own headquarters, but also to the Saivite math at Kambaconam. The Vaishnavite Brahmins, followers of Ramanuja, looked to the Ahobilam math in Kurnool: in time, this was transferred to Kambaconam as well. Just as influential were maths managed by non-Brahmins, the so-called adhinam temples, small in number, but wealthy. The mathapadi, abbots of these monasteries, were great religious personages. We need to have a sense of just how different were the roles of monk and priest. Many would chose a monk, or swami, as their guru or teacher. A priest, on the other hand, was but a reciter of prayers, or mantras, a guardian of the temple. Missionaries were invariably blind to such distinctions, tending to aggregate all such figures as priests. Here was a rich religious culture, in many ways still able to meet the ritualistic, emotional and intellectual needs of Hindus.

Were there here social tensions that the missionaries could exploit? Maybe it was out of an Orientalist perspective that colonial accounts tended to accentuate Brahmin dominance. Brahmins had indeed been encouraged to settle in Tanjore, especially under the Cholas. One in fifteen of the population was a Brahmin. They were versed, we learn, in the sacred law, performed Vedic sacrifices on the river banks, chanted 'in a manner rarely rivalled', published philosophical treatises in Sanskrit verse. Here was the great centre of the Tamil Brahmins: 'preeminently industrious, thrifty and intelligent'; prosperous landowners and also dominant in the professions.[7] The Saivite

Smartas comprised three quarters, the Vaishnavites the remainder. But were they an oppressive caste elite?

Oddie plays down the idea of tensions based on social hierarchy and emphasises, instead, a socially integrated society. Admittedly there were quarrels, e.g. between sections of the Vaishnavites: on the one hand, the vadegalais or northerns, more Sanskrit orientated, and the tengalais, the southerns, more Tamil orientated. The latter were beginning to lose out in the control of the temples from the 1830's onwards. A far more serious potential divide lay between Brahmin and non-Brahmin, but it is just here that Oddie sees social harmony. Non-Brahmins exercised considerable patronage over temples and maths. Besides, a common religious culture drew high and low caste together. We are, of course, very much more aware of this kind of hybridism or synthesis. Even the colonial officer, whilst claiming that non-Brahmins were dependent in so many ways on the service of Brahmin priests, to the extent that domestic ceremonies 'are tinged with Brahminical observances to a degree which is unapproached elsewhere', and that 'Brahminical Hinduism is a living reality and not the neglected cult shouldered out by the worship of aboriginal godlings, demons and devils which it is so often in other districts', conceded that 'even Brahmins do not scorn to propitiate the devils and village deities especially when they are ill'.[8] However, one should not gloss over genuine divisions. There was the clean sudra caste, the vellalas, imitators of the Brahmins but edgy at a sense of ritual inferiority, and often contemptuous of other sudra castes. There were the kallars, a former robber caste, though here was no cause for shame. Inevitably there were losers. There were the out-castes, the parayans, the majority labouring caste, and the pallars, a minority, but a community which considered itself the superior.

Oddie sees in Tanjore a society where property and wealth, rather than caste, dominated its religious life and this is the explanation for its stability. With the fertility of the delta, Tanjore was largely spared famine. As a result of rich salt deposits of the Kaveri, here was a prosperous, largely rice-growing, agrarian economy. The mirasadar peasantry (akin to a ryotwari settlement, together with its defects of absenteeism and sub-infeudation) were its beneficiaries.

None of this looked promising to the missionaries, where converts often came from social antagonisms and out of the wretched circumstances of famine. But, of course, inevitably there were losers. If it is just that hybrid religious culture which leads one to identify Tanjore as a ' peculiarly stable society,' nevertheless, the depressed classes were 'in a state of almost perpetual minor crisis': 'the potential for a change of religion was there even before the Protestants became active in country areas'.[9] So there was room for missionaries to manoeuvre. Yet, significantly, in mid-century, Tanjore was not to witness mass conversions similar to those in Tinnevelly. This was to give this old mission a poor reputation at the time.

Alongside and emerging from the religious life of the temple was a court culture.[10] Here was another, often unacknowledged and not clearly perceived, obstacle in the way of Christianity. Out of the temple came poetry, dance, art, sculpture and music. If Brahmin influence always imposed something of a traditionalist and ritualist ·character on this culture, there were to be new and modernising influences at work on this evolving court culture of Tanjore, from Vijayanagar and its successors, the Naiks, to the Marathas, who came to power in 1676. Probably the most persistent influence was *bhakti*, itself encouraging an uncritical devotionalism. Its art, much influenced by folk art, essentially eclectic and heterogeneous, drawing on Telugu, Maratha and Tamil traditions, was in time to open itself to European styles. By the time of these events, with those overornamented figures of the gods, those strangely plump and sumptuous figures of Krishna, epithets of 'overblown', 'ripe' and 'decadent' are not inappropriate: 'the last phase of craftmanship whence life had almost fled'[11] Here, in a sense, with the end of one Indian style and no clear new one to follow, was a time of vulnerability of Indian art to outside influences.

One would not be so pessimistic about the vitality of music. In Tanjore there was the flowering of the Karnatic style. Rather portentously, Dr Seetha states; 'of all the arts it is music that has preserved continuity and growth throughout the cultural history of India.'[12] Here again there was a fusion of styles, Tamil, Telugu and Maratha. With that trinity of Sri Thagaraja, Sri Mutthuvami Diksitar (1776–1853), and Shama Sastri (1762–1827), Tanjore, from the late eighteenth century onwards, was to enjoy a golden age of music. This court culture also kept alive the dance tradition of Bharat Natyam.

The Maratha rajahs played a major personal role. Shahji (1684–1712) has been described as 'the most cultured and scholarly of his line'.[13] Tulaji II (1763–1787) patronised music. Under Sarobji II (1798–1832), there was to be a greater exposure to the West, with the Rajah's interest in western-style portraiture and western music; it was now that musicians added the piano and the violin to their repertoire. If Indian rulers had always taken an interest in the arts, under paramountcy – Tanjore came within the system in 1799 – Indian princes, robbed of any meaningful political role, became even more absorbed in the arts. Court patronage in Tanjore in the nineteenth century paralleled that of Awadh. Missionaries had the option of either trying to work through this court culture or else ignoring it. George Pope chose openly to challenge this culture in his confrontation with one of its most distinguished representatives, if also its critic, the Tanjore poet, Vedanayagam Sastriar.

OLD MISSION: LUTHERAN

The nineteenth century evangelical missionaries followed on two very different earlier missions, Lutheran and Catholic. If the Catholic brought about a much larger Christian community, the evangelicals in Tanjore were to be much more entangled with the legacy of the Lutheran and with its revival in the 1840s, and hence it warrants closer attention here.[14]

If the Danish Admiral Ove Giedde acquired permission from Ragunatha, the Naik of Tanjore, to set up a trading station in 1620, it was only in 1706, in the persons of Bartolomeus Ziegenbalg and Heinrich Plutschau, that a Protestant mission was to be started. In her atmospheric account of Tranquebar today, Georgina Harding provides a marvellous pen-portrait of Ziegenbalg: 'all accounts have him as a difficult character: zealous to an extreme, intolerant and bad-tempered: this exacerbated by the terrible prickly heat he suffered in India and his refusal to leave off his black wool overcoat or his periwig'. She continues: 'he was voluble in his disgust at his fellow Europeans and dismissed the majority of the natives as lazy and indifferent, reserving respect only for the brahmin pundits with whom he studied the Tamil language and discussed theology – and annoying his superiors in Europe by suggesting that Indian philosophy might actually surpass that of the Ancient Greeks'.[15] Ziegenbalg himself was never to visit Tanjore. On his first attempt he was arrested on orders of the Privy Council: on his second, he got no further than Perumalei; he could not proceed without formal permission of entry from the court at Tanjore. He died, 23 February, 1719, his early death at 36 almost certainly brought on by the unfair charge from the Mission Council in Denmark that he had neglected his primary apostolic role of spreading the gospel e.g. itinerating.

The decisive link with Tanjore came through Rajanaiken, son of a Catholic catechist and under-officer in the King's service, who had accompanied a Brahmin on a visit to Tranquebar on the King's behalf. He converted to Lutheranism in 1728. Another Lutheran catechist, Aaron, had visited Tanjore in 1727, followed by a missionary, Presser, the year after. (He had been invited to attend the wedding of the Rajah's son.) An indication of Lutheran attitudes to caste is that Rajanaiken, a successful catechist in Tanjore, but a pariah, was never ordained (it would not have helped that he had taken to drink again) but Aaron, a Vellala, did become a priest, December 1733. With Pratip Singh (1741–65) as rajah, the barriers were raised again: he looked on Europeans as 'notoriously bad characters'[16]: he imposed a heavy entrance fee on any would-be visitor. In a way, all had still to be won, and the man to do so was Christian Frederick Schwartz.

His is a well-known story. For Stephen Neill, through 'the beauty of holiness . . . the superlative purity and integrity of his life', he was 'without doubt the greatest of all the Tranquebar missionaries'[17]. Born 26th October 1726, to a 'respectable family'[18] – his mother dedicated him to God – he moved to Halle in 1746, was ordained there, 8th August 1749, and arrived as a missionary in Cuddalore, 16th July 1750. On 23rd November, he preached his first sermon in Tamil, in Ziegenbalg's New Jerusalem Church in Tranquebar. We can visualise him through this contemporary portrait (1767) by William Chambers, Master of Chancery at the Court of Calcutta: 'Figure to yourself a stout well made man, somewhat above the middle size, erect in his carriage and address, black curled hair and a manly engaging countenance, expressive of unaffected candour, ingenuousness and benevolence'.[19] The early years were unremarkable: 'by his gentle and modest manners he won the love and respect of his colleagues but during the first ten years of his stay in India there was nothing to distinguish him particularly from the rest.'[20] Others anticipated Schwartz's visit to Tanjore: one, Wiedenbroch, went as an interpreter in 1753, another, Berg, as Captain in 1762.

It was Berg who invited Schwartz as chaplain to the garrison at Trichinopoly in 1765. He then played truant for a year. On the 10th July, 1766, he wrote to Tranquebar: 'I have now been absent a considerable time from Tranquebar and have lived here in Trichinopoly and now and then in Tanjore. The hope of soon having something certain to say has delayed me so long that I must now with shame ask for forgivance for my negligence and promise in future to be more careful of my duty'.[21] Did rumours of supernatural powers – his words of rebuke had seemingly precipitated the death of a hostile Captain in Trichinopoly – bring him to the attention of both the Naub of the Carnatic and the Rajah of Tanjore?[22] Through his linguistic skills and his natural talent for diplomacy, Schwartz became an increasingly indispensable intermediary between the warring parties of South India, the Company, Hyder Ali of Mysore and the Rajah of Tanjore.

Key was his relationship with Tulaji II. He first preached in his hearing, 17th April 1769. Did he surmise that' the conversion of so prominent a person, if it could be affected, would benefit his mission work greatly'?[23] From now on the Rajah granted him free access to the Fort, though not without opposition from Brahmin officials: 'the great about the Court saw with regret that he was desirous of detaining me being fearful that corrupt practices might be exposed.'[24] He mastered the court language, Maratha. Schwartz became most useful to Tulaji as an intermediary with the British: 'Padre, I have confidence in you because you are indifferent to money'.[25] Tanjore now experienced a painful time, invasion by Hyder Ali, temporary annexation by the Company, 1773–76, and grave misrule by the Rajah. Some 7000 left the state in despair. In no way was Schwartz blind to Tulaji's abuse of power; 'my friendly intercourse with the rajah from his accusers shall never bias me to be regardless of the injustice he has done his people.'[26] Schwartz's presence did something to lure them back. The Company now paid Schwartz £100 a year to act as their interpreter.

On grounds that it would be beyond his powers to deal with the court feuds that would follow, Schwartz refused Tulaji's request that he look on his adopted son, Sarabhoji, as his own. But he did act as his guardian and on his succession in 1798, following the quarrelsome Regency of Ameer Singh, he might well have hoped that here, at last, was his Christian prince; he had gone to great trouble to obtain validation of his right to succeed from the Brahmin pandits in Benares. Admittedly, Sarabhoji broke major taboos by attending Schwartz's funeral service – 'to be in the vicinity of the dead is pollution; to remain in his house where a corpse lies is the essence of pollution; but to bow down and touch the dead is the intensity of pollution and defilement'.[27] 'No son', wrote Revd. 'Gericke, 'can have a greater regard for his father than the good Hindoo had for Mr Schwartz and still has for his memory'.[28] But there was to be no conversion. On the contrary, he was to be a good protector of dharma. When he met Bishop Heber, he was doing so on his return from pilgrimage to Benares. Following recognition of the Company's paramount power in 1799, the Rajah was little more than ruler of the Fort and its surrounding area and maybe he hoped, were Heber to take his own son under his wing at Calcutta, he could do something to strengthen his cause with the British. But the Rani objected – she did not think her sickly son would survive the journey – and Heber was not keen.

Had Tulaji all along been the better prospect? Was it the Company's siding with the Naub of Arcot against Tanjore that had destroyed this prospect?[29] But according to Schwartz, Tulaji saw Christianity as 'too directly opposed to the corrupt propensities of human nature to be readily complied with while the sacrifice not merely of caste but as they erroneously apprehended of princely revenue and possibly even of life, ... too formidable to be overcome by anything short of that divine grace which can in spite even of opposing influences bring every thought into captivity to the dominion of Christ.'[30] Was this a better explanation?

William Hickey, apologist for the princely rulers of Tanjore, branded the generation of evangelical missionaries in the 1830s onwards as deplorably neglectful of the spiritual welfare of the royal family: 'mixing as they did with the local magnates of authority; they counted these personages as below their notice and classed them with the common mass of people.'[31] Certainly the last Rajah, Shivaji (1833–55), did not feature in the same way in missionary endeavour and one charge subsequently to be brought against Pope was his contempt for the Court. But, as in almost all relationships between Indians and Europeans, and with the power structure of Empire it was predictable, the court of Tanjore had been opportunistic: dangling the prospect of conversion before the Lutherans was but one device to get the

Lutherans to work on their behalf. Maybe all along, the missionaries had been but pawns in a desperate struggle for survival by the house of Tanjore. Here was one Lutheran legacy the new missionaries chose to reject.

If they failed in their attempt to convert the Rajahs, the Lutherans were, nevertheless, comparatively speaking, successful missionaries. We have to define their strategy. They saw no ideological divide between the merits of proselytising and teaching: both were encompassed. According to the 1735 instructions from the S.P.C.K., Schwartz had, anyway, to encourage teaching. Most striking was the enormous care the Lutherans took over the instruction of converts. Most controversial was their notoriously permissive attitude towards caste. In fact, Schwartz did not favour caste. His, however, was a non-coercive approach: 'I have carefully avoided all unnecessary restraints'. Down to 1778, in the communion service, sudras and pariahs could use different chalices; thereafter, sudras still drank first. Better to bring castes together by the slow process of a change in mores. Let the castes, for the meanwhile, sit apart in church. Try to persuade the low castes to give up unclean practices, such as feeding on dead cattle: 'I have always expressed the utmost abhorrence of such a custom and positively declared I would not allow it and accordingly I hardly know of any instance of it here'. His mild and forbearing approach to caste, Pearson believed, was far more conducive to its gradual disappearance than 'the rash and intolerant spirit' which was to replace it.[32] In Schwartz's time there was a higher percentage of high caste converts, if only they went on to become priests.

Maybe even more significantly distinctive about Lutheran mission was its willingness to explore Indian culture. Missionaries both mastered the local languages and studied Indian religions. Ziegenbalg read widely and wrote extensively: 'taken together', as one commentator has it, 'all these works represent nothing less than an encyclopaedic inventory and analysis of what contemporary South Indian Hinduism was like in theory and practice.'[33] Schwartz had already learnt Tamil whilst at Halle, helping to prepare a Tamil Bible. If he did not go on to be a great translator, he did spend the first five years in India mastering Hindu texts. Both were embattled men. Here is Schwartz's account of the Brahmins of Tanjore: 'it is remarkable that within the narrow limits of Tanjore a hundred thousand vigorous young Brahmins might with very little trouble be collected. With the exception of their daily ceremonies and ablution they do nothing: living in voluptuousness and corrupting sloth. They possess the best land and give away little or nothing, besides which the numerous pagan festivals are eminently profitable to them.'[34] But the secret of Schwartz's influence lay in the tact and sensitiveness of his approach; 'the zeal of Schwartz was untinctured by fanaticism and unbiased by extravagance, eccentricity, intolerance and harshness, whether of spirit or expression.'[35] Graul, in the mid nineteenth century, was to reveal an even keener sense that, without insight into the content of Hinduism, Christianity would not progress. His was almost an anticipation of an inclusivist theology. Here, in all, was a gradualist approach to mission which the Evangelicals were loath to follow.

Conversion stories from Tanjore are rare. One in Schwartz's time, if in fact the work of Huffemann at Cuddalore, was of Tondeman Mudaliar, a priest of the Saivite Isuran sect. Born 1737 in Madurai, he decided at the age of 14 to become a priest, a decision strengthened by the death of both his parents. He came to Tanjore to study. In time he became disillusioned by the character of temple worship and the personal stories of the Hindu gods, and under Huffemann's instruction, converted. The priests in Tanjore could only explain his apostasy in terms of a crime committed in some previous incarnation: they warned him: 'your change is like a king turning pariah.' He replied: 'fourteen years have I been witness to the infamous worship of your pagodas and I am convinced in my heart that you are on the road which directly leads to hell and eternal ruin.' Revealing of the non-intrusive nature of Lutheran conversion was denial that he had lost his Indian identity: 'by becoming a Christian I did not become an Englishman – I am yet a Tondeman. This priest of this place never desires me to eat cow-flesh, nor have I seen him eat it or any of the Tamilian Christians.' Here was Schwartz's gradualism and tact at work.[36]

OLD MISSION: CATHOLIC

Tanjore itself never became the headquarters of any Catholic mission.[37] Yet Catholics vastly outnumbered Protestants, by 9 to 1. In the mid-century, Catholic mission was primarily concerned with the revitalisation of this community rather than its expansion. In terms of conversion, this was a decadent phase in Catholic mission. Some effort went into reclaiming Protestant converts, but there were swings and roundabouts in such poaching.[38] In the meanwhile, all the running on conversion was with Protestant mission. Not until the end of the century were there to be spectacular high caste Catholic conversions and the beginnings of a mass Catholic conversion movement. But this very much larger Catholic Christian community was a constantly provocative presence to the nineteenth century Protestants and made them wonder if they were correct in their own missionary strategy.

Intra-Catholic rivalries gravely weakened Catholic mission. Most crippling was that between the Portuguese Padroado, centred on Goa, and the Vatican's Propaganda Office, its Vicars Apostolic rivalling the Portuguese ecclesiastical hierarchy. In the mission field, this surfaced in rivalry between a Goanese priesthood and the Catholic missionary orders, above all, the Jesuits. Here were conflicts that could be exploited both from above and below. With some 40% of its British troops in India Irish Catholics, the Company certainly had cause to take an interest in Catholic affairs, but, increasingly, its policy was to wash its hands of these squabbles, and leave them to the courts to resolve. Indian communities from below did not hesitate to turn these quarrels to their advantage. With the dissolution of the Jesuit order and the collapse of its Madurai mission in the eighteenth century, the Société Des Missions Etrangeres (SME) did something to fill the gap(and sheltered some of the Jesuits): the Goanese were quite unable to maintain similar standards of priesthood. The Madurai mission had extended to Trichinopoly, to Tanjore south of the Kaveri and to Puttokottai: the SME had covered north of the river, above all at Kumbaconam. The Jesuit order was reconstituted, 7th August 1814. Through Gregory XVI, in so many ways a reactionary Pope,[39] the Vatican in the 1830s once again sought to seize the initiative.

On Abbé Dubois's advice, 23rd December 1836, he revived the Jesuit Madurai mission. Father Garnier came to Trichinopoly, his church the forerunner of St Mary's Cathedral: Father Ranquet to Palamcottah (Palayankottai.) Neither seepage to Protestantism nor any large-scale apostasy to Hinduism is seen as the explanation for the failure of Catholic numbers to match population growth: 'what is more likely is an increase in non-practicing or indifferent Catholics. We have also ample evidence that from neglect, bad handling and habits of insubordination or caste rivalry, many catholics needed a sort of reconversion.'[40] This was the challenge the Catholic orders addressed. Maybe the most significant Jesuit development was the setting up of a college (though the name flatters it at its start, with but two fathers and 15 pupils) at Negapatam(Negpattinam). In 1866 it became a high school, affiliated to the University of Madras; 18th August 1882 it transferred to Trichinopoly and as St Joseph's College was to be the venue for some highly controversial Brahmin conversions in the 1890's.

Imposing any common discipline on Catholic India was a struggle. Gregory appointed new Vicars Apostolic. One, Mgr. Bonnard, who only very reluctantly took up his appointment as Bishop of Pondicherry, 8th November 1833, did make some considerable impact; through a Synod at Pondicherry in 1844 he began to impose his authority; in 1871 he was appointed a Vicar Apostolic with a watching brief for the whole of India. But new divisions arose. There were quarrels with the Irish Catholics, under Bishop O'Connor, appointed in 1835, Vicar Apostolic to Madras. And nothing bridged the old divide between the Goanese and the Vatican. Mgr. Bonnard superseded the jurisdiction of the Portuguese bishops by the vicariates of Pondicherry, Mysore and Coimbatore. The Concordat of 21st February 1857 was still-born. Not until another, 23rd June 1886, were these disabling conflicts over authority and spheres of influence resolved. The scale of the sacrifice to Portuguese Mylapore in the area is in some dispute; the river Vetter became the frontier between the Jesuits, to the south, under the Bishop of Madurai, the SME to the north, under the Bishop of Pondicherry.[41]

Given interests so plural and so divided it is surprising that there were any common characteristics to Catholic mission. Catholics paid considerable attention to their convert communities. These were divided up into some 120 square miles, incorporating some 4 to 7 villages each. One consistent theme in Catholic writing is the greater material sacrifice of Catholic missionaries over Protestant: those from the Jesuit noviciate in Trichinopoly, set up in 1846, for example, made a life time commitment to India. Catholic missionaries did not live in comfortable bungalows: some 200 days a year they itinerated their villages in bullock carts. The death toll in the Madurai mission in the 1840s was disturbingly high. Here was an asceticism that drew them close to India's own yogic and sanyassin traditions. Not that there was anything democratic about the organisation of the missions. Control remained firmly in European hands. Nor did they favour any policy of Europeanisation. This, the French believed, merely gave Indian Christians ideas above their station. But they were far more tolerant of merely material reasons for conversion. In Houpert's words 'it is neither good Christianity nor good sense to offer the pariah the stone of theological speculation or purely spiritual gifts and let them lack the bread of humanity.'[42] Protestant mission was to charge them with softness on caste and endless collusion with Hindu practice. The Goanese showed the greatest sympathy towards the poor and low caste. M. X. Miranda has presented a case as early as this for a progressive Jesuit social policy: 'a Jesuit commitment to the transformation of society;' 'dynamic and egalitarian values were infused into a tradition-ridden society.'[43] If true of the Jesuits today, for this period it seems special pleading. There is reference to a Vellala colony at Idaikallur in North Tanjore in 1860, organised around betel production; shades of the famous Paraguay reductions. Here was evidence of a certain pragmatism which Protestant missionaries found both threatening and disturbing.

But no signs of Robert de Nobili's inculturation policy remained. This had been inspired by a genuine regard for the intellectual strength of Hinduism. A mere collusion with Hindu practice was quite different. One nineteenth century Catholic voice wrote off Hinduism, both of the high and low castes, as mere idolatry.[44] One from the 1930s was just as negative: 'the Hindu literature dating from perhaps 1000 BC down to our days unfolds the long and weary tale of part of mankind grasping after truth without success.' 'It was a religion without a morality'.[45] In many ways, Neill's judgement on this phase of Catholic mission can stand: 'the second birth of the Roman Catholic Church in India,' but one very much in 'the spirit of restoration', and under the dead hand of Rome.[46]

A TROUBLED SPG MISSION AT TANJORE

This is a story of a major conflict in one of the old missions, so called through this earlier Lutheran and Catholic presence. Following Schwartz's death, 14th February 1798, John Kaspar Kohloff, his adopted son, took over the mission. In 1819 it passed to the S.P.C.K., in 1825 to the S.P.G., an untroubled series of successions. In 1845 the Company purchased Tranquebar. But the history of the SPG in the 1840s and 1850s was to be far from peaceful. The Leipsig Evangelical Lutheran Society, a breakaway neo-Lutheran group from the Basel Mission Society, saw itself as the legitimate heir of the Tranquebar mission, took it over in the 1840s and did so in a spirit of confrontation with the Anglicans. The opening of the Jesuit college at Negapatam was yet another danger signal. Secretary of the Madras District Committee, Symonds, had this to say of the perceived Jesuit threat: 'they insinuate themselves into the good graces of Europeans . . . have been only too successful in obtaining countenance and assistance for their pleas and projects.' On their permissive attitude to caste: 'they adapt themselves with great craft to native habits and prejudices and leave untried no expedient that worldy policy can suggest to augment their numbers.' The heathen 'with comparatively little effort become a Romanist, so much is he allowed to retain of heathenish habits, feelings and practices'. The Goanese were just as bad.[47]

Into this somewhat moribund Anglican mission came in 1851 George Uglow Pope. There is an air of Greek tragedy, of hubris, about Pope's years in Tanjore. All that emphasis of his on the need for discipline and authority which had marked his years at Sawyerpuram in Tinnevelly, seemed to rebound against him. Here we can see key aspects of mission ideology and strategy in contention: the battle against compromise with caste, itinerating versus education. With the former, Pope was up against the countervailing influence of the Lutheran and Catholic mission and the entrenched attitudes of Tamil Christians and he was to fail: with the latter, as a pioneer of education, he was ahead of his time and was to pay the price.

But there was another equally serious divide, over theology. In a memorable metaphor, John Clive writes of 'British India as a distant stage on which an English touring company came to act plays that had created some stir at home.'[48] Tractarianism reached India and here was another area in which Pope was to intervene to his own self-destruction.

Clearly something had to be done about the Tanjore mission. A set of interlocking bodies, whose responsibilities were not clearly delineated, hammered out policy: the Home Committee, in Pall Mall – Ernest Hawkins became its Secretary in 1843 and is described by the Society's official historian as 'perhaps the greatest that the Society ever had'[49] – the Madras District Committee, itself under the authority of the Bishop of Madras. The composition and powers of the MDC were hotly debated: it was, in fact, open to anyone prepared to pay an annual fee of 15 rupees; it was dominated by Company chaplains and laymen; members need not be Anglicans, nor indeed, Protestant. Its Secretaries were SPG: Shortlands, who resigned in despair 19th February 1845 at the mayhem of its quarterly meetings and the hostility shown to the Society, though he was to continue for a while; Symonds then took over. Bishop Spencer, Corrie's aristo-cratic successor, was Bishop 1837–49, Bishop Dealtry, his successor, 1849 to 1861. Missionaries in the field felt increasingly margin-alised and alienated from this structure of power; they passionately resented the interventionist and, in their eyes, arrogant role of Company chaplains, desperately hoped a new Bishop might be appointed with exclusive commitments to mission, and continu-ally laid claim to greater powers of personal initiative. None of these aspirations was to be fulfilled in Pope's time.

During his rare descents from the Nilgiris, Bishop Spencer, aided by the Secretaries of the MDC, sought to restructure the Tanjore mission, largely along Tinnevelly lines. Divided into three counties, with Tanjore itself a separate station, only in 1843 was the parish system introduced. Newly appointed Symonds took stock of the mission, 23rd September 1848: Tanjore itself had 5 villages attached, Canendagoody, 13 villages, Vediapuram, the Seminary and 15 villages, and Kambaconam, 16 villages (Trichinopoly had 9.) But this was a time of retrenchment, missionary salaries were under review, and with carefully nursed funds, Tinevelly was always to be privileged over Tanjore: this does much to explain the cantankerousness of its missionaries. Spencer sought to wean away those Lutherans still attached to Tanjore: following J.C. Kohloff's death, 27th March 1844, he no longer felt the Society should retain the services of his son-in law, F.W. Schnitz; he was too suspect on the question of caste. Not that Kohloff himself had passed this test: 'indeed, I may say he was altogether more indulgent to the Tanjore Christians than was compatible with the maintenance of Christian discipline.'[50] The Bishop was even less disposed towards the East Indians; 'generally speaking indolent, weak-minded, dawdly persons.'[51] European missionaries were always preferable. (Here there is scope for confusion; East Indian normally implies those of mixed European and Indian descent, and was probably so used here, and, if so, the Bishop was very unfair to the gifted missionary, H. Bower; but it might also apply to those Europeans born in India, and here it might be best to apply the term, 'Anglo-Indian'.) Tanjore Christians, in Symond's eyes, had exaggerated expectations of the power and wealth of the MDC: 'some of the older congregations in Tanjore are disposed to claim as a right what should be regarded as a favour and to question the justice of any of their demands being declined.'[52] The mission fell down through inadequate provision for widows.[53] Its most serious fault lay in attitudes to caste: 'the principal cause of reducing our old missions to the lowest state of spirituality if indeed spirituality be not altogether extinct.'[54]

This was clearly put too strongly. Good work was being done. Brotherton and Bower struggled on. At Canendagoody, Brotherton had a personal triumph, with a Brahmin convert: 'this interesting convert from the priesthood of a corrupt worship tore off his Brahminical string as he stood beside the font.'[55] On his first tour, Symonds reported the Revd. Coombes's new village, Anaycade, as 'one of the most pleasing and promising of our missions.'[56] Maybe its freedom from cholera had something to do with its success. Hubbard, also at Canendagoody, came up against caste insistence that pariahs should take communion separately: 'the Hindoos can do nothing without immense chattering' and the caste Christians refused communion unless Hubbard reverted to the old practice of their preceding the pariahs.[57] At least these new appointees were struggling against the old order. Symonds emphasised how much more intractable in its way was the city of Tanjore than the villages.

One special institution in the mission was the seminary at Vediapuram, (the town of religious teachers). Situated four miles north of Tanjore, on the road to Tiruvedi, on the banks of a tributary of the Kaveri, it was at the centre of the mission. Since his ordination in 1843, Brotherton had been in charge. Bower, the distinguished theologian and translator, a Tanjore missionary since July 1843, was to join him. Both tended to highlight opportunities for evangelism. But Symonds valued the academic side of both Sawyerpuram and Vediapuram: 'a sound scriptural education accompanied both mental and moral training of a high order is being imparted in them to numerous youth.'[58] By 1856 there were 51 students. In their first year they studied such works as the Kural and the Gita: in the second, the story of the Passion in Tamil. Here lay the possibility for training a native clergy.

But the demoralised state of the mission prior to Pope's appointment becomes clear from studying the correspondence of two other missionaries, Wiltshire and Fletcher, though, as both were to fall out with the Society, their views may be jaundiced.

Wiltshire got off to a bad start by arriving in Madras in July 1842 without an official letter of introduction to the MDC from the parent body, this in itself a bar to ordination. Madras, itself an old mission, did not impress: 'a gay and luxurious capital, thronged with gay and luxurious inhabitants . . . a business of life as it were occupying the thoughts of all giving a colour to the actions of all from the humblest to the highest.' It lacked those 'quieter more clerical shades of character' to be found in Europe. If 'religion has assumed a fashionable guise at Madras which is perhaps somewhat better than being quite unfashionable', there was no intimacy between European and Indian Christian, and 'the influence of European manners is also by all accounts banefully undermining every good quality among the natives. I have a low opinion of their piety altho not so low as some who think there are not two Christians in the place. As far as one may judge from rumour and appearance Christianity does not progress in any satisfactory mode in Madras.'

Tanjore was no better. Company chaplains, the white clergy, as they were named, are at loggerheads with the black, the missionary. If the missionaries, however hurt, have learnt to live with the social exclusiveness of the chaplains, 'they do regret this notion being so popular that it becomes a bar to their usefulness. Their own converts sometimes neglect their authority to appeal to some passing chaplain.' Catholics do not despise their missionaries and in consequence 'they meet with greater success than we: I do not doubt that had France obtained the dominion instead of England the whole peninsula would by this time have been converted.' Robbed of any powers of initiative, missionaries 'find by experience that it is immensely easier to let things go on quietly, than to attempt to do their duty of improving their several districts . . . the sum however is that the veriest vital and most devoted portions of the clergy are fostered into languidness.'[59]

Initially appointed a catechist at Cuddalore, he moved to a station near Negapatam, allowing further insights into Catholic mission: 'Romanism is so closely and apparently with study and design assimilated with Heathenism that a large part of the people do not themselves know the difference between the worship of Krishna and Christ and so the whole animosity of the land is directed against the profession of Reformed Christianity.'[60] From thence, in April 1845, he went to work under Bower in a Kallar community at Boodalor, 'fruits of the apostolic labours of the excellent Schwartz'. Many had apostasised on his death 'to the dark and brutish idolatry of their fathers' but whilst itinerating, living in the now dilapidated and squalid small churches built by J.C. Kohloff, he and Bower had met many seeking readmission, 'that their infants may become partakers of the priveledges (sic) withheld from them so cruelly by their parents.'

Wiltshire gained some considerable insight into the workings of caste: 'low caste as the Kaller themselves are, they are almost as much filled with contempt of the Pallahs and Pariahs and Chucklas and others below themselves as the high Vellalas and Brahmins. Each caste, however despised itself, seems to regain its self-respect in caste contempt to some other, and even the pariah, outcaste as he is, forbidden to appear in the Brahminical street, denounced as a wretch whose very touch is pollution will yet break his cooking pots and utensils if polluted by the shadow of certain other natives.' On asking a Catholic pariah to enter his church, all but two of his congregation walked out, and only his blackmail tactic of threatening to withdraw both catechist and schoolmaster had lured them back. But he was not despondent: 'if not so bright as Tinevelly in Tanjore also there is a degree of activity and fruitfulness which is truly refreshing altho not so brilliant as in the semi-Christianising south.'[61]

But a much gloomier assessment was to follow. Tanjore was up against far worse odds than Tinnevelly. 'The inhabitants are of high caste, wealthy landed property, splendid and age-honoured temples, are bound up with Paganism by the influence of numerous Brahminical colonies settled everywhere thro city and country.' Brahmins have amassed 'every possible Government office of any influence thus having a power (by a fatal policy of the Company's agents too long upheld) of insisting on a rigid observance of all the outward marks of deference due from them to the sacred caste, the favoured children of heaven.' 'The Court, or rather the wealth of the present besotted Rajah is directed by the Brahmins who surround him to give a life, joy and activity to the old religion.'

Missionaries are up against this 'worldy mindedness every-where.' Missionary strategy was misguided. In the villages are 'uneducated nominal Christians, attendant on heathen faith, receivers of heathen demons into their own homes, ashamed of Christ, deliberately determining that their children should grow up heathen and closing by in many cases themselves apostatizing.' This has not been addressed. He wrote scathingly of those who offered material inducements: 'a few missionaries in Tanjore have endeavoured to make Christians of an ignorant worldy brutish village population by purchasing land for them, or redeeming their mortgaged property, by levelling bounty among them, providing them with clothes and cattle inducing the people to assemble in miserable mud hovels, for purely intellectual worship, without the slightest attempt to alter the poor sensual human feelings and imagination of the ignorant converts in favour of the Christian religion.' If there was still a steady trickle converting, he delivered a warning the likes of Pope would have been wise to heed: 'for my part I do not wish under the political and ecclesiastical circumstances of this country that any rash move-ment should take place in Tanjore – the Church is not prepared to meet it and it might create future difficulties.' At most, Wiltshire sought a missionary bishop, which would lessen dependence on the chaplains.[62] .

Wiltshire's critique was fatally impaired by his poor progress in Tamil. This had prompted Shortlands's comment that the CMS had got it right with its policy of lower pay but provision of a munsif.[63] Wiltshire had both been kept on in Tanjore to improve his Tamil and denied ordination until he did so. When he failed for the second time, he wrote an aggrieved letter, pointing out that Tamil was 'the most difficult living language in India', that Bower had passed him in the written examination, and 'that an intimacy with the vernacular is not absolutely necessary for the success of all missionary efforts, as the experience of the Scotch missionaries at the time and that of many eminent missionaries of various societies may show.' Besides, the catechists undertook so much of the mission work. In his own self-defence, he pointed out that he'd spent his first five years learning Telugu, the next two in charge of an English and Portuguese congregation, and the last two in a newly formed district, 'still without a house, where most of my time is engaged with buildings or the organisation of the district.' 'From the first day of my arrival,' he complained, 'I have met with an ever damping and depressing unkindness.' We will not understand the limitations of Indian mission unless we know both about those who failed its demands, as well as those who in the eyes of contemporaries, succeeded. Wiltshire requested a transfer to the Caribbean; at least there Tamil indentured labourers would welcome someone who knew their homes and families, and he could even pray with them in such Tamil as he knew.[64] In fact, he was to be sent to the Cape.

The Revd. Fletcher proved even more quarrelsome. He arrived in India, August 1845, briefly joined Caldwell in Tinnevelly, prior to taking on the mission school at Canendagoody in Tanjore. His was an even more scathing account of Madras. It was riven by factionalism: an ultra-evangelical party, 'vehemently opposed to our society', headed by John Tucker, Secretary of the Church Missionary Society; high church Evangelicals, including Shortlands, favourable to the SPG; those opposed to both tendencies. If Tucker kept his cards to his chest, 'there can be little doubt that he and his party are watching closely and the least false step would injure us extremely.'[65] Fletcher nursed ambitions of taking charge of the Vepery Grammar School in Madras, and of turning it into a training school for catechists. Taylor's dismissal as its headmaster, he speculated, was on grounds of his attitude to caste: 'of course he could not make his people renounce caste for none but an almighty power can change the heart of man.'

From Tanjore he vented his anger against the Company chaplains: 'it is certain that some few of the chaplains have within the last few years treated the missionaries with a hauteur not becoming the relation which one clergyman bears or ought to bear another.' There followed a personal tale. 'On my first arrival in the country I was the guest of a chaplain of some literary attainment who one day expressed himself to me in the following manner.' My dear Fletcher, how is it that you whom I perceive to be a gentleman and a scholar could think of becoming a missionary. Your knowledge of Hebrew, Arabic and Syriac will be completely thrown away. The missionaries are a vulgar and illiterate set of people and the black people so stupid that they are six month's learning the Lord's prayer. Admission of East Indians – 'half-caste as they are termed here' – was deemed another liability: drawn from 'the lower and humbler classes' bringing into their new profession, 'a degree of vulgarity and ignorance, which makes them contemptible not only in the eyes of

Europeans but even of natives. The latter generally designate them by an epithet of the utmost scorn. It implies that they have assumed the European dress without being entitled to wear it.' Fletcher himself at least rejected such aspersions: 'many of them are gentlemen and scholars and would be treated as such in any part of England.'

There is a familiar sound to his complaint at SPG subservience to the MDC. How could the parent body, which does not possess itself the power to do so, have delegated such power?: 'Many missionaries have become so vexed and disgusted with the system that they wish to leave this country and go to the colonies where the principles of the Society are really carried out.' He likewise felt a purely missionary bishop for South India was the answer.

Fletcher expressed imaginative ideas on the respective roles of a native clergy and the European missionary. He was not impressed by Bower's control of the Vediapuram seminary: although a good Tamil scholar, he was 'not a man of sufficient education to train up men on whom depend the future destinies of the India church. It is becoming more and more evident that if we wish to make the Native Christians anything better than miserable defendants and grossly interested adherents not to a system but to its emoluments we must seriously think of raising up at once a native ministry.' Were European missionaries required for any other role than teaching?: 'the example both of the Apostolic and the Primitive Church argues strongly for a ministry almost exclusively native.' Europeans can cope neither with the climate – they can only go out early and late in the day – nor the local dialects: they take four or five years to master these, and even then their accents and ideas expressed remain foreign. In the villages they are isolated. Even the German missionaries kept to the cities and left the villages to the catechists. There was no social intimacy: 'the low cunning of the Hindoo cannot appreciate kindness for he normally attributes it to your desire of overreaching him.'[66] So why were modern missionaries so ineffective compared with those of the past?: 'The modern work seems like a rope of sand. A few come over today to Christianity and they go back tomorrow. My impression is that if the missionaries were withdrawn the whole of the congregations would become heathen or semi-heathen in a very short time'. Maybe the Abbé Dubois was right to suppose that the Almighty for some inscrutable purpose had chosen to delay the conversion of the Hindus. Missionaries were wrong to put their faith in the catechist: 'as he is generally an ignorant (comparatively speaking of course) and sometimes unprincipled man it is easy to perceive how much mischief may ensue'.[67]

The answer lay in creating some superior college, 'something akin to colleges at home with their ceremonial will attract Indians', and here he meant the high castes. Seminaries such as Sawyerpuram and Vediapuram provided an education scarcely superior to that of an English charity school: 'they will never fit men to go out as well grounded and solid teachers of Divine truth.'[68] He warmed to his theme. Here, in the running of such a college, was a proper role for European missionaries. They should be of a special temperament, and celibate. 'Clever men merely will not do for India', he averred. 'You must get men of ascetic habits, men whose health will bear the climate and who have been unaccustomed to what is called good society. There is a peculiar sensitiveness in men of the higher and middle classes that shrinks from contacts with the natives of India. But they must be learned and studious, apt at acquiring foreign habits and customs. In fact they must resemble as nearly as possible the mission monks of the Church of Rome. If you would shake the gigantic idolatry of India you should send out Augustines and Wilfreds'. The earlier Lutheran missionaries had been celibate: 'this has produced an admiration of and respect for celibacy among the Hindoos.' However, no-one can be expected to live alone in an Indian village without 'most hurtful results (I speak from experience)': 'the earlier missionaries lived much together and travelled together and therefore did not feel the want of wives.' Here, in his idea of missionary brotherhoods, Fletcher was ahead of his time, and, of course, recruitment of missionaries was coming from just that polite Oxbridge society, though some of his ideas on training a native clergy were in line with those of Pope.

If attracted to Catholic models, Fletcher was even more conscious of the virtues of the Lutheran: 'the best and most flourishing state of the Tanjore missionaries was during the times when the Lutheran system was in vogue . . . They built splendid churches, ornamented with high altars, with a crucifix and lights. High views of blessed sacraments were carefully inculcated and confession made a necessary prerequisite to communion. They made much of church festivals. The native processions and rejoicings at marriages and baptisms were tolerated'. On the issue of caste: if seen as an evil, it was 'one which must be eradicated only by a more advanced knowledge of the gospel and a gradual realization of the injunctions of Christian charity. Yet the Lutherans inculcated the strictest moral discipline.' In contrast came the Evangelicals, thought to be differentiated from Anglicans: 'fanatical missionaries imbued with the gloomy spirit of Calvinism which abolished the ceremonial connected with festivals, forbad processions and looked with an evil eye on anything like innocent mirth and religious festivity.' Once Schwartz's church in Tanjore had been left open all day, so that 'pious natives might like the Primitive Christians pray at the tomb', now it was closed. 'Saints days and daily practices were discarded as superfluous.' 'Confession was abolished as popish.'[69]

Fletcher had some interesting relativist insights into Hinduism. Admittedly, he had a poor opinion of Hinduism: polytheism had led to 'the almost entire annihilation of the moral sense and the sanctioned practice of the most fearful abomination.' 'Their literature is a mass of absurdity and superstition unredeemed by the noble genius which cast a halo over the fable and mythology of Greece and Rome.'[70] But 'Committees and missionaries,' he warned, 'have forgotten that they were dealing with a people immersed in the corruption and degradation of centuries. They could not understand the nature of that love of symbolism and allegory which distinguished Hindustan and indeed all semi-barbarous people. They mistook assent for faith and silence for an acquiescence and comprehension of their doctrine.' In different societies ideas came across differently: 'Present to an Englishman the doctrine of predestination and though he receive it in theory it makes no difference in his moral conduct or holiness of life. Preach the same to an Eastern mind he at once degenerates into a fatalist if not a sensualist'. The Evangelicals had gravely misread Hinduism. It is 'a religion which recognises above all things sacerdotalism, tradition and ceremonial, a religion imaginative even to absurdity.' Contrast 'the cold intellectual Evangelical system with its gloom, its exclusivity and its hatred of the imaginative and the symbolical, its distrust and contempt for antiquity and its dogma scarcely intelligible to the initiated, consider these things and you will scarcely feel surprize that while the Lutherans and Romanists are flourishing and successful we are gradually decreasing.'[71] Few more powerful statements could be made in defence of old mission against new.

Here was another disillusioned Tanjore missionary. He rallied to Wiltshire's defence: 'Every species of annoyance and indeed persecution was directed against him . . . it is not wonderful that he could not apply himself to the close study of the language. He is fanciful and eccentric but laborious and active.'[72] He was himself a good linguist and Symonds had entertained every hope that he would be a good missionary.[73] Fletcher was likewise to be transferred to the Cape.

THE GRIEVANCES OF THE TANJORE POET

Tanjore's most distinguished Christian was the so-called Tanjore poet, Vedanayagam Sastriar. Symonds had met him on his tour through Tanjore in 1848; 'the Tanjore poet is quite a character in the mission. He has a fine tall figure and is without exception the most intellectual native I have ever met.'[74] Born 7 September 1774, his father a Catholic catechist, whom Schwartz had met in Palamcottah and persuaded to let him take his son back to Tanjore, he became an official court poet to Sarobhoji II, at a salary of 70 rupees a month, though subsequently dropped to 40. At this stage there was no incompatibility between employment by a Hindu court and his Christian practice. For example, 2 February 1826, he sent out a circular requesting subscriptions for the Nizam Sadir, an annual meditation for 45 days during Lent. 'In this year I intend commencing the same again, because not only members of our congregations but also most of the Roman Catholics are very desirous to hear it'.[75] The Kohloffs were among the subscribers. Nor did Vedanayagam experience any qualms of conscience at taking on such a role. But under Sarabhoji's successor, Shivaji, the court was not so pliant, and when Vedanayagam refused to write a poem in honour of the Hindu gods, he was dismissed. 'It is strong proof of sincerity', Symonds rather caustically observed, 'when a native will lose his salary rather than abandon his convictions.' He had now to earn by teaching, though voluntary contributions were forthcoming from former pupils and congregations: 'he has rendered good service in the cause of Christianity among the people by his poems, many of which are of considerable merit.' Here was a culture where work was enlivened by song, previously, in Symond's estimate, on the bawdy side, but Vedanayagam's were 'wholesome and profitable poetry', including one a hundred stanzas long, a narrative of the scriptures, sung to accompany those drawing water. When Symonds had first met the poet, heading a considerable number of people singing his songs, Vedanayagam had spoken warmly of the benefits conferred on Tanjore Christians by Schwartz and Kohloff, 'expressing the hope that the Society would be enabled to carry out their benevolent designs.' Symonds noted that 'like most of the Tanjore Christians he was a great advocate of caste which is a sad bar to their growth of Christianity'; 'he is I hope really Christian.'[76] This was the man Pope chose to cross. In 1851 Symonds was to receive from him a quite extraordinary Petition, One Regarding Caste Distinctions, and in 1854, a second, an even more embittered, Afflictive Letter.[77]

Caste was the ostensible issue. In the light of our knowledge of Lutheran permissiveness, the poet's litany of grievances is predictable. As a vellala, Vedanayagam was characteristically opposed to missionary policy of mingling castes, in his view, one of degrading all castes to the level of the outcaste. If caste were indeed the explanation for evil action, could you prove, he queried, that caste was the cause of murder, drunkenness, adultery and fornication? Where is it stated in the Gospel that to be baptized or saved 'all men should all unite in one caste?' The poet looked back to Schwartz. If caste were heathen, how to explain his readiness to convert 'without interfering in their caste distinctions?' He had no truck with the claim that Schwartz did not in fact preach against caste. How could those who spread such ideas know as they were not born at the time of Schwartz's death: 'why do you then allow this falsehood?' He sought to annexe Heber to his cause. He had selected six boys, from the high castes only, as trainee priests: but the missionaries 'in spite of the said lawful order selected the children of paria and then of Tamilians who ate the food dressed by a paria and engaged themselves to ordain them only.'

There was much on the celebration of Communion. 'The recent missionaries at this time administer the Lord's supper not for the remission of sins but for the trial of caste.' Old forms are abandoned. No longer does one kneel on a footstool before the communion table: 'all kneel down upon the ground under the rails.' If you mix Tamil Christian and Valenkamattars(pariahs), one will be filled with grief, the other with pride: 'and that in consequence the both parties lose the remission of sins.' He pointed to double standards. Did not Europeans remain separate and would anyone seriously suggest that were cooks and their employers to take communion together, this would break down rank?: 'Why do you labour in vain for that which cannot be affected?' Clearly, he was scandalised by the way the bread and wine were now brought down beyond the altar: Ziegenbalg and his successors would never have administered the communion 'so irreverently.' 'Yet do not they wish heartily that the Tamilians should go to hell' for their 'unwillingness to sit promiscuously with Valenkamattars.' 'The dishonour and degradation with which was consisting of four houses of Vellala castes are treated on account of having embraced Christianity are greatly increased.' The upshot was vellala reluctance to take communion.

Early church history was drawn on to show that the disciples had not dined with gentiles. He was not persuaded that missionaries did not eat beef prepared by parias 'from piety, from brotherly love.'

Now, more specifically, Pope came under attack. It was he who locked several of the gates of the church during divine service, clearly with the aim of enforcing a common entrance; but women felt ashamed 'to go and come rushing amidst the men indecently.' There were several charges against Pope's conduct of marriage: the bridegroom is forced to remove his turban; the bride to break taboo by naming her husband; the couple are not allowed, again in breach of custom, to visit their own house after the service, but had to attend Pope's, there to sign the Register. There they have to stand for another half hour. 'Men of rank' were afraid to have their marriages performed by Pope. Out of 'feeling for his cruelty', some go to the Catholic priest instead. Even tombs had been vandalised and the remains of Tamilians and parias interred together. The poet was ready to petition Queen Victoria to protect Tamil Christians from 'the molestations which we suffer under the tyrannical controul of the recent missionaries.'

The second letter revealed a greatly intensified struggle between Vedanayagam and Pope. Clearly Pope had tried to undermine his role as teacher. He was no longer allowed to teach his tunes to other Christians. After he had successfully petitioned the Bishop, Pope insisted on a letter of apology for sending the petition: 'as it was contrary to conscience Vedanayagam Sastriar has not complied with his demands. In consequence of which Rev Pope in his vehemence of anger began to entertain hatred against him more than before and continued to molest him and his children since two years.' Various benefactions to the father and to his daughter and younger son were blocked: 'he prevented him and his songsters from singing in the Church the songs which he continued to sing in the church for the space of 60 years in the presence of many missionaries for the edification of the congregation.' Not even in the compound in front of the church could he do so. Pope had scratched out the last verses in his published collection of songs and replaced them with those by younger poets. Malicious attempts to hurt the poet and his family were cited. After requesting that he and his family should come near the altar to receive communion, Pope, 'without giving them he carried the blessed Bread and Wine out of the altar and gave to those who sat at distance leaving the former in kneeling posture for one hour and after disgracing them he gave them at last.' For so highly status conscious a society this was clearly an intolerable insult. Three houses that the poet had purchased from a widow had been razed to the ground by Pope, 'stating that they belonged to the mission.' His younger son's marriage was branded as heathen, on grounds that he had failed to attend Pope's house after the ceremony. 'Thus the cruelties of Rev Pope having been gradually increased against him, he found no means to live at Tanjore and being informed that the congregation at Tinavelly as promulgated trusted that the Lord will perhaps show him a way for his support by them and sent all his children to them with his songs.' What sort of a man could inflict such humiliation and hardship on so distinguished an Indian Christian?

POPE AT THE NEW MISSION OF SAWYERPURAM VARYING ASSESSMENT

Pope had acted out his father's ambition in becoming a missionary.[78] Unable to become a Wesleyan missionary through the Society's lack of funds, John Pope had joined his brother's timber business in Nova Scotia. Here George Uglow (his mother's name) had been born, 24 April 1820. He came from a large family, five brothers, four sisters, and family was always to be important to George. He drew both his younger brothers, Richard and Henry, into the SPG Indian mission, though anxious that his father might see him as asking too much: regarding Henry, he wrote, 'I am afraid to mention the matter to my father lest he should accuse me as Jacob did.'[79] He used to stay with his father in Plymouth during spells of home leave. In August 1839 he came out to India as a Wesleyan missionary, but transferred to the SPG in 1842. He was ordained deacon, Easter Day 1843, and took charge of the new Sawyerpuram seminary in 1844. Oddly enough, he was even then thought of for Tanjore, but extraordinary events were to intervene and he did not go there till 1851. He was ordained priest, 1848. By exploring his Tinnevelly years, a new mission, we will find interesting markers for his future behaviour in Tanjore, an old mission.

Sawyerpuram, named after a merchant, Sawyer, who had purchased the site for Christian converts, a forest area that had had to be cleared of its palmyra trees, lay just north of Tuticorin. Pope came as an educationist but was to make his name through one of those mass conversion movements of the 1840s. We are today more aware of their economic origins, of the way missionaries found themselves as intermediaries in struggles between peasants and landowners. Such a movement occurred in Sawyerpuram in 1844. To give Pope his due, he was initially sceptical: 'such movements are often temporary and even now I think we should rejoice with trembling and be prepared for disappointment though I trust we will not experience this'. This is how he saw it: 'For the lowest classes to come over to Christianity is comparatively easy but for the middling and higher classes of Hindoos to abandon the worship of their forefathers, to assimilate themselves to the lowest caste by the abandonment of the peculiar customs and ceremonies connected with marriages and funerals and to attach themselves to a "a sect everywhere spoken against" is indeed difficult and the struggle probably not yet over in the case of the people.'[80] Key was the role of the zamindar. 'In the south of the province almost every man has his own little spot of land, but here the land is generally in the hands of zamindars and extensive farmers. These men are almost universally sensual, tyrannical and turbulent and universally their influence and example are very prejudicial to the welfare of the infant church.' One such, the Zamindar of Mentaxshi in Putukatti, at one stage the bully of the Christians, 'has become their friend and supporter.'[81] On this occasion, the converts were Retties, a sudra caste superior to and deemed more intelligent than the Nadars, and it was difficult for Pope not to give way to millenarian expectations: 'I think we shall have large accessions until the whole of the north of my district is under Christian instruction. I judge from a very intimate knowledge of the dense population between this place and Ramnad that the feeling towards Christianity is peculiarly favourable.'[82] Shortlands became anxious at the strain on Pope's health: 'in danger of sinking altogether under the unceasing anxiety of mind and labour of body to which he has been exposed during the past trying season.'[83] For Shortlands the conversion was 'no transient feeling but proceeding from rooted and well established conviction of its superiority and of its infinite value to them as the revelation of the true and living God.'[84] Nor indeed should we be sceptical of a genuine religious character to these low caste conversions: Duncan Forrester has strongly defended such an account.[85] But such stories had, nevertheless, to be milked of all possible propaganda value for home consumption.

Not all were convinced. Another luckless Tamil learner, Mr Lovekin, under Pope's supervision, belied these expectations: the Retties, he reported, 'were seeking only assistance from the missionary and they, having all without exception gone back to heathenism, my removal from the district became necessary.'[86] Lovekin exaggerated and the local SPG authorities, Pope included, simply registered Lovekin's lack of moral fibre; Pope observed: 'he appears to have taken a decided prejudice against the missionary work, against the natives and the language and his health has sunk under the disappointment.'[87] Lovekin persisted: 'It has often struck me,' he confessed, 'as being my duty to communicate with the Society concerning the state in which I found the so much talked of district in which I was sent. I have not done so hitherto as I knew that the most helpful accounts that I could write would be very distressing to the Society. Of the 96 villages that are stated to have come over imploring Christianity I found not one man – the writings published in England concerning the mission I am sorry to say are such as to excite nothing but disgust in the minds of those acquainted with the facts who read them.' This had been, after all, but a dispute with the zamindar, a long standing one at that, in which the earlier CMS missionary, Rhenius, had ignored their pleas. Such is the population of Tinnevelly that there is 'little temptation to keep them from our humiliating doctrines except in the towns of Tinevelly and Palamcottah, and there missionary work is at a very low ebb.' 'No spirit of Christ' moved the Retties 'but an evil spirit.'[88] Shortlands saw Lovekin as 'greatly misinformed and from his faith and missionary inexperience quite incompetent to form a correct opinion.'[89] Lovekin was sent back to England.

Fletcher was even more damning. 'I have been informed on good authority (by a Collector) that nearly the whole of the 96 villages in Mr Pope's part of Tinevelly have gone back to heathenism. Their motives were only ever self-interest.' The late conversions were 'something very inferior and commonplace.' Pope had merely intervened at the crucial juncture when they were pressing their law-suit against the landowner. 'I may say', he continued, speaking as a Tanjore missionary, 'that the Tinevelly movement, which seems to have raised so much stir in England is very little thought of here on the spot and Mr Pope's name is hardly known except for some few who do not, to say the truth, give him a very good character for politeness and gentlemanly behaviour.' Certainly, he behaved towards Lovekin 'in a very brutal manner. They represent him as a very conceited, superficial man with no pretensions to scholarship in anything but Tamil, exceedingly vulgar and a bigotted low churchman.'[90] This was to get Pope wrong in at least two counts; he was a considerable scholar and he was high church. But maybe some alarm bells should have rung in London, and one wonders what indeed Hawkins made of these conflicting reports. Clearly in the Tanjore mission field Pope would not with everyone be a popular appointment.

Iconoclasm came easily to Pope. As temples were converted into churches, their effects had to be disposed of: brass to the brazier, gold to the goldsmith. In one village he visited, three images of the Hindu gods had already been 'ground to powder and thrown into the tank', two others 'they dragged out and demolished with a spirit and energy which was quite refreshing.'[91] Against caste he was adamant, though here he was but implementing Bishop Wilson's very stringent policy. Overall, Pope was pessimistic at the prospect of conversion: 'it would be expecting figs of thorns and grapes of thistles to look for elevation of feeling and motive among the great mass of those who have been nurtured in a system which debased the intellect, destroys the moral feeling and confounds all distinctions of Good and Evil.'[92]

He began to question both the personnel and the strategy of mission. He doubted the competence of the catechists. Often up to twenty miles from the mission station, they could not be properly supervised. If would-be converts could not be adequately supervised, he would rather turn them away: 'my difficulty here is in guarding against the admission of improper and insincere persons rather than in retaining those who have joined me.'[93] He had little faith in the Anglo-Indians(he referred to Eurasians): 'our colleagues are no churchmen at all . . . without energy or without enlargement of mind.'[94] Nothing could replace European missionaries. Interestingly, Pope was also a signatory to a joint letter protesting at any drop in salary. But Pope was primarily an educationist, was in charge of a seminary, and was beginning to have heretical views on the way forward.

The seminary was but a fledgling. By 1845 there were only 35 boys, 6 from each of the 5 districts which made up the Tinnevelly mission. It offered but a rudimentary education. For Pope it was vital that a thorough Christian training should be provided for the children of converts: 'if the motives for the conversion of their parents be doubtful, though not as far as I know in any case improper, . . . their children are the children of the church and if judiciously trained the next generation will present a different aspect from the present.'[95] But the SPG was insufficiently concerned with its development: 'it is a thing which lies at the root of all missionary work. For want of it our missions have long been crippled and our missionaries have been and are working with inefficient and untrained native helpers.' Should there not be a diocesan college? The Jesuits at Negapattam had set an example. But numbers grew. By February 1847 there were 121 students, by November, 144. Under Pope's management, it was recognised as an Arts College and a Seminary.

There was a strong personal dynamic in Pope's commitment to education. He very much regretted his own lack of an university education: 'I came out to India when my brother went to Cambridge under the impression that to study the language was better than to graduate. This has compelled me to work hard and after all I feel the want . . . of standing as a University man. . . . It has cost me much painful study to obviate some of these disadvantages.'[96] Wistfully he observed: 'we have none of us much time for writing or for literary pursuits, except in immediate connexions with our work.'[97]

Pope displayed considerable insight into the nature of local Hinduism. 'Devil worship does not prevail so extensively and exclusively here', he reported, 'as in the southern part of the province.' Folk and sanskritic cultures were admixed. He conversed with the Brahmins of nearby Saivite temples. 'They are quite ignorant and live contetedly on the revenue of their temples and by cultivation. They manifest no hostility to Christianity as a system and when spoken to on the subject invariably answer, "all this may be true but our living and our caste compel us to remain in the religion of our forefathers". I see in these parts very few traces of the superstitious fear which enslaves so many of the poorer Hindus.'[98] No doubt something of the higher Hinduism at nearby Tiruchendur had rubbed off on the neighbourhood, but Pope had not really grasped the merely functional role of priests and little here would have prepared him for the sophistication of Tanjore.

In many ways the missionary who returned on sick leave to England in 1849 was not the model missionary the authorities believed him to be. Pope himself had definite expectations of a missionary; he should be entirely susceptible to order and discipline: 'in such a place as this the slightest appearance even of insubordination would greatly injure the native institution. If a man be not naturally very patient, if he have the least predisposition to irritability, he should not come out to India, at least not as a missionary. Calmness, patience and self-command are most essential here.' These were not qualities Pope was to display in Tanjore. There was equally a need for strong faith: 'without communion with God I do not know how any man can hold out for even a month. With it, no work can be done more pleasant.'[99] In Tanjore even his faith was to come under review, though not to break.

CONFRONTATION IN TANJORE

On leave Pope could not leave mission affairs alone. He railed at the news of the ordination by the MDC of Indian catechists: thus 'converted into an indifferent missionary . . . utterly spoiled'.[100] Highly significant for his time in Tanjore, if he exonerated Symonds was his lambasting the MDC: it exercised a control contrary to SPG principles, promoted inferior agents and prevented 'men of independent minds from going out' and 'gave all our affairs the air of a government department.' It was 'decidedly a party committee.' In the depths of Devon he took some comfort from sensing that the prejudice against the SPG had lifted, though many still believed 'that where the CMS had obtained a footing our Society had no claim for support.'[101]

On his return in 1851 his posting had not yet been decided, though Tanjore seemed likely. There were plans there for another seminary. There had to be someone 'to influence the other missions roundabout and that in fact I am the man. If all agree I can be more useful in Tanjore I suppose I must go.' But he did not relinquish his plea for greater autonomy: 'my convictions deepen that you must aim at giving self-government to Tinevelly and Tanjore circles of missions at least.'[102] In Tanjore his greatest achievement was as an educationist, to build up 'an elementary school in a sorry state'[103] into a High School, St Peter's College, the first in the Presidency to be government aided. He himself became a recognised Tamil expert. But it was a career over-shadowed by three great conflicts, his handling of the Tanjore Christians, his controversial report on the Tanjore Mission, submitted in 1857, and a major theological row prompted by his translation into Tamil of a seemingly innocuous text on the Eucharist.

Harbinger of the last surfaced almost immediately on taking up his new post. At two points in the communion service Pope used to bow. He informed the Bishop of this. In reply, Dealtry threatened to withdraw his right to preach; 'for a quiet, unostentatious common act of reverence in the house of God, an act familiar to me from long habit – can I lawfully and rightfully be subjected,' Pope queried, 'to this treatment at your lordship's hands?' Rashly, he questioned the legitimacy of such powers, 'for if so is it not time for every clergyman of honourable and independent mind who belongs to no party in the Church and wishes but to do his duty in peace to seek refuge in some more favoured diocese.' Grudgingly he surrendered, whilst still seeing the bishop's injunction as ' partial and arbitrary'. Dealtry withdrew his threat.[104]

The next conflict, Pope's attempted show-down with the Tanjore Christians, does not appear in the records. Maybe Pope, recognising the price of honesty with the Bishop, thought it wise to keep such matters from the authorities. Catalyst was the renewed threat from the Lutherans at Tranquebar. Pope was less than candid in his reports: 'I have little to tell of Tanjore. Daily services, weekly communion, daily examinations and catechisings of girls and boys, etc. My plan is to look out for any little atom of good in anybody or anywhere and labour to develop it.'[105] In actuality he was indulging his very considerable polemical powers against the Lutherans.[106] From day one there was confrontation. The Lutherans had enrolled one Pakkyanathan, whom Pope had expelled. For a man of Pope's authoritarian temperament, it was clearly insupportable that a Mr Wolff, who had visited him as a friend, proceeded both to hold a service in his mission and build a church: 'in the midst of my people, on my own ground, I have families who do not acknowledge my authority and do not obey yours, who gather around them all who are discontented and disreputable and who practise with immunity all that I seek to wean my own people from.' This had been going on for three years.

Lutheran attitudes to caste were, of course, the issue. But Schwartz had not, he claimed, defended caste: 'he denounced caste as sinful . . . he proposed to eradicate it.' Heber was on his side. 'In opposing caste,' Pope declared, 'we do not wage war with an abstraction. There are definite manifestations of an evil principle. . . . If caste be only equivalent to what we call rank, let it be maintained in the same way. If it be anything *real* and worth having it cannot be injured or broken by eating food cooked by another or occasionally associating with another. Nothing but heathen caste could be affected by such accidents. We do not strive to degrade our people, but to elevate them by inspiring a consciousness in them of the true dignity to which Christianity has raised them. But in fact I have found that this incomprehensible and impalpable phantom against which we contend is admitted by all to be sin.'

Tanjore Christians were worse offenders than elsewhere. Bishop Wilson had seen this. There are some 'sensible and earnestly minded men among our native folk' but, in general, 'many of them would rather forego anything than aid us in the least in preparing the way for their own emancipation.' He listed the various steps he had taken, especially regarding the communion: 'no one shall come to the holy table who would there manifest by any gesture or act, by sitting apart or by communion before or after his brethren, any feeling of disgust towards his fellow Christians. This is a thing which must be *tested* We must be on the watch to repress any indications of a temper of mind that would convert the gifts of God into a means of condemnation to our people.' Schwartz, besides, had accepted Anglican services and liturgy; the new Lutheran missionaries were not his true successors.

Admittedly it was, averred Pope, their catechists, rather than they, who did the poaching: 'to gather a congregation is to secure a livelihood for themselves.' With so many permissive attitudes, e.g. on caste, 'nothing is required but what can be evaded easily', on marriage, laxer rules on consanguinity and 'no questions asked about the ceremonies and tamask in their houses', infrequent visits by missionaries, 'so that the utmost laxity of discipline is tolerated', they have a head start. Not that we regret the loss of such Christians: 'we have seen the utter worthlessness of a system built upon such foundations' and they would have been excommunicated, anyway. In conclusion: 'I pray you before the whole Christian community in southern India, for the sake of Christianity which is disgraced by these disputes, to refrain from this interference with our people.' Clearly, Vedanayagam Sastriar was directly replying to this tract. The confrontation continued to fester during Pope's Tanjore years and in large part was to drive him out in 1857.

Meanwhile the work of mission went on. The Society was concerned at an apparent drift in strategy: 'it cannot be disguised', reported Symond's, 'that the operations of the Society are too much of a merely pastoral character – that they consist too exclusively in the care of Christian congregations already gathered whereas a missionary society ought to be mainly and prominently an evangelizing body, making forward and aggressive movements in the territory of the great adversary of souls.'[107] Tanjore had to be strengthened: 'with this view it was that they recommended the Rev. G. U. Pope to Tanjore and they fully contemplated a still further accession of strength whenever the means might be placed at their disposal.'[108] But this was at a time of retrenchment and a hopeless muddle ensued of both laying off missionaries and seeking new ones. One missionary pointed out how savage this could be: 'we are taking from them the occupation to which they have been solemnly set apart and dedicated, the very profession of which legally and practically debars them from entering every purely secular employment and their long training in which would virtually disqualify them from success in any of the very few careers that may still be open to them.'[109] Just as well Pope had a proven track record as a teacher when the crisis came.

There were property disputes and these may well explain the tensions between Pope and the Tamil Christians. Sarabhoji II had donated the village of Seydengal to the mission, but 'the cultivators frequently defraud us and it will relieve the Mission of a vast amount of anxiety and secular occupation.'[110] were their payments in kind to be commuted. C. S. Kohloff proved to be the beneficiary of the original bequest to his father, not the mission, but he was happy enough to sign a formal transfer to the Society.[111] Not that this solved the problem. Pope still found such arrangements impossible to manage and requested the land be given over to the government for a fixed annual payment of a 1000 or 1200 rupees.[112] Many cultivators occupied mission land and Pope was for their buying up these plots.

Meanwhile, Pope kept quiet about local conflict: 'the Committee are thankful to learn that unanimity of sentiment now exists among the Revd Missionaries of Tanjore with regard to the measures adopted for the eradication of caste from their mission and trust that by God's blessing their united efforts to remove this fearful evil from their congregations will be attended by success.'[113]

Matters academic and educational began to surface. Pope failed in his request for a local printing press. He was appointed to a translation committee for a new Tamil Bible. Brotherton could not be spared. Various plans, none implemented, were entertained for Vediapuram: translating it to Vallam, (headquarters of the Collectorate), closing it down. Pope sought to strengthen the teaching staff of the Mission High School: The Rev. Adolphus – he was in disgrace through his neglect of itinerating in Puttokottai – was transferred to the school and in 1856. Rev. Percival was a welcome addition. Pope would not agree to the promotion of John Areevandelu from catechist to teacher. Request for trained teachers from England was turned down. It was in this situation that Pope made use of the provisions under the Government's new education policy and applied for a grant-in-aid. When applying for leave, 1 September 1856, he asked that his brother, Henry, should be his stand-in, but this was not to be: Richard, however, was later to replace Bower at Vediapuram. None of this hints at the furore that was to break out when Pope submitted a report to the MDC, 11 February 1857, on his years in Tanjore, 1851–56.

No copy of the report has surfaced in the archives but from its extensive discussion and quotation it is possible to assemble its main elements. C. S. Kohloff was standing in at the time for Symonds as Secretary, absent on home leave. In submitting the report, Pope admitted, 'parts may seem strange but wished it may be taken into consideration as a whole', and requested permission to print it for private circulation among friends.[114] The MDC's response was to send a copy to Brotherton and Guest for comment, refuse permission for its circulation and return it to Pope.[115] Not until 27 July 1858 was a copy sent to London. There had been a furious discussion in the MDC. Clearly Pope went ahead anyway and circulated the report, and for this he was to be roundly condemned by Underwood: 'to publish a paper giving an account of the Mission of so unfavourable a character keeping all these circumstances from the knowledge of the Committee for six years is as unprecedented as it is improper but the proceeding becomes in my mind reprehensible when the statements are either untrue or highly exaggerated.'[116] Guest and Brotherton shared this outlook, but Revs. C. W. Drury and J. D. Sim submitted minority reports, and these should be taken together.

Pope's errors were numerous. He was faulted for his harsh words on the Court of Tanjore, to quote: 'the vicinity of a Native Court peculiarly corrupt (which) has aided in reducing the moral standards to the lowest level,' and for branding the Native Christians as antinomian: 'I cannot consent (this is Underwood) to allow this to go forth with the concurrence of the Committee. If it be so it should have been informed of and the matter would have received the consideration it deserved.' Pope was also wrong to use the report as a way of criticising the catechists. Here Drury was not so sure and cited Pope's views that catechists acquired powers above their station, failed to challenge caste and that many had been sacked for 'fostering caste and other evils which the missionaries were striving to eradicate.' Since their dismissal, Pope had reported, 'moral offences have been brought to light which owing to catechists were not known before.' The situation had become out of hand: 'there were no caste catechists for no caste people and caste catechists for the caste people.' Drury was clearly sympathetic; 'it has been replied that for some time past caste prejudices have been gradually discouraged. This means I suppose censured and protested against, and in some measure from motives of expedience . . . winked at. . . . Discouraging caste prejudices does seem to me to be doing very little towards eradicating them', and he was impressed by Pope's 'great ability and zeal.'

Underwood gave short shrift to Pope's ultimate objective: 'I have but one wish indeed with regard to my plans for the future and that is really efficient native clergy men could be appointed to take the pastoral work of my mission while my colleagues and myself devote ourselves to that which we are better fitted.' This was education. But Pope was ahead of his time: 'the Report impresses on my mind Mr Pope looks more to secular instruction and translation of books than any other means of conversion of the heathen. This is beginning at the wrong end and converting the missionary into the schoolmaster.' Drury demurred: 'I must say that I feel deeply anxious for the permanence and full development of our school system. It affords us here the very best means of doing our missionary work. It is not improbable that future years may show that it is one of the most effectual tools we have for promoting the conversion of the heathen.' Could Pope not be allowed to concentrate on education?

The majority verdict on the report was damning: 'I disapprove of it in toto. It does not breathe the spirit of a missionary in any part of it. His statements are controverted by others. The condemnation of proceedings of his predecessors and the early missionaries is as open to objection as they are unprecedented and unjust. To my mind the whole report is a laudation of himself and a condemnation of others. It exhibits an undue partiality for pursuits which should be secondary in the mind of a missionary. It has an insubordinate tendency which the letter to the parent society (see below) aggravates.' Only reluctantly did Underwood agree that it be sent to London; Drury was much more emphatic: 'the English public has a right to know the full truth. There is I fear a growing impression at home among many persons that the Missionary reports circulated among them give too favourable a view of missionary work among the heathen. They will I think be glad to learn from this report the difficulties and drawbacks which Missionaries have to encounter and take more interest in Missionary work.'[117]

Meanwhile Pope, granted sick leave, had been to England, returned to India and taken himself up to Ootacamund. From here he tried to justify himself to Hawkins. How could he have contacted Pall Mall when the MDC 'had both privately and publicly shown such an extreme enmity that no "agent" should communicate directly with the parent.' 'My position as a Missionary SPG is a very insecure one and I wish that you should know it.' He had foreseen the rumpus, but how other than 'openly' could he have written the report? The MDC have not explained their anger. Rather disingenuously he continued: 'I printed it for private circulation and missionaries all denominations – old tried men – and laymen of good repute – continually assure me of the fullest sympathy in my views.' 'If the MDC do not know it to be the true they alone in the diocese are ignorant of the fact.' He then summarised their reasons for rejection: its tone; its tractarianism; its complaint against the Tanjore Christians – 'this is the truth regarding Tanjore, I can't say more or less'; its critique of catechists – 'the monster evil of our Tanjore missions'; condemnation of past missionaries – 'not guilty'; neglect of preaching, again unfair; time misspent on translation – 'never more than leisure hours'; his examining – 'I have marked for the Government, it has been at odd times and for good ends, besides I have published more books for the tract society than all the other Tanjore missionaries put together.'[118]

But Pope's hubris deepened. So concerned was the MDC by the report that Caldwell was dispatched to report on Pope's teaching in his school. Theological alarm bells rang at the content of Pope's translation of an English tract on the Eucharist, the Gold Casket. Eventually Pope's suspect ideas were to be assembled in a pamphlet, Summary of Doctrines. Clearly the critique of Pope as an educationist and as a theologian are interconnected, but here we will try to keep them apart. By now Bishop Dealtry had become involved.

Caldwell's visitation stung Pope into a long self-apologia to the Bishop. How could Caldwell have sunk to such espionage, to so invidious a task? In which mission station would he now be welcome? (In fact, Caldwell was becoming accustomed to the role of trouble-shooter, having sorted out the 1852 scandal of headmaster Ross's pederasty at Sawyerpuram – Ross had fled the country to escape arrest).[119] Besides, Pope continued, Caldwell had visited the school when it was shut for holidays and his informant had been an 'exceedingly inexperienced and uncertain young missionary in temporary charge.' (Presumably Percival.) Education had not been promoted at the expense of other missionary tasks. Nobody had preached more than he: 'every Sunday I have had three Tamil services and two discourses. Every morning and evening we have had prayers in Church and I have rarely failed to catechize once each day.' Daily did he attend the sick and poor. Nor had he neglected itinerating: 'often, very often have I gone into the streets thus to speak of Christ. Bower and myself have spent days on this work'.

Now he went onto the attack. Better that this be done by those better qualified, such as Ragland: 'what I feel is that in Tanjore at present – other work is more pressing.' This was not the way to reach the Marathas, Tanjore's élite. Qualified Indians are best for this role of evangelism, but they are lacking. Even catechists – and here a rare commendation from Pope – can do good work among non-Christians. With the new grant-in-aid system, he could draw on funding always denied by the MDC: with their refusal to pay for another teacher, 'I became one myself.' 'It was and is evident that missionary societies must either make a great effort to maintain their position as educators of the country or allow the youth of the land to fall into the hands of others whose system excludes all religious teaching'. And, yes, he had translated works of a merely secular character, but then the Society did not pay him enough to educate his children and he needed the money.

He had then to rebut Caldwell's charges against the content of his education. Here was Pope the moderniser: 'I will freely acknowledge that I have pursued a system of secular training very far. I believe that a sound, rational education brings men in one sense nearer to God. I am not afraid to say that I view every attempt to expand the faculties of young men with unfeigned and hearty satisfaction.' He then panned the conventional missionary schooling: '. . . I have no sympathy with the so-called education that consists simply in teaching the Holy Scriptures unintelligently, the geography of Canaan, the Church catechumen and Fabricius's hymns. I know that it has been found to fail utterly'. He came back at Caldwell's charge that the Bible was not taught: in fact, each alternative afternoon there was a two hour lesson; in these he sought to convey the truth of God's revelation. 'The Bible lesson became I think the most popular of the whole. And this is saying much when it is remembered that the elite of Tanjore and the neighbourhood were there.' Here Pope was expressing arguments that were not to be adopted till the 1880s. 'Is not this method,' he continued, 'preferable to making of the Bible a daily parsing and spelling book?' Pope had clearly discovered himself as a teacher. 'The happiest and most useful hours of my life have thus been spent among these boys, many of high rank and of great intelligence, whose eyes beamed with interest and sometimes glistened with tears too while the truth was preached in our lecture room'. And well they might, for Pope's fare was Christian poetry from Milton to Pope. This, of course, was to mainly Hindu boys. But the Christian, who made up a third of the school, were specially catered for; they attended morning and evening prayers, besides Sunday services. With a rhetorical flourish he concluded: 'I think it must appear that Dr Caldwell's statements and the MDC's interpretation are rash and unwarranted.'[120]

On his return Symonds tried to impose some order on the situation: 'as soon as possible I carefully perused the several papers . . . anxious if possible to heal the breach between the committee and a very zealous missionary'. [121] Tanjore was evidently in trouble: 'there is so much that is stagnant and stationary and where bold and vigorous efforts should be made to arouse and quicken by sending forth evangelists of strong faith and hallowed belief and by establishing schools of a superior order.' (This was to hedge his bets on strategy.) But Symonds was concerned at any erosion of his own authority and when Hawkins seemingly permitted missionaries in the field to contact London direct, he was quick to point out that such by-passing of the MDC was 'contrary not only to general usage but to the understanding already come to that communications of this kind should pass through them.' Did he fear that Hawkins would take Pope's side? He gave a somewhat different, blander, account of Caldwell's visitation. He had 'urged the maintenance of the strengthening of his school,' but 'noticed some defects, one being the inadequate Christian teaching as it appeared to him in a book written by Mr Pope and used in his school.' He would first have preferred Pope's comments, but the Committee had referred the matter to the Bishop, and 'as an avowed High Churchman Mr Pope ought not to have taken offence at being left to deal with his Diocesan only.'[122] On the contrary, as it happened Pope felt that the MDC should have taken responsibility, and that the Bishop had been 'impelled.'[123] But matters theological were clearly in the Bishop's domain.

Any hint of Roman leanings was cause for concern. The great Tractarian debate had reached India.[124] Pope had already come under suspicion of Catholic practices on his arrival in Tanjore. Now there was his pamphlet on the Eucharist. 'I wish it to be in every sense "Catholic",' he told the Bishop. 'I have no wish to say, write, or teach anything but the plain simple Scriptural doctrine of the English Church which I believe to be the faithful guardian and interpreter of holy writ.' But there was a distinctly Catholic flavour to his claim that Christ was 'invisibly present, he is revealed to the faithful in the feast of His Body and Blood as in general he is not revealed elsewhere and at other times.'[125] (18 July 1857) Dealtry felt he had no alternative but to ban the book. 'We think the whole tendency of the tract is in a wrong direction, it is unprotestant if not papistical: the substance, the style and the animus strongly remind us of Roman Catholic teachings and sympathies.' The Communion was priveleged at 'the expense of true repentance, conversion of heart to God, living justifying faith in pardon of sin.' Two CMS missionaries had been asked to comment and Pope saw their critique as but 'railing accusation' and insisted on his 'liberty of prophesying': 'I cannot give up the right to teach, preach, print and circulate what in England is allowed in every diocese.' 'At least let me represent my own party as an Evangelical High Churchman.' (31 August 1857) Such indiscipline for Dealtry was in breach of Pope's ordination vow. Liberty to prophecy he saw as 'licentiousness': 'I am resolved to take every lawful method to put a stop to the propaganda of these semi-popish errors whatever trouble or opposition I may meet in doing so. I confess I should have expected from you a very different conduct.' (7 September 1857) Pope appealed to the Archbishop (without success).

Against Caldwell's more wideranging catalogue of errors Pope went on the offensive. 'I have yet to learn,' he mockingly observed, 'that "the most essential doctrine of Christianity is that of the sinner's forgiveness and access to God through his own conscious realisation of God's atonement."' This smacked of 'the newest Hegelian fountain of German metaphysics.'[126] In fact, here was that crucial difference between an evangelical focus on the crucifixion and the Atonement and a High Church on the Incarnation and the Sacraments. But Dealtry was to be just as intransigent. Here were views 'entirely at variance with the teaching of the Protestant Church.' He specified 'the Romish doctrine of mortal and venial sin, a fine passage of scripture distorted and limited to uphold the erroneous idea.' But the MDC backed away from his insistence that the book be banned: to do so 'would have been on their part an invasion of private right and could have been at once set at nought by the author.'

However, they could legally forbid its use in missionary schools.[127] Interestingly, though Pope did not cross the line to Rome, his brother, Richard, did,[128] and the son of Thomas was to be Professor of Sacred Scriptures at the Vatican.

The parting of the ways with a missionary of Pope's stature was grievous. Everyone wanted to wash their hands of the responsibility. Pope resigned 15 May 1858. In forwarding his resignation the MDC felt 'bound to disown wholly the imputation of their being actuated by any personal prejudice against him.'[129] More elaborately, Symonds wrote of his regret: 'you are aware that I sought to make peace between him and the Committee, I considered that he had been somewhat hardly dealt with.' But he stood by his action: 'neither as a personal friend nor as a member of the society can I vindicate Mr Pope's resignation. It is a cause of deep concern to myself that any act of mine should have contributed to bringing about Mr Pope's separation, but after reviewing the matter again and again I cannot regret the course I pursued how much I may lament the result'.[130]

Pope was in no doubt of his harsh treatment. As he explained to Dealtry, hardly his friend, 'I can no longer remain their missionary. I cannot retire from a work which I have been engaged for nearly twenty years (from August 1 1839) without pain, but must do so.' 'The stay at Tanjore had been one of anxiety and excitement arising from the conduct of the MDC towards me.' He rehearsed all his grievances over the way his report had been handled: 'the exceeding unseemliness and unfitness of the whole procedure must I think strike everyone.' The report had been returned with half-erased, pencilled comments, together with the signed initials of members of the committee, but 'to this day I have not the remotest clue for its contemptuous rejection.' 'From all this it is abundantly evident the MDC are determined to get rid of me.' 'They have my hearty forgiveness but I cannot continue to work under their guidance.' He returned to the need for greater autonomy: 'I could not conduct the Tanjore mission without originating plans and doing much in which I should require the entire confidence and sympathy of both my Diocesan and the Society by whom I was appointed.' He ended on a sour note. Caldwell's belief that the Tanjore Christian community could support a native priest was ridiculed: 'there is but one man in the congregation who earns an independent livelihood and is not in debt.' He was a catechist.

'He is a bitter enemy to our system on account of caste.' 'Were they to be asked to support a priest, they would reply, "we are poor, pay us, Schwartz's legacy is ours, restore it to us, give us a caste minister, allow us to follow our own devices in all things". The MDC know all this well enough. But the current runs in that direction: the times changes and we too change with them.'[131] Even were this true, not so for Pope, and, in the end, we would probably be right to conclude that it was more exasperation with the local Christians than his battle with the MDC that drove him to resignation.

WAS POPE ALONE?

How isolated was Pope in his struggle? Clearly Pope saw his new assistant in the school, Percival, as less than loyal, and indeed his attitude to education subtly varied from Pope's. He taught the history of India, Geography, physical and general, English grammar, Mathematics including Arithmetic, Algebra, Geometry and Trigonometry: 'it may appear strange,' he admitted, 'to some that a Christian Missionary's time should be devoted to pursuits such as those now mentioned which are per se essentially secular.' Whereas Pope gloried in this secularism, Percival, in contrast, 'ever regarded such studies as merely secondary. They are in fact the bait by which we endeavour to attract as large a number of heathens as possible. I would further observe that every study however apparently secular is made an instrument for the conveyance of Christian truth.' The boys, many of them Brahmins, 'answer questions put to them regarding the word of God' and all castes mingle together in the school. Had Pope reported in this style maybe there would not have been the same fuss. Percival recognised the barriers missionaries in Tanjore were up against: 'Tanjore is peculiarly the hotbed of heathenism and whatever may be effected here will take time.'[132] In class, in his pre-Darwinian innocence, he drew comparisons between the Bible and the Vedas: pagan and infidel e.g. Muslim had failed to invalidate the Bible, but many statements in the Vedas were 'plainly repugnant to modern science.' They admit that their geography is false, with the earth 'represented as a vast circular plain surrounded by the oceans of salt, water, sugar and juices, spiritous liquors, ghee, curds, milk and sweet water,' but cannot answer the question 'how came it to pass that it should form part of the system they believe to be divine, God being the author of truth only.' Similar scorn was poured on the Hindu version of the eclipse. 'I find it important to dwell on subjects such as these,' he explained, 'in as much as the Hindoo connects all knowledge with his system'. 'They see no distinction between sacred and secular knowledge'. Percival went on to make all the right noises about strategy: 'much of the school work now required of me might be well performed by a secular master, thus giving the missionaries of the place the opportunity of itinerating amongst the heathen which I cannot help but feel is my more legitimate duty.'[133] Not that he fared any better against the Lutheran and Catholic tendencies of local Christians. To the list of local difficulties, he added: 'the pernicious example set by the soldiers who have recently been quartered in this place . . . patterns of drunkenness and low debauchery.'[134] (An extremely rare reference to the Rebellion in missionary records from the south.)

In nearby Trichinopoly another young missionary, also under Pope's supervision, Holden, battled both against rival missions and the great Hindu centre of Srirangam. Here was a missionary whose career pointed to the commonsense of Pope's approach. There was a community of some 8,000 Catholics in and about Trichinopoly. 'Romanism,' he reported, 'is practically little more than a substitution of the saints for the Swamis and the romish chapel for the heathen temple. I have seen even the heathen marks made of the holy ashes on the face of a romanist.' This prompted some insight into Hinduism: 'the heathen are loth to give up a religion of external rites which rites many of themselves term sport, for one which imposes a spiritual worship, adapted to the nature and character of him who is the object of it.' He hardly dared proselytise the great temple complex of Srirangam and its surrounding villages. Here he would encounter those undergoing various forms of self-inflicted penance: to someone who had an iron-frame around his neck the time it took him to complete the building of a temple cart, he remonstrated 'on the utter uselessness of his seeking salvation in this way.'[135]

His next station was Kombaconam. Here he would engage in fruitless conversations with Brahmins: 'it is impossible to find them in or get them in a serious mood. They admit every charge made against them – if one were to believe all they say, image worship is becoming quite obsolete, the swamy processions have lost all their religious character and are to be looked upon as mere sport and everything else heathenish comes under the denomination of "custom", by which they seem to mean anything which though bad cannot be given up.' One local Brahmin, an English speaking vakil in the sessions court, conceded: 'there was one great advantage in Christianity: it does not force us to believe any doctrine without giving some proof or reason for it. There is no concealment in your religion.' To Holden's reply that this was to reject his own religion, came a typical pantheistic reply: 'all religions are like gold, gold you know may be moulded in different shapes but if you melt it down it will become one.' Holden's best was to reply, 'yes, that will hold good if all religions be like gold but you know that there can be but one religion pure and precious – that religion is Christianity which could never coalesce with heathenism.' His was a good description of Kombaconam, with all its many small idol temples, and, at its centre, 'three great swamy temples, with great cobarums (gopurams)', which 'look like so many pyramids. If Heathenism and they are to fall together Christianity has to struggle on for hundreds of years yet.' This was a virtual admission of the bankruptcy of the itinerating strategy.

Christians were subject to caste. Given a ratio of 250 Hindus to one Christian, how could one be surprised at its influence. However, a Judge he spoke to, believed: 'that in fact their attitudes to caste were not simply modified but entirely changed from those of the heathen'.

In the villages Holden met real hostility. 'You say we are not to have any Gods made with men's hands', retaliated one angry villager, 'what are we to do then? Are we to shut eyes and say Lord Lord? We are better off than you, but then we have something to look at, show us God and we will join you.' Holden had few expectations of village Christians. Could one be surprised 'that the poor village Christians so full of superstition, so easily attracted to externalism, and so much in contact with Roman Catholicism, attach great importance to the mere reception of the outward and visible signs of the sacrament.'[136] It was just this hopelessness in proselytising the adult generation that led Pope to see the way forward in the education of the younger generation, if, in his case, its elite.

A. F. Caemerrer, son of a Lutheran pastor, succeeded Pope at Tanjore. The Society had sought a 'missionary of matured experience . . . Mr Caemerrer was selected as the fittest person.'[137]

Here was a battle-hardened Tinnevelly man, from Nazareth. He had come up against Arumainayam (1823–1918), inspirer of the Nadar based separatist movement, the Hindu Church of the Lord Jesus.[138] Here was an itinerating missionary in the classic mould, unlikely to endorse Pope's preference for education. When Caemerrer first visited the Fort Church, he discovered that Schwartz's house had fallen into ruin; bats had' entered some aperture in the brass wire which covers the ventilators to obviate such a nuisance':[139] a symbolic commentary on Pope's attempt to shed the legacy of Schwartz, and here, at least, an approach Caemerrer could share.

CONCLUSION

Anglican mission, in terms of its own objectives in mid-century, largely failed in Tanjore. As Oddie has concluded, 'during the second half of the 19th Century Christians in the Kaveri delta were in some ways not much different from Hindus'.[140] Most continued to respect caste practices. However, by other criteria, the age of marriage, widow remarriage, there was greater change. Vedanayagam Sastriar persisted in his non-attendance at Communion, but his will had prevailed. Each Christmas and Easter he held his sudders: 'a kind of open air meeting attended with a great deal of singing and a lecture.' On such occasions, held in honour of Schwartz and his successors, Tanjore took on 'the appearance of a little Jerusalem. Thither may be seen Tamil Christians wandering their way from distances of 20 or 30 miles around'.[141] Both the poet and his family had withstood Pope's attack and continued to prosper.[142] The poet died 24th January 1864.

Pope himself was far too robust a character to be put down. His Ootacamund High School became a highly successful ICS preparatory school for Europeans living in India. From 1870 to 1880 he was to be Warden of Bishop Cotton School in Bangalore. (His square, rather severe, bearded face still stares down at the dining hall.) He ended his days, 1886 to 1908, as Lecturer in Tamil of the University of Oxford, and Chaplain of Balliol College, dying in post, 11 February.

In a wider sense, who had prevailed? In his more recent study, Oddie suggests a growing demoralisation of the Hindu community in the nineteenth century. Once the Company had devolved in 1841, in response to outraged evangelical opinion at European support for Hindu institutions, the management of temples to their traditional trustees, 'a sense of foreboding and unease' had spread as to their efficiency and vitality, and this had not been allayed by the setting up of new supervisory Temple Committees under the Religious Endowment Act of 1863. Would not this parlous situation, Hindus feared, let in Christianity?.[143] If such were indeed the case, had the missionaries missed their opportunity and do the besetting quarrels of the SPG, both within the Society, and with Lutherans and Catholics, explain their failure?

There is a strong case for arguing that Anglican mission in mid-century was locked into a mistaken strategy of proselytizing the adult population and would have been better advised to pursue Pope's pioneering emphasis on education. Clearly, alternative Lutheran and Catholic strategies, a greater collusion with caste and Hindu practice, had demoralised some Anglican mission-aries. In terms of high caste conversion, the Catholic approach belatedly brought dividends. In September 1894 a sizeable number of Brahmins in St Joseph's College, Trichinopoly, converted, though did so with the proviso that they preserve caste practice. Christianity should not signify, they asserted, 'drinking, wearing hats, boots and trousers or the surrender of caste dignity but a vivifying influence which raises man to the highest perfection of his moral nature.'[144] Oddie seems to be saying that Hinduism only recovered its nerve through the Hindu revival movements of the 1880s. But I am reminded of Swami Ranganathananda's insight that Hinduism is always strong, just stronger at certain times, as under the impact of a Vivekananda or Gandhi.[145] Its customary way of life and its traditional institutions seem to have been well able to resist this the most vigorous assault to date, from evangelical Protestantism. But the Tanjore Christians had also held their own.

Notes

1 Rajaiah D Paul *Triumphs of his Grace*, (Madras, 1967), p. 20.
2 It was fascinating to see this story taking shape. I began by looking at the USPG records in Rhodes House Library, Oxford, both the file on Pope, C/Ind/Madras/9 and the collections of Correspondence Local Received (CLR). But it was only amongst the USPG papers in

the archive of the United Theological College, Bangalore, that all the conflicts of Tanjore began to emerge. There were the astonishing documents in the Vedanayagam Sastriar papers, K2A 3. If this showed up one hidden struggle of Pope's, with the Tanjore Christians, another, with the local Missionary authorities, became clear through consulting the Madras Diocesan Committee Correspondence 1 12 A 12–16, bringing this story into even sharper focus by looking at the Proceedings of the Monthly Meetings of the M.D.C., SPG 51. On a return visit to Rhodes House I was able to find further relevant information in Original Letters Received D4 Madras 1850–59 (A).

This might best be the place to apologise for inconsistency in my use of Indian proper names. Sometimes I favour their 19th Century spelling, sometimes present day. I just feel it is going too much against the primary materials not to use such spellings as Tanjore, Trichinopoly, Tinevelly, etc. I have adopted the same approach for village names.

3 H.P. Thompson, *Into All Lands.* (London, 1951), p. 190.

4 Stephen Neill, *A History of Christianity in India 1707–1858,* (CUP, 1985), p. 228.

5 I've pieced together this brief account of Tanjore and Trichinopoly from T.P. Hemingway, *Madras District Gazetteer: Tanjore,* Madras 1907, *The Imperial Gazetteer of India,* entries on Tanjore District and Tanjore City, Vol XXIII, on Trichinopoly City, Vol XXIV, on Kambaconam City, Vol XVI, Reprint Edition (Original 1908). Another source, a lament for the demise of the state of Tanjore in 1855, is William Hickey, *The Tanjore Mahratta Principality in Southern India. The Land of the Chola: the Eden of the South,* 1873. Reprint Edition, (New Delhi, Madras, 1988). I am seriously in debt to Geoffrey Oddie's, *Hindu and Christian in South-East India.* (London, 1991).

6 Christopher Tadgell *The History of Architecture in India.* (London, 1990), p. 95. A scholarly account, with superb photographs.

7 Hemingway's account, *op. cit.,* pp. 60–82.

8 *Ibid,* p. 68,69.

9 Oddie, *op. cit.,* pp. 222, 223.

10 Here I consulted Jaya Appasamy, *Tanjavur Painting of the Maratha Period.* (New Delhi, 1983). Dr S. Seetha, *Tanjore as a seat of Music,* (Madras, 1981).

11 Appasamy, *op. cit.,*p. 96.

12 Seetha, *op. cit.,* p. 1.

13 Appasamy, *op. cit.,* p. 96.

14 For the Tranquebar Mission and the story of Ziegenbalg and Schwartz, I have consulted: J. Ferd. Fenger, *History of the Tranquebar Mission on the Coast of Coramandel,* (Tranquebar, 1863); Rev E.W. Grinfield, *Sketches of the Danish Mission on the Coast of Coramandel,* (London, 1831); Revd Hugh Pearson, *Memoirs of the Life and Correspondence of the Revd Christian Frederick Schwartz* Vols. I and II. London 1831. There is an interesting article by D.I. Wright, Schwartz of Thanjavur: Raja Guru? *Indian Church History Review,* Vol XV, No. 2,

December 1981. Stephen Neill's *op. cit*, is an excellent and very warm-hearted summary. There is a more general account of Tranquebar by Karl Pedersen, The Danish Settlement on the Coramandel Coast, in *The Indian Ocean Review*, Vol. I, No. 3, September 1988. I have uniformly adopted the spelling, Schwartz.

15 Georgina Harding, *Tranquebar. A Season in South India*, (London, 1994), pp. 55–56.
16 William Hickey, *op. cit.*, pp. 78–79.
17 Neill, *op. cit.*, pp. 46,47.
18 Pearson's account.
19 Pearson, Vol. I, *op. cit.*, pp. 162–3.
20 Fenger, *op. cit.*, p. 201.
21 Quoted Fenger, *Ibid.*, p. 208.
22 Discussed, only to be scornfully rejected by Wright. *op. cit.*, p. 125.
23 Wright's interpretation, *Ibid.*, p. 143.
24 Pearson, Vol. I, *op. cit.*, p. 208.
25 *Ibid.*, p. 295.
26 Vol II, *Ibid.*, p. 82.
27 William Hickey, apologist for the fallen house of Tanjore, makes much of this. *op. cit.*, p. 95.
28 *Ibid.*, p. 100.
29 So Hickey claimed.
30 Pearson, Vol. II, *op. cit.*, pp. 404–5.
31 Hickey, *op. cit.*, p. 121.
32 Pearson, Vol. II, *op. cit.*, p. 104.
33 Hans-Werner Gensichen, Daring in order to know, *Indian Church History Review*, Vol. XX, No 2, December 1986, p. 94.
34 Pearson, Vol. I, *op. cit.*, p. 192.
35 Pearson, Vol. II, p. 437.
36 Revd. Greenfield, *op. cit.*, pp. 92–98.
37 For Catholic Mission I have consulted J.B. Piolet S.J. *Les Missions Catholique Francaises au XIX e siècle* Vol II (Paris, 1901–03), Stephen Neill Chapters 4,6,13, *op. cit*, Joseph C Houpert, *A South India Mission: The Madura Catholic Mission 1535 to 1935*, (Trichinopoly, 1937), Kenneth Ballhatchett's, Priests, Peasants and Fishermen(in manuscript).
38 Houpert claims but 590 Catholics converted to Anglicanism. However, Kaj Baago argued for a substantial transfer of Catholic catechists to Protestantism in the 1820s and 1830s: 'The Protestant Mission would never have had the flying start they had but for these conversions'. But the Catholics were to fight back in kind in the 1880s. See his essay, Sheep Stealing in the 19th Century *Bulletin of the Church Association of India*, No.10 November 1966, p. 22.
39 He condemned, for example, Lamennais's attempt at fashioning a liberal catholic movement.
40 Houpert, *op. cit.*, p. 70.
41 See Imperial Gazetteer, Vol. XXIII, p. 231. Houpert argues that Mylapore made considerable gains in the cities.
42 Houpert, *op. cit.*, p. 304.

43 M.X. Miranda, The Social Apostolate of the Jesuits of the New Madurai Mission 1838–1938, Ch. 10 in Ed Anand Amaledes, *Jesuit Presence in Indian History,* (Madras, 1988).

44 Piolet *op. cit.,* pp. 107–9.

45 Houpert, *op. cit.,* p. 13.

46 Neill, *op. cit.,* pp. 305–6.

47 Symonds, 13 December 1848, USPG CLR 48 (Rhodes House) p. 227.

48 John Clive, Macaulay. *The Shaping of a Historian,* (New York, 1973).

49 H.P. Thompson, *op. cit.,* p. 111 Unless otherwise stated, all correspondence quoted is addressed to Hawkins.

50 Spencer, 17 June 1846, CLR 46.

51 Spencer, 17 June 1844, CLR 46.

52 Symonds, 23 September 1848, CLR 48 p. 192.

53 Shortlands, 15 July 1844, CLR 46 p. 289.

54 Shortlands, 17 August 1844, CLR 46 p. 297.

55 Shortlands, 22 October 1845, CLR 47 p. 113.

56 Symonds, 22 February 1849 CLR 48.

57 Symonds, 22 February 1849, CLR 48.

58 Symonds, 14 April 1848, CLR 48, p. 116.

59 Wiltshire, 20 October 1843, USPG C/Ind/Madras 10 (Rhodes House)

60 Wiltshire, 10 September 1844, *Ibid.*

61 Wiltshire, 7 May 1845, *Ibid.*

62 Wiltshire, 8 August 1846, CLR 47.

63 Shortlands, CLR 47 p. 139.

64 Wiltshire, 8 August 1846, CLR 48 pp. 30–31.

65 Revd J. P. Fletcher, 29 August 1845, USPG C/Ind/Madras/8 (Rhodes House).

66 Fletcher, 8 December 1847, *Ibid.*

67 Fletcher, 29 January 1849, *Ibid.*

68 Wiltshire, December 8 1848, *Ibid.*

69 Fletcher, 29 January 1849, *Ibid.*

70 Fletcher, December 8 1847, *Ibid.*

71 Fletcher, 29 January 1848, *Ibid.*

72 Fletcher, 29 January 1848, *Ibid.*

73 Symonds, 12 April 1847, CLR 48 p. 3.

74 Symonds, 14 April 1848, CLR 48 p. 192.

75 Circular Letter to the Benevolent and Charitable Ladies and Gentleman. It went on: 'In order to defray the necessary expenses for a pandal to the audience, oil, candles, servants, washermen, clothes to the children assisting and songsters, it will require at least 1/2 pagoda or two rupees a day. Therefore I request you will be so kind as to give out of the treasure God gave you in order to promote his glory.' The Vedanayagam Sastriar Papers K 2A 3 (UTC: Bangalore)

76 Symonds, 15 April 1846, CLR 48.

77 Neither letter is dated, and no mention of it appears in the SPG records. Did they prefer to keep quiet about it? Damp has begun to make parts of the document illegible and maybe, for this one, the

new air-conditioned archive at the UTC has not arrived quite in time. See K 2A 3.

78 For biographical information on Pope I am indebted to John Jones, Archivist of Balliol College, for sending me his c.v in the College Register, 1833–1933, and to my friend, Jesu Prasad, for directing me towards information on Pope in A Short History of Bishop Cotton's Boys School, in *The Centenary Cottonian*, Vol. LV, No.1–II 1965.

79 G.U. Pope, 25 June 1848 USPG C Ind/Madras/9 (Rhodes House).

80 Pope, 25 August 1844 C/Ind/Madras/9.

81 Pope to Bishop of Madras, 4 June 1845 C/Ind/ Madras/9.

82 Pope 25 August 1844, *Ibid.*

83 Shortlands, 20 September 1844, CLR 46 p. 309.

84 Shortlands, 22 October 1844, CLR 46 pp. 314–15.

85 Duncan Forrester, The Depressed Classes and Conversion to Christianity Ed. G.A. Oddie *Religion in South Asia: Religious Conversion Movements in South Asia in Medieval and Modern Times*, (London, 1973).

86 Lovekin, 4 October 1845, CLR 47 p. 109.

87 Pope, 22 October 1845, CLR 47 p. 113.

88 Lovekin, 12 October CLR 47 p. 123.

89 Shortlands, 12 February 1846, CLR 47.

90 Fletcher, 6 May 1847, C/Ind/Madras/8.

91 Pope, 20 September 1844 C/Ind/ Madras/9.

92 Pope, 5 June 1845, *Ibid.*

93 Pope, 7 February 1846. *Ibid.*

94 Pope, 13 January 1846. *Ibid.*

95 Pope to the Bishop of Madras, 4 January 1845. *Ibid.*

96 Pope, August 20 1846. *Ibid.*

97 Pope, 28 December 1847. *Ibid.*

98 Pope, 5 June 1845. *Ibid.*

99 Pope, 12 May 1847. *Ibid.*

100 Pope, 11 April 1850, SPG Madras 1850–59 D4(A) (Rhodes House).

101 Pope to Bridport, 9 August 1850, *Ibid.*

102 Pope 11 March 1851, *Ibid.*

103 How The Cottonian put it. *op. cit.*

104 Pope, 5 August 1851, USPG Original Letters Received Madras 1850–59 D4 A.

105 Pope, 2 June 1853, *Ibid.*

106 G.U. Pope *The Lutheran Aggression. A Letter to the Tranquebar Missionaries, regarding their position, their proceedings and their doctrine.* Dated 14 October 1851. American Mission Press: Madras. This was in reply to a Lutheran pamphlet and followed on an article in the *Madras Quarterly Missionary Journal.* The pamphlet was missing from the shelves of the UTC Library, but I tracked it down amongst a collection of Lutheran Tracts in the Cathedral Library, Canterbury, CCL31662H.

107 Symonds to Bishop of Madras, 26 November 1853, Madras District Committee Correspondence SPG 1 12 A 14 (UTC: Bangalore).

108 Symonds to Bishop of Madras, 4 June 1853, MDC SPG 1 12 A 13.

109 A note of dissent from Mr Kidd, 15 April 1856, Proceedings of the Monthly Meetings of the MDC SPG 51 (UTC: Bangalore).
110 Symonds, 11 May 1853, SPG 1 12 A.
111 Symonds, 24 September 1853, SPG 1 12 A 14.
112 Pope, 18 November 1856, Proceedings SPG 51.
113 24 July 1856, Proceedings SPG 51.
114 See Kohloff, 26 December 1857, SPG Madras D4 1850–59 B (Rhodes House).
115 Kohloff, 17 February 1857, Proceedings SPG 51.
116 This was Underwood's Minute and I assume this was the Secretary of the Baptist Society, then on a visit to India.
117 SPG Proceedings 15 December 1857.
118 Pope, 24 November 1857, SPG D4 Madras 1850–59 (B) (Rhodes House)
119 Symonds, 11 August, MDC Correspondence 1 12 A 12. This is an issue that will have to be returned to in discussing the educational context of conversion.
120 Pope to The Bishop of Madras, 10 April 1858, SPG D4 Madras 1850–59 (B) (Rhodes House).
121 Symonds, 27 July 1858 SPG 1 12 A 16(UTC).
122 Symonds, 8 July 1858, SPG 1 12 A 16.
123 Pope, 24 November 1857, SPG Original Letters Received D4 Madras 1850–59 A (Rhodes House).
124 To acquire a feeling of 'inwardness' for these theological issues one cannot do better than read David Newsome's *The Parting of Friends*. (London, 1966).
125 This debate on Pope's attitudes to the Eucharist was assembled in a pamphlet, which is in his file C/ Ind/ Madras/9. Rhodes House.
126 Pope to the Bishop of Madras, 10 April 1858, D4 Madras 1850–59 A (Rhodes House).
127 MDC, 25 October 1858, SPG 1 12 A 16 (UTC).
128 The Society became aware of his Catholic sympathies whilst he was at Trichinopoly in August 1858. The Society treated him generously, funding his return to England 'without difficulty or embarrassment.' Symonds to the Bishop of Madras. SPG 1 12 A 16 Was this as an act of reparation for their treatment of George?
129 15 June 1858 Proceedings SPG 51 (UTC).
130 Symonds 8 July 1858 SPG 1 12 A 16(UTC).
131 Pope to the Bishop of Madras, 10 April 1858 SPG D4 Madras 1850–59 (A) (Rhodes House).
132 S. Percival 4 September SPG C/Ind/Madras/9 (Rhodes House).
133 Percival, 31 March 1858. *Ibid.*
134 Percival to C.S. Kohloff, 5 January 1858, *Ibid.*
135 Holden, 22 January 1856, SPG C/Ind/Madras/8 (Rhodes House)
136 Holden, 8 October 1857. *Ibid.*
137 Symonds, 27 August 1858, SPG 1 12 A 16 (UTC).
138 For a brief account, see Stephen Neill, *op. cit*, pp. 230–33.
139 Caemerrer, 20 September 1857, SPG C/Ind/ Madras/8 (Rhodes House).

140 G A Oddie, Christianity in the Hindu Crucible: Continuity and Change in the Kaveri Delta 1840–90, *Indian Church History Review,* Vol. XV, No. 1, 1981, p. 67.

141 Perceval, 31 March 1858, SPG C/Ind/Madras/9.

142 In the Sastriar papers there is a note, dated 26 May 1882, from one Syriantrapohtan of Malabar: 'It gives me much pleasure to certify that the services and sacred songs conducted by Noah Nyanadra Sastri and his family have been highly appreciated by the people.' Though this appears to be in Tirichur and not Tanjore. K 2A3 (UTC).

143 G.A. Oddie, *Hindu and Christian in South-East India, op. cit.,* p. 78.

144 This was the occasion when 5 Brahmin converted. Piolet suggests 30, but he must be referring to a longer time-span. See Rev Louis Lacombe S.J, Rao Sahib V. Mahadeva Aiyer. *A Great Indian Convert,* (Trichinopoly, 1932).

145 In a personal conversation, Hyderabad, November, 1990.

Index